The Sun Struck Upwards

Finding fifteen different Spains

Luke Darracott

Printed by www.lulu.com

ISBN 978-0-9544919-2-5

Published in 2011 by
Brian W. Darracott
6, Medallion Place
Maidenhead
SL6 1TF

To my dearest Elena,

for living with a *guiri*...

Foreword

Let me tell what this is not.

This is not a travel guide, though it could, at a stretch, be used almost like one. This is not a history book, though it does contain information here and there that could, strictly speaking, be considered history. This is not a travel journal, though the chronological journey aspect of it could appear as such. This is not a deep, psychological or philosophical insight into the Spanish people, though I dip my toe in. This is not a social commentary, though, by its very nature, it has elements of that. It is not a "Bill Bryson" book, though I wish it were. It is all of these things and at the same time none of them.

It is also not the epic tale of a twee, middle-class couple that leave their life behind and start up a farm in the south of Spain, full of whimsical confusions and hardships as they bumble through it without any Spanish, but three years later are happy and functional. My adventure could be seen as a glorified holiday. I went where I wanted to go, full stop. In a fairly short period of time (June 4th – August 3rd 2010) I did my best to get to grips with the identity of a country in which I had already been living. Using buses and trains I visited more than fifty-five places and covered over 10,232km. The actual theme of the trip will soon become apparent but it was slightly more than merely a way to string together a two-month voyage of discovery; or rediscovery.

Contents

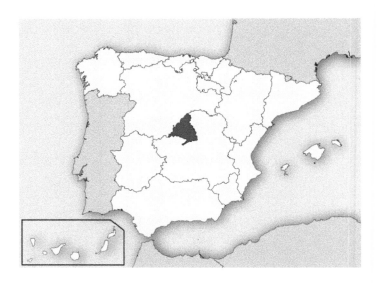

Capital Planning...

I was sweating a lot and suffering under the limp efforts of the tragic air conditioning unit. I was at table number 5, which wasn't in direct line of the air current produced.

'Yesterday I go to the village.'

'I go, Juan?'

'No, no. Yesterday I went.'

'Very good.'

My hands were blue and black with marker pen dust. I was drowsy and my eyelids were no doubt heavy-looking. Outside in the thick streets horns were blazing, people were shouting and sirens were whizzing past. Students were sighing as they tried to remember their conjugations. It was always fun to hear about the village...in whatever tense.

'What are you going to do this weekend María?'

'I going –'

'Mmm?'

'Sorry. I *am* going to go out, take a drink –'

'Take?'

'Ah! Have a drink!'

10 o'clock and the class was over. It was dark outside and the alleys were full of tourists, street-sellers and Spaniards starting to go out for the evening. It didn't matter what night it was, it was always busy. It was Thursday.

'Pub?'

'Yeah. Couple of pints.'

A small band left the school and clipped down the steps minding not to touch the static metallic banisters that *always* shocked them. *La Solera* was waiting at the top of the road, a giant barrel outside. Smiles all round and past the door and into its wood-panelled belly.

'Hola Diego!'

'Hey guys!'

It was useful to know the owner.

'Hola Flo!'

'Hola!'

It was also useful to know the waitress. Cheap drinks and free nibbles. Beers guaranteed to land you with a stinking hangover and ciders and wines at dangerously reasonable prices. The tapas would always improve with every round. Peanuts or crisps; then olives or ham; then tortilla or mayonnaise concoctions; finally, if we were lucky, and probably drunk enough, we would get grilled *morcilla*, salmon or garlicky potatoes. Olive stones were spat to the floor and cocktails sticks and chorizo wrappers were tossed as well. It was never a couple of beers. The walk home softened the effects of the booze and then the week would roll on. I could get up at 12pm if I really wanted.

In the two-bedroom flat, Elena, my housemate from Extremadura, would sonorously sing hellos from her room as I bumbled in at the end of my days. She was on a very stressful Nuclear Engineering Master's degree course and would usually be glued to her computer screen reading some graphics about radioactivity levels or half lives or she would be sat in her pyjamas, bleary-eyed, nibbling cheese or cured meats in front of some appalling television programme. I would then cook my dinner, always too much, and then maybe watch a programme I had downloaded in my room. There was nothing worth watching on Spanish telly except the occasional programme with Elena, with the aim of improving my language: *Física o Química, Gran Hermano, Sálvame Deluxe, Ana Rosa*. The box was always on – as was her iPhone – full of minor celebrities angrily discussing other celebrities and other non-celebrities. Often her boyfriend, Carlos, would be there on *his* iPhone or iBook, lounging around working or checking the football as his girlfriend berated him.

Pronouncing my name 'Lú-keh' instead of Luke she would tell me she was off to bed, rubbing her eyes with the stub of her palm. I soon would go to my own creaky bed. Only occasionally did I return home to find that a party was minutes away from welcoming its first guests and then I, dead on my feet, had to be present. It was a tiny flat and I couldn't hide. I would sit, trying to be the interesting *guiri* – white foreigner – and impress them all with my Spanish. When Elena had got bored of puppy eyes and I had been fully accepted as more than just a part of the furniture I would be let to bed and they would, at 12 o'clock or 1 in the morning, go out on the razz. Peace. Only once did Elena, and Esther, another friend, decide it would be funny to enter my room at four in the morning and wake me playfully, giggling at my angry, sleepy protests.
'I'll do breakfast if you get the hell out.'
That morning I got us *churros* – a deep fried, light doughnut ring – and brought them home. The brown bag had developed little opaque windows where the grease had taken hold. Not angry, just

irritated. This seemed to be the way I was with Spain and its people. It so rarely made me angry. It *was* irritating sometimes, but that's natural of anywhere.

Weekends were hallowed territory. Working until 10pm every day and working four hours every other Saturday morning, free time, *proper* free time, was sacred. Day trips out to nearby towns, going out for a night on the tiles, lounging around at home or in a park, having dinner parties, or popping to the local market to buy fresh vegetables and cheese were all savoured moments. One thing I was never able to do though was to go away for the weekend. Finishing late on Fridays somewhat put a damper on that process. When I had come to the end of the first year there with the company I worked for, I was toying with the idea of going to Russia to teach and try and improve my Russian. The niggling thought kept floating through my head: 'you've been living in Spain for a year…but you haven't even seen it, have you!'

It was true. I had been to a few places – see appendix – but I didn't have a firm feeling of what Spain meant: either to its people, or me. I knew it had *communidades autónomas*, autonomous communities, but I didn't know where they all were or what they contained. 'This isn't good enough', I thought to myself. I had just over two months to play with before I really had to return to England to start sorting out the Russia problem, so I started to plan a trip.

A quick word about the regions: the first thing to know is that there are seventeen of them, each with their own flag and identity and, often, language:
Andalucía
Asturias
Aragon
Balearic Islands
Canary Islands
Cantabria

Castilla La Mancha
Castilla y León
Cataluña
Extremadura
Galicia
La Rioja
Comunidad de Madrid
Región de Murcia
Comuidad Foral de Navarra
País Vasco (Basque Country)
Comunidad Valenciana

I instantly ruled out the islands. The Balearics consist of four: Ibiza, Mallorca, Menorca and Fomentera; and the Canary Islands ten: Tenerife, Fuerteventura, Gran Canaria, Lanzarote, La Palma, La Gomera, El Hierro, La Graciosa, Alegranza, and Montaña Clara. I would have loved to have visited them but wouldn't have had the time to visit each one. That left me with fifteen communities, including the one in which I lived.

The second thing to know is that they vary wildly in size and development. Castilla y León, for example, is the largest region covering an area of over 94,200 km² - an area comparable to the size of Hungary. Alternatively La Rioja, one of the most celebrated regions, clocks in at only 5,045 km² - more like Trinidad and Tobago. Size, however, doesn't denote population. The fairly small region of País Vasco has twice the population of Extremadura – a region almost six times the size.

This made the planning stage trickier than I would have hoped. Spain is not a small country by any stretch and travelling through it on public transport was affordable but not quick. Throughout my trip I often had to, on the fly, strike off destinations from my itinerary or rush around certain places so that I would make a certain bus, perhaps the only one that day.

The third thing to know is that the climate, both meteorological and political also varies between the regions. Murcia, Andalucía and Extremadura, despite their green enclaves, are fairly dry and heat-beaten regions; Castilla y León and Castilla La Mancha are the lands of the great high plains; whilst the regions along the north offer forests, rivers and lush, verdant peaks. Hills and mountains are present almost all over the country. Indeed, it is one of the most mountainous countries in Europe with various ranges sprouting up all over: the Picos de Europa and Pyrenees in the North; the Sistema Central that cuts through the centre from Portugal and across Madrid; and the Baetic Cordillera in the south that follows the coast.

The regions are often proud places with proud people and strong regional characters. Spanish is the country's official language but then there is *Galego* in Galicia; *Vasco* in the País Vasco and Navarra; *Catalan* in Cataluña; *Valenciano* in the Comunidad Valenciana; *Bable*, used by some in Asturias; *Aragones* in Aragon, still spoken by between 10,000 and 30,000 people; *Llengua llionese*, still used in some places in Castilla y León; and to a lesser extent *Estremeñu* and *Fala* in some areas of Extremadura. For the tourist however, only Basque and Catalan could pose a problem and Castilian Spanish is still the most prominent of all the languages.

This pride can, however, take on a more nationalistic air when some members of the regions go radical. The Catalans are very outspoken about their position, and, as a result, have historically been given the most autonomy of all the regions. Many have called for full autonomy, which has led to protests and strikes against government legislature. This is nothing, however, compared with the problems that have emanated from País Vasco, where the regionalist face has become one of aggression, violence and fear with the terrorist group ETA at the forefront. These are, of course, exceptions and the majority of displays of regional pride are positive, with flag flying, promotion of local products and conservation of regional sites of importance.

'Oh yeah, two months is lots of time to see Spain,' said one of my Spanish friends. He couldn't have been more wrong. A few weeks in each region would have helped me to really start getting to grips with the country as a whole. I didn't have endless months though. Two months is still a considerable amount of time and, with the occasional trip back to the capital to clean clothing or re-start another leg, I did manage to get to every region before the day of my final flight back to the UK.

Armed with my "Rough Guide to Spain" and a slightly undersized backpack that I borrowed from Anna, a friend from work, I was ready to leave the security of my flat and venture out and discover the country.

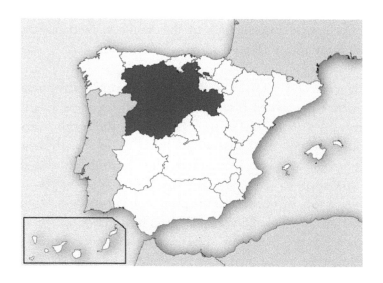

Mighty Spires

Salamanca – Zamora – León – Vallodolid – Peñafiel

I found myself journeying through that Welsh-style countryside of
the community of Castilla y León west of Madrid. It was an area I
had visited prior to this trip, to Segovia and Ávila. This time,
however, I passed through Ávila and pressed on towards the
historic university city of Salamanca. As we left the small turreted
town we started to sail through green lands dotted with reservoirs
and views of the then far off Sierra de Guadarrama. Although my
trip technically started as I bundled onto my train at Madrid's
Chamartín station, I felt inside that it started then, on that metallic
bullet wiping through the countryside. Unknown lands littered with
unknown places, little towns no one ever visits and with people and
everything ahead of me.

The craggy, sheep-spotted land near Ávila eventually gave way to golden and green seas of shimmering wheat. I could see different industries just by looking out of the window. Jaen has its olives, Ávila its meat and the land further on has cereals.

Palpable heat and a lot of walking formed my first impression of Salamanca. I needed to find my first hostel. Its name was Lazarillo de Tormes – Tormes is the river that cradles the south of the city. I was following the map that I had tried to fix in my head from Google images. About 40 minutes after having left the station I found the spot where I thought the hostel was supposed to be. There were lots of children and some adults outside so I guessed I had the right place. I didn't. I very much didn't. I had just walked, sweating and tired, into a four-star old-people's home. Pulling myself together I squeaked over the shiny marble floor and walked up to the reception. A smiley, but slightly bemused looking woman looked me up and down as I dumped my rucksack hoping it wouldn't leave a mark.
'Hello, is this the youth hostel?' What an idiot.
'No.' There was a surprise.
She pulled up Google Maps on her computer monitor and then directed me to a nearby 'friendly' hotel that then was kind enough to point me to my youth hostel.

The lady inside the big, orange, brick hostel was charming and sorted me out within minutes. I settled myself, washed my face and decided to go and explore for a bit. I backtracked to the knobbly Roman bridge that takes the visitor into the city and headed for the old buildings I had previously seen from afar. The air was spongy, full of pollen and smelled of hot flowers. The first old building that arrived was the 'Catedral Nueva y Vieja de Santa María', an enormously dramatic and spiky, combined 12-17th century cathedral. It was deliriously pretty, much like the whole area surrounding it. The guidebook calls Salamanca the 'most graceful city in Spain' and

I was already starting to see why. Inside was like many similar grand cathedrals of the style. Big, bold columns, impressive arches, lots of space and surprisingly light. Not like the gloomy ones you find towering over the low roofs in England.

I left the building to the sounds of a Spanish guitar singing to itself in the afternoon by the university. The sun was still fairly high and fairly hot; 'yes, it is definitely time for a beer'. Twittering French, loud Americans and some quiet English surrounded me as I sipped from the cold glass at a tiny, outdoor café. Even though I had lived in Spain for more than a year I was still very much a foreigner. I wanted to be accepted or, if not accepted, not viewed as a *guiri*. My wish was not helped by the presence of my much-needed shorts, flip-flops and guidebook.

As I finished my drink the sun began its trip to bed. Sat next to me were a group of young Americans and their Spanish culture teacher. I ordered another beer and some olives, continuing to listen to the students as their teacher did the rounds. She asked them questions in Spanish about where they lived and where they studied. They answered confidently, as is the nature of the American, but with some inaccuracy. I had some flashbacks to when I was studying and at once felt sorry for them and excited for the journey they had decided to undertake. At one point she asked a Chicago girl what the typical food was from her area. There was no answer. This was a question from a woman whose country is so steeped in the culture of food and where practically every town has a local dish, and she had directed it at a young girl who came from a country where steaks and burgers and twinkies are king. The kids showed off their great accents; just Spanish words in American. I called my parents in the UK and then Elena, half to check in that I had started OK and half to show these tourists that I could speak Spanish. Give them something to aim for. Inflate my ego.

I mistook the university building for another opulent cathedral and wandered aimlessly around the city's deliciously glamorous *casco histórico*. It is a hub of small, light, café-lined streets that suddenly give way to expansive architectural delights only for them to immediately sink out of view again. As rewarding as aimlessness was I thought I should head back to the striking plaza mayor in order to find a '*turismo*'.

'Do you have some timetables for León?

'To where?'

'León.'

'No.'

'Oh, OK.'

'You need to go to the bus station for them.'

'Is it close?'

'Well…20 minutes walk out of the city.'

'Great.'

Shrugs and smiles.

I entered the Cathedral Nueva/Antigua again, partly to escape the heat. The '*nueva*' part was holding a classical music concert at the time so I couldn't enter.

'To be honest, it'll look better tomorrow,' said an officious looking man in a little ticket kiosk noticing that I was eyeing up the entrance. He then bent forward and offered me another option. There was a pay-to-use staircase that led up into the towers. It was a part of the building that was oddly hidden away. The internal ones spat me out mid-way up the wall inside the cathedral giving a grand view of the nave. This walkway, known as a *triforium*, was originally used, as in all these buildings, as either a viewing platform or as an elevated position for monks and clergy to attend to the condition of the building. The external ones, of differing heights, offered an unparalleled view of the city and of the detail of the spires and domes.

Another splendid building was the Iglesia de San Esteban. The building itself was nothing to shout about, but the façade was sculptured beyond belief. Animals, trees, saints, and even a lucky frog adorned the front. You can stare at it for quite a while and not see anything. Legend has it that if you can find the frog unaided amid the mess you will be granted a wish. I couldn't find the bloody thing and I felt a momentary anger at the whoops of the German tourists standing next to me as they located the little beastie. Amphibians generally do a good job of evading me; in water, on land, in the garden, and now in stuccowork.

Salamanca in general felt like a Spanish version of Bath, for amid all its history there is an obvious and thriving student population. As I tucked into a dinner of typically un-Spanish *'pasta arrabiata'* I got a sense that the younglings were coming out to play. Café Erasmus was the place I had selected for the sake of a chuckle, but it turned out to be rather good. Erasmus, by the way, is the European scheme that sends university students abroad to study. I did it. It felt strange eating dinner alone in a restaurant. I kept writing in my notebook so people thought I was busy and important and not just friendless. 'Get used to it,' my conscience told me. I told my conscience to bugger off and pester somebody else. I sat awkwardly as passers-by stared at my food as they searched for somewhere to eat.

After a post-dinner trek I could barely keep myself on my flip-flopped feet so I decided it was time to call it a day and head back to the hostel. I walked through a sunset with its pastel pinks and purples. A brace of ducks and furry clouds of dancing flies were silhouetted as blurry runners ghosted past. I met my roommate later that evening as I prepared myself for a 9-hour corpse impression. He was an excitable primary school teacher called Ignacio and he spoke with a rapidity that made me feel good. He wasn't slowing down for poor Johnny Foreigner. He was taking a Master's in the city and was in the middle of having his exams. I asked him why he was staying in a hostel.

'I come every weekend. A lot of the people here are students. Either there's no space; it's too expensive or they live too far away to stay in the centre, so they stay and study here.'

We then talked a little about the weather. I showered, he went for a walk, I slept, I woke, and I never saw him again.

*   *   *   *

Steeling myself for the heat I strolled slowly back into Salamanca, keeping to the shade as best I could. For a couple of hours I walked around and tried to track down as many little churches and cathedrals as was possible. I paid a €3 entrance fee and had a guided tour around the old university building. Due to it being a Spanish language tour I was the only *guiri* there. Walking around I felt like I had stumbled onto the set of 'El Harri Potter: Y la Busca de la Paella Dorada'. It was a Hispanic Oxford, very prestigious and founded by the *Reyes Católicos* – Catholic Kings – in 1254. The university is comfortably the oldest in Spain and is the fifth oldest in the world. At one time, and for a long time, it was held in the same esteem as Oxford or Bologna. During the War of Independence twenty of the twenty-five colleges were destroyed and the university logically, and tragically, lost its position. Nowadays the results don't compare to those of the capital, but to say you studied at Salamanca still holds a lot of weight socially.

Inside the enormous chapel was the only piece of religious art to have ever affected me. It was a model of Jesus Christ after a whipping by his persecutors. The effect it had was two-fold:
1. It was shockingly life-like. Perfectly sculpted muscles, a worn-out expression on his face and veins in his glistening hands and arms.
2. I looked at it the moment the guide said 'here he is picking up his clothes after being whipped'. The brutality was so casual.

I don't believe in God or religion. Good consequences and bad consequences of belief aside I think it is just not true and, frankly, naïve. That even in this modern age people believe in a three-part magic man in the sky who oddly won't stop war or pestilence but will take time to talk to a crazy American in a dream seems astounding to me. But if there *was* a Jesus – and I think there is a fair chance there was some forward-thinking 'prophet' or social activist at that time – what he *may* have suffered at the hands of bestial and inhumane people *was* terrible. I know the story behind Jesus but this was the first time it hit me about what might have happened to a man who might have existed. It was nasty. Or might have been.

After a considerable period of aimless wandering I decided it would be best to flee the heat. Keeping as best as I could to the shade I absconded to the old cathedral yet again – a sanctuary of cool and free temperatures where I could give some peace to my flaming soles. I sat for maybe 40 minutes relaxing on a pew, planning the next few days of my trip.

I awoke from a siesta wanting wine and tapas. I had a cold shower, put on my shirt and entered a spot-lit Salamanca. Out were the tour groups and in were the cool and young again.
I sat down outside the 'Gatsby' bar.
'Ribera please,' – the wine of the region
'We only have Rioja.'
Confused, 'OK.' No tapas came.
It was then I noticed the 'I ♥ La Rioja' flag outside the entrance. Whether it was a special place or a random spot of wine-based nationalism I didn't know, but I was a little miffed at what I was drinking. Part of the reason I wanted to do this trip was to sample the regional cuisine of Spain. Food fuels both my gut and my obsession. And here I was in Castilla y León drinking a product of somewhere else.

There are nine wine regions within Castilla y León that also include the popular Toro and Rueda wine varieties. Though the region only received its *Denominación de Origen* status in 1982, wine has been made in the region for over 2,000 years. We all know those drunk, Bacchus-loving Romans couldn't resist a drink. Its rocky, green fields and fine tasting produce helped the area set up trade with other parts of the country. The increasing importance of the Ribera wines then resulted in the country's first quality regulations: the 'Ordinances of Castilla y León' in the 15th century. All this historical hype has ensured the persistent quality control of the region's sloshy output and the continued joy from the mouths of those who drink it.

I drank it faster than I perhaps should have, paid what I owed to the great American classic, and searched for somewhere tastier.

I called my friend Euan back in Madrid who I knew had previously taken his girlfriend to the city for Valentine's Day. An affable, funny, stoic Glasgow boy, it was nice to see he had it in him to be a romantic, although if pressed about the city he would probably just say 'aye, well, there's nice cathedrals and that'. He couldn't remember where he had eaten with his girlfriend, only that it was good. In the end I found a cheap and cheerful and, importantly, Spanish populated, little tapas bar called the 'Ruta de Plata', the Silver Route – an old Roman trade route that connected Mérida in Extremadura with Astorga in the north of Castilla y León and originally used to ferry tin from city to city. Despite its name, it was mostly just food on offer.

'I'll have a glass of Ribera and a menu please.'
'*Muy bien.*'
I extracted my notebook from my bag and proceeded to create my image. Glug went that smoky sanguine liquor. The effusive waiter twisted the bottle with a flourish and looked at me.
'Ah! You are writing a book?'
'Yes. My trip around Spain.'

He smiled, 'I'll get your menu now.'

I was sat near the back door of the bar. I heard the word '*toro!*' shouted to the kitchen. That would be my dish of dead bull. Waiting in the sultry air I was glad I wasn't surrounded by tourists. I know it sounds haughty but I felt I deserved to be surrounded by Spanish people and to be sitting opposite the neon-lit 'Jacko's Bar' offering litre drinks of beer without the need to be lumped in with the 'others'.

'I'm just gonna see if I got any money in my American account,' slurred a West Coast drawl.

'Nathan shouldn't have reacted in that way though,' added a staccato English accent.

'Well you know man, usually you can drink in a hostel but you can't get shitfaced.'

I wanted to join in with a witticism as the young guys used the ATM next to me, but I didn't. They staggered off. As I found eating alone an already fairly uncomfortable situation I decided to draw a line between me and litre beers at Jacko's and instead return to my lodgings.

*   *   *   *

The countryside that flickered past outside the windows of the 'Fecalbus' I took on the way to Zamora was a little different to what I had seen previously. There were still the same creamy wheat fields but they had opened up into vast endless plains. It looked like we were driving through the prairies of Middle America. Dotted around the plains just north of Salamanca were large, expensive looking family houses, sprinkler systems and stains of coloured flowers. After thirty minutes the bus was spat into England with hundreds of bushy trees and lolling hills blanketing the scene. Ten minutes after that we were again swallowed up by the US. We pulled into Zamora and I, with my overly small, light blue, girl's backpack digging into my shoulders, followed my guidebook's directions down to the centre of town.

Zamora is one of Castilla y León's provincial capitals although it didn't feel like one. I was walking through ugly suburbs and then smart old streets from about 10 o'clock in the morning onwards. And for the first while I barely saw anyone. The town was hushed and sleepy and quiet. I tried to walk with light footfalls so as to not disturb the bricks. Those people I did see were silver-haired and had walking sticks. For an important city it felt more like my little town in England. That's Maidenhead if you want to check my roots. When I did some research I found out that the populations of the two are actually quite similar. Maidenhead has around 60,000 people and Zamora around 67,000. I walked – with my backpack weighing heavy on my shoulders – past lots of tiny, hidden churches and a convent until I arrived at the plaza mayor, which had a church stuck right in the centre of it.

Whatever serenity slept in the city was soon obliterated when I got there. Out of the *ayuntamiento* – town hall – streamed traditionally costumed people with drums, trumpets and bagpipes, as well as people dressed as giants and dwarves. Suited children and parents were hurrying away to some other location and noise was all around. I had no idea what was happening so I decided to follow them. I managed to wedge myself in between a float of some female saint standing triumphant over a vanquished serpent and a band of jolly pipers. The road on which I walked, well, plodded, along was thickly strewn with lavender, the smell of which danced lightly on the still, cool air. Little old ladies were tossing fragrant petals from bags, shooting colours on the honey cobbles. More was revealed to me as we reached the end of the lane. Opening up in front of the human procession was the cathedral of Zamora around which were large crowds of people. There was the band that the earlier people were hurrying their children to form, there were the dressed up people and over there were scores of families looking resplendent: dads in suits, mums in skirts, grandparents in their finery and little boys and girls in shirts and white dresses holding baskets of petals. There was one final piece to the puzzle.

'*Perdona*, what is all this for?!'

'It's the fiesta de Corpus Christi.' – the catholic celebration that honours the Eucharist – the Holy Communion. This is my body, this is my blood etc. After a bit of people watching I peeled off, explored the ruins of the city's old castle and dozed for a while on a granite bench in the shade of a tree.

Walking back to the plaza mayor I had to make several diversions in order to avoid the long post-service procession that was slowly bulldozing through the centre of town as it marched from the belly of the cathedral. It was a strange thing. The dressed up traditional band were still playing as the human train snaked its way along the streets back to the main square. The snake passed people perching out of their windows, old women weeping lightly on the side of the road and a speaker system that was churning out choral music that some were singing along to. And there was me trying to squeeze by, looking inconspicuous with my baby blue rucksack on. Blending in was out of the equation.

I finally escaped to a little bar where I could have something to eat, something typical. I opted for *sopa de ajo* – garlic soup – a typical Zamoran dish. It was not as I expected it to be. I thought it might be some 'cream of garlic' style puree affair. It was in fact a lot more like the regional dish *sopa castellana*. It was an oily, thin, watery soup with soggy bread, bits of egg, ham and paprika floating about it in. And, of course, a lot of garlic. It looked like someone had evacuated themselves orally into a brown ceramic bowl; however the taste and smell were delightful. A subdued but present surge of garlic wheeled its way around my gums. Part soup, part mouthwash. The great social commentator Victoria Beckham once said in her infinite wisdom that Spain smelled of garlic. Although her frankly bad-taste remark was clearly offensive and wrong, the Spaniards do love the stuff and use it in an impressive quantity of dishes. So much so they have their soup as an edible love letter to the thing.

The place – with its creaking chairs, marble tables and humble wood panelling – started to fill up, mostly with old locals, so, fearing the colossal extent of bad damage one could do to the old dears with a swinging bag, I paid and left. I then spent over an hour waiting in the Zamora bus station – a depressing and unsettling place full of pathetic characters. One man was sleeping face down on a bench with his hairy arse cleft showing; one was slinked up in a corner holding a cigarette weakly and looking forlorn; another man was looking for cigarette butts in the dust swept up by a cleaner – 'you'll smoke nothing from that, asshole!', 'I can try! I am going to eat'; and one woman, who kept filling up a baby bottle with milk, adding a flavoured powder and knocking it back, kept spitting out sporadic outbursts of profanity all directed at some unknown 'wanker'. I took my bus and half-slept my way up to León in the North West of the region. The landscape became more scruffy and arable and all usefully sized spires and pylons were topped by storks and their nests. Other than that my two-hour trip north was a bit of a gluey blur.

I decided I was fed up with buses and so I scoped out the Renfe station as soon as I arrived. Having found a couple of handy evening trains available I trekked into the town. From the stations it is a more or less straight line over the river Bernesga via a bridge guarded by four stone lions and up. León had a very stately air to it. It was neither constantly beautiful like Salamanca nor ever ugly. The buildings were all very large and very tall, often with elegant facades. They entombed me as I walked up the pedestrianised streets into the historic quarter. León was a famous city in Spain both culturally and historically, but it wasn't blowing me away. I started to wonder what all the fuss was about until I reached the top, turned left into a square and then WHAM! There was an enormous and overblown cathedral standing there in an open square, proud as a...*león*. Two vast spires backed by a large atrium and coloured grey, it actually made me gasp. By gasp, I mean I swore to myself. Inside was equally as resplendent. Old-school bible bashers did have a knack for architecture. Stained glass windows, two tiers of them, splashed little pearls of multicoloured light over the walls whilst the hall and columns themselves were hit by dusty, yellow beams. This almost aromatic image, mixed with my hunger and fatigue, was quite heady.

There were two things I had wanted to try in the city but couldn't. The first was visiting the *barrio húmedo*, the 'wet quarter'; probably named for all the booze sloshing about. It is the bar area after all. The second thing was to try some *cicena*, a dried meat typical of the area. But because it was a Sunday mostly everything was shut up, apart from some cafés and bars. I huffily walked back through town, passing Gaudí's turreted, neo-gothic and, of course, modernist town mansion. I dejectedly decided to just move on to my last destination of the day and find a place to sleep. I took a late afternoon train – smelly and sweaty from toil and unfortunately sat next to an attractive Italian girl – southeast down to Valladolid.

The landscape was unremarkable except for the far off mountains of the northern regions. They would have to wait. The train trip itself was uneventful but full of characters: there was a little old lady with a wildly panting dog in a basket, she would warble motherly sounds to it and tap it on the nose when it attempted a bark; also a young boy who pretended to be asleep to (unsuccessfully) avoid paying and the ticket inspector herself whose 'posh' and distinctive Valladolid accent seemed to know half the train passengers as she clipped their tickets.

In Spain there are a variety of different accents. They aren't as marked or as varied as those of England or the US but they are present. The first major difference is the famous north/south divide between Andalucía and, well, pretty much the rest of the country, although the Andalucian accent does have a little in common with that of Extremadura. In Andalucía the basic and most obvious change is that they drop the 's' and gobble the ends of their words. So *'buenos días'* becomes *'bueno día'* and *'malgastado'* becomes *'mal ga'ta'o'*. According to some Spanish people I quizzed on the subject, the people from Galicia also talk a little differently. Apparently they are more like the British, with a more sonorous, sing-song intonation instead of the usual fairly monotone Castilian. I can't say I noticed this too much when I finally got there, but I tend to think it's best to listen to the opinions of the indigenous population. Finally, speed seems to differ. I have noticed, definitively, that peoples from the south of Spain speak far faster than those of the north. I don't know why, but it seems to hold true. Perhaps it's to ensure they spend as little time as possible out in the punishing sun. However, that isn't to say the Asturians all speak slowly. By standards of spoken English the Spanish generally all speak at a faster tempo, but I definitely noticed a difference between the fiery southerners and their more placid northern cousins.

I was trying out a website called couchsurfing in order to find some free accommodation for Valladolid. Couchsurfing is described as a 'hospitality exchange' network. At the time of writing it has well over 2.5 million members across 246 states and territories. The general idea is that if someone has a 'couch' or spare bed they offer it up as a free alternative to a traveller instead of them staying in a hotel. As well as a bed hosts often take time out of their days to show the visitor around their town, cook meals, lend maps and brochures or, at the very least, have conversations. In general these people go above and beyond the call of normal hospitality. The traveller pays nothing, but it is good practice to offer to cook or, if nothing else, keep the place clean.

As of 20:20 I had received no news from either of the two guys I had messaged and my train was to pull into Valladolid at 20:58. I called Euan again and he told me that there was a message on my webpage that translated as:

'I have just left my girlfriend and have no desire to see people these days.'
Poor bloke, I thought to myself, but still, not very useful for helping
me find somewhere to sleep!

Irked by the fickle nature of love I pulled into Valladolid and walked
in the direction, as usual, of the *plaza mayor*, came across the tourist
information centre and found it was shut. Outside – a sign of how
modern the regional capital was – was an enormous touch screen. I
pressed the accommodation section and scrolled down to the one
star options. With my phone camera I took photos of some of the
details and set off hunting and feeling quite confident in a 21st
century kind of way. After about twenty minutes I found the first
hostel. Some lights were on. I started first by ringing the contact
number I had in the photo. It rang out. I then tried buzzing on the
telecom system on each floor. Again, no answer. A little
disheartened I picked up my bag, huffed whimsically, and pressed
on to the other one. I spent another twenty minutes trying to find
the road *Ramón y Cajal* but to this day I am certain it exists on maps
only, and not in real life.

It was beginning to darken up above me and I started to worry a
little. I started walking around aimlessly in the area around the *plaza
mayor*, three-star, four-star, until I came across a jumble of yellow
street signs directing road traffic towards various hotels. One caught
my eye, 'Hostal Lima'. Not a hotel, a *hostal*. The signs then took me
on a twenty-five minute, seemingly endless, rabbit warren route until
finally I lumbered and creaked up to the right place. Smiling
triumphantly I hobbled up to the door. It was locked and all the
lights were off and there was no button. Hostal Lima was dead. It
was 10:30 on a Sunday, and I had yet to find a place to lay my head.
For the first time in many years I whimpered to myself. I also didn't
know where I was in the city, which didn't exactly help my situation.
Even though it was a modern city and civilization was everywhere, it
was momentarily scary. I phoned Euan.

He did some quick Internet research for me. The only result – that may have not even had rooms – was a three star hotel, at €32 a night. I decided to give the area around plaza mayor one last go before parting with so much money so early on. My feet were hot with fatigue, my neck burned from the bag straps and my heart and sense of adventure were sinking quicker that a certain doomed ship. I saw one place hiding in an alleyway, checked the book, four star, and then another dark little building, five star. Finally I returned, desperate, to the one star hostel again and all but leant on the intercom system. Flats one through six were receiving the buzzes of my frustration. I didn't care. In the reflection of the window a few families were enjoying the last of the evening's warmth at the *El Rincón Del Val* restaurant, a couple of kids were playing football with the waiter and a middle-aged man was amusing his little daughter. How lovely for them I thought, sardonically, as I picked up my bag to continue the search.

'Excuse me, were you trying at the hostel?' It was the man with the little girl.

'Yeah, I was.'

'And they didn't answer?'

'No.'

'This is always happening! I'm from across the road.'

He pulled out his phone, told me to wait, and spent a while trying to get hold of them for me.

'They are my friends…' he whispered to me as waited on the line

They didn't answer.

'Are they stupid or what!?' he said to himself.

He regarded me in my white t-shirt, shorts and ill-fitting bag and then tried another person nearby who he knew had a hostel. There was no answer there either.

'I don't understand this. They're all idiots!'

After multiple buzzings at the hostel we managed to get some invisible Samaritan to open the front door; probably some innocent tourist plucked sludgily from their bed. Thanking the man I trudged up the steps to the third floor and rang the bell. I then rang a further three times. Flumping my head into my chest and exhaling noisily I descended the staircase and opened the front door. The man who had been helping was no longer there. I suppose he thought I had succeeded and left me to my own devices. Dilemma: do I close the door and hope to find him again or do I stay inside, curl up on the stairs and hope the patrons come back and feel sympathetic towards my dire situation? I closed the door and wandered forlornly over to the little restaurant of the tiny square and sat down on a nearby stone bench.

After a couple of minutes the man reappeared from inside and a brief euphoria bloomed inside me.
'No luck?'
'No.' I answered, adding a sad face.
'I don't believe this. One moment.'
He went back inside for a couple of minutes and then materialised with a pushchair, a baby, and a wife.
'We are going to see if they are in the bar, wait here.'
I did what he said and sat. Shivers began to frill over me as my sweaty t-shirt took in the evening chill while the restaurant bid farewell to its last customers and started to pack itself away. The man returned.
'It turns out they have gone to the theatre tonight.'
'Ah...so do you work in the restaurant then?' I enquired.
'It's mine, I own it.'
He tried his friend again, this time with success. He smiled and held up a finger, nodding positively. He hung up and clicked his head sideways signalling to follow.
'There's a hostel just up here. The guy's like family and it's a similar price to this one.'
We walked up to my new home.
'I told my friend he owes me a wine!' he laughed.
'After this I think I owe *you* a wine!'
'Ha! Don't worry about it.'

At the door I was buzzed in.

'There you go.'

'Thank you so much for this.'

'No problem.'

'What's your name by the way?'

'José. This guy's called José too.'

'I'm Luke.'

I smiled as genuinely as I could as we shook hands and then I disappeared inside. I paid and greeted José number two, got to my room, disrobed and fell, half-dead, onto the bed.

*   *   *   *

I slept deeply and well and awoke to the sound of a tiny dog's footsteps tapping past outside my door. I surveyed my room a little more. It looked like it had taken its own initiative and left my grandmother's house for sunnier climbs. Floral curtains, a general hue of off-yellow, some peeling posters on the walls and lots of wooden furniture. Under normal holiday circumstances it would not be considered 'attractive' but its homeliness was comforting.

Returning to the station, this time thankfully without my big bag, I took a local bus to the town of Peñafiel. I had a conversation with a gentle, old man who got on at the dusty town of Tudela de Duero. He, in that old person way, bent himself into position, lowered a little, and dropped into the seat with a content sigh.

'Good day,' he said.

'Hello.'

We sat in silence a while.

'Where are you getting off? I don't want to be any trouble for you to get out.'

'I'm heading to Peñafiel.'

'Ah, well that's ok, that's after me. I'm heading to Quintanilla de Arriba,' he smiled wistfully.

'Do you know how many stops before I get to Peñafiel?'

'Oh yes of course. You want to stay on another two after Quintanilla.'

Thirty minutes after leaving Valladolid and one really is in wine country. The first hint was that all the villages had *'venta de vino'*, 'wine on sale', painted on the side of buildings or slapped across signs and banners. I would have loved to have had a car that day and zip around the little towns and wineries loading the boot up with bottles. We had entered the land of the *bodegas*. Miles upon miles of elegantly lined grapevines, light green and juicy, spread out from the road like a blanket. They perched on hillsides or marched their way up to colossal and overblown wineries with names like Casa Vega, Casa Sicilia and Viña Mayor; each of them obviously trying to out do the other with regards to making themselves attractive to visitors. Alcoholic peacocks. It was very appealing countryside. My first thoughts on Peñafiel however were of intrigue and sizzling disappointment.

We swung into the silent village of Quintanilla de Arriba. My silver haired companion heaved himself up on his cane and patted me on the arm gently before leaving.

'Remember, another two stops.'

The town itself was not particularly nice looking – although it did sport a few churches – and, as seems to be the wont of Spain, everything seemed shut. The most visually sumptuous thing in the area is the castle, el Castillo de Peñafiel. Laid out like some stony crest (or 'beached ship' as is the preferred description), it stands overlooking the whole wide plain from every angle. The amazing thing is its dimensions: 210m long but only 25m wide. A tube of castle. I had read, on the bus because I am an idiot, that the castle and corresponding *'museo del vino'* were open Tuesday to Sunday. It was a Monday. I walked up the side of the hill following an unofficial and often self-made route panting in the heat, startled by blackbirds and smiling at butterflies, until I reached the summit. It was expectedly shut. However, at the top I was sweetly rewarded to some extent by great views of the area and a nice, cooling breeze.

Following the signs for *'información'* I reached the *plaza de coso*. This little nook perked me up a little. It was a broad square expanse lined by pretty wooden houses, hidden from the outside and with a view of the castle sailing nowhere in the distance. I wasn't going to allow my trip to become blotched by disappointments any longer so in the *información* I bought a winery *'abono'*, voucher, for five euros. It entitled me to a session at one of eight bodegas the following day. Also the castle and its wine tasting area were open the following day too so things were picking up, I thought.

The Gothic-Mudéjar Iglesia y Convento de San Pablo sat squat and covered in brick arched windows. Inside, even though they were closing, the man cleaning up let me have a quick walk around then gave me a bit of history. In the church (with sections from the 12th, 16th, 17th and 18th centuries) there was a pretty chapel that he insisted was interesting for two reasons:

1. Before the War of Independence it housed the tomb of the 'Señor de Peñafiel' or Don Juan de Miguel whose uncle was the great Spanish king Alfonso X. The Don in question was the chap who had ordered the building built in the first place. His tomb was later looted by the French during the war as they wanted to steal the sleeping man's gold sword. We shared a 'God! French eh?' set of raised eyebrows.
2. It also contained some artefacts that eventually ended up in the Louvre. The man told me excitedly that he had gone to see them there and got a real sense of pride on seeing *'origene: Peñafiel, Espagne'* printed on the little plastic caption cards.

I promised I'd check the following day, though I never did.

Searching for somewhere to eat and drink wine in Peñafiel was a harder task than I would have imagined. The first place I entered was a local dive with flies and pollen clouds flitting around inside. However I *had* entered and, due to my debilitating politeness, sat down and ordered despite not wanting to. I had a quick glass of cold Ribera there and then, as quick as I could, spat the fluff out of my mouth, paid up and briskly strode over to another, still local, but more charming place called Bar La Glorieta. For €3.20 I had a glass of cool wine – for red wine should never be served warm in Spain – a small dish of mixed olives, cocktail onions and pickles and some (stale) bread with ham and tortilla.

Back in Valladolid I relaxed in my hostel for a while as I tried to soothe a heat-induced headache that was no doubt slightly exacerbated by the large glasses of red wine. I also left a message on an answering machine for the marketing director of the Zifar winery. As I was snoozing to my mobile phone's tinny speaker's best efforts to produce some of my favourite music the phone itself rang. It was an unknown Spanish number.

'Hello,' I answered groggily.

'Hi there Luke? My name is Diana. You rang Zifar earlier. Sorry the phone was in the car and I couldn't answer.'

'Uhuh, yeah.' I tried to remember how my mouth worked.

'Basically all I need to know is when you want to arrive for the visit.'

I rubbed my eyes and tried to quickly come to my senses and understand what was happening. Oh yes, the wine people.

'Is four o'clock OK?' I asked.

'How many are in your group?'

'Just me.'

'Ok. Your name?'

'Luke, as in Skywalker.'

'Ok, so that's Luke as in Skywalker for four o'clock. You know how to find us?'

'More or less.'

'Perfect. See you tomorrow at four. Bye.'

'Ciao.'

In English we could say 'bish, bash, bosh'. In Spanish we could say 'bien atado', well tied up.

I dined in a small, and very popular, place called *'Taberna sabor taurino'*, Tavern of the bull flavour. It was cheap so I ordered two dishes, *salchichas de Zarantan en vino de Toro* and *patatas rellenas con salsa Taurina*, thinking they would be small portions to go alongside their fairly small price tags. The first, the sausages, had a subtle taste of red wine and were served with chips and a fried egg. That alone would have been enough to see me through the night but then I got my potatoes. A house special, they were deep fried balls of mashed potato stuffed with meat served in a sauce similar to *bravas* (a sort of spicy tomato syrup). The bar girl, noticing the ever messier nature of my eating, brought me some paper napkins. Nice.

Quite unexpectedly my little tavern took on quite an international flavour. Outside and across from me sat a group of pretty French girls who had the air of Erasmus about them. Passing me and then *entering* my little tavern was a group of maybe five Brits from the north of England. I once again fought hard to suppress my mouth from letting a greeting slip out. Shouts and laughs briefly erupted as the tavern's door swung open. Feeling the soft sting of loneliness and boredom I initiated a chat with the waitress.
'So, do you get many foreign people here?'
'Yes.'
'Where are the majority from?'
'We get a lot of English and French.'
She told me how there were some tourists but that the bulk were Erasmus students and that this area was a typical one for 'going out'. We talked a little about Valladolid and I mentioned how it felt different from the other provincial capitals.
'It feels like a mini Madrid,' I offered.
'Exactly!' she pounced 'I mean it *is* the capital of the entire Castilla y León region so it is bigger, and I guess feels bigger.'
'They say Valladolid is the place with the best spoken Spanish.'

'Well this is the home of Castilian Spanish, so technically this *is* where it is spoken best,' she smiled, 'but every time a little worse eh!' She picked up some plates and went inside leaving a space where I noticed that the French girls were all looking at me. They quickly went back to eating their plate of chips as I met their gaze. Two gangly American boys with a jug of sangria came out and starting talking loudly and overly using the word 'dude'. My calm bubble burst. So after dropping a few extra coins on the receipt I left.

*   *   *   *

In the morning I walked through town past the grey, monolithic and still unfinished cathedral to the bus station. My route took me once again through Valladolid's small, but pretty, park. A group of young school children were giggling at pigeons; water trickled peacefully down chutes or out of fountains; septua and octogenarians were taking mid-morning strolls or sitting on benches twirling their canes under a blanket of vibrant green while peacocks splayed their plumage and called their attractive squeezed-cat call. I was reminded when walking through there just how fine the Valladolid people were. The women, like Salamanca, were impossibly beautiful; the old folk were smart; and all ages were elegant. I could see Valladolid's wealth in its people. Of course I was in the centre, but as centres go it was doing very well for itself.

Yet another disappointment waited for me in Peñafiel that day. The wine tasting part of the *museo provincial del vino* ticket was only held at weekends. This absolutely vital piece of information was not mentioned in the guidebook so I paid six euros and walked around the museum. I had a guided tour of the castle itself but wasn't given any wine. It was very interesting but not much when compared to some of the great British ones: Windsor, Conwy or Bodiam for example. The most interesting part of the tour was when the lady pointed out to us the Protos winery down in the valley on the outskirts of the town. Protos was a firm favourite of my mouth and belly back in Madrid. I had previously thought that Protos' *bodega* was far out of town so I was surprised and a little miffed when I found out it was only a fifteen-minute walk away.

The building itself was designed by the English architect Richard Rogers and resembles four wave-like undulating roofs, all terracotta red. Opposite was a castle-style entrance that presumably led into the hill where their barrels were kept. I rang the number and left a message with them in the vain hope that I would be able to fell two wineries in one afternoon. I wasn't hopeful as on my little *abono* voucher it read for Protos: 'groups of at least 8 for the tour' and I didn't think I could pull that off even with a variety of voices and some sticks stuck up into old t-shirts. I had time to kill. I chickened out of going into a local, busy sounding restaurant in fear that silence would lay itself down and all eyes would turn on me. Instead, I sat in a little park and listened to the birdsong until it was time to visit my *bodega* – Zifar.

The building was closer than I had expected and, with everything naturally shut, I waited outside. It was windy and I felt cold. At four o'clock I rang the doorbell, waiting patiently like a schoolchild to see the headmaster. A door further down the building squeaked, opened and a man stepped out and hailed me. His name was Sergio, the current owner. I was ringing the wrong bell.
'Good morning! This is the exit' he smiled.

Sergio was maybe mid-forties and greying. He had a longish ponytail and wore a rumpled blue shirt, some jeans and a pair of scruffy trainers. He looked neither wealthy nor financially needy. Just a normal bloke in charge of a vineyard. The building itself was the ex-Guardia Civil headquarters. It was a large cream-coloured, official-looking, brick building that loomed authoritatively over the tiny street it was on.
'We are a small bodega. We produce maybe 60,000 bottles a year. The average for the Ribera region is 120-150,000 and a large one

may produce 300,000 bottles or more,' he said casually, waving his arm lethargically in a Mediterranean manner.

'Is that a lot?'

'Well, even a small producer in La Rioja can produce one million.'

This may account for the fact that in the UK almost all Spanish wine is Rioja: we are the biggest buyer of the wine, claiming about 36% of the total exports and buying almost thirty million litres a year. At Zifar, despite the space the region offers, they don't have pretty fields of grape vines surrounding the factory with teams of South American workers in gloves plucking the juicy fruit from their homes. Instead they have scoped out and bought various plots of land all within a 50km radius of their headquarters. The best land with the best soils. Zifar is a quality, not quantity, brand.

'Unfortunately the good, and natural, materials cost more' he said, matter-of-factly.

Bright, straw-coloured barrels made of American and French oak, gleaming fermentation tanks, a watered and treed garden above the cellar to regulate humidity and temperature, combined with a small harvest equals an expensive wine. Those barrels are important and the effect they have on the wine was greater than I had previously thought. The barrel actively affects the wine. It cleans it. Leaving the wine in the barrel allows a natural filtering process to occur as any sediment or impurities sink to the bottom. The slightly porous nature of the barrel also allows a slow process of oxidisation to occur. Then there is the wood itself, which alters and adds a distinct flavour to the wine.

'I see the barrel like the chef's spices, it adds a little flavour.'

After five, twelve or eighteen months in the barrel you have wine ready to go into the bottles. It's quite a process.

'Everything affects the wine,' he began as he surveyed his underground barrelling hall, one hand on his hip, the other rubbing his stubble, 'the type of soil, the weather, the variety of grape, the efficacy of the fermentation process, the number of pips in the

grapes, the quality of the skins, the barrels, where the trees are from, the length of time in the barrel, the temperature, everything!'
'Have you ever had any bad harvests?'
'Of course. Almost every year we lose a lot of good fruit when there is an unpredictable freeze.'
'What do you do with the freeze-ruined grapes?'
'Make wine.'
'Oh.'
'But not good wine,' he smiled.
We moved from the cold, atmospheric cellar upstairs to the tasting area.
'How do you deal with the competition then?' I asked.
'Well there are over 350 winemakers in the region; almost 200 in Ribera del Duero. So it's *always* a struggle.'

The tasting room was like a very fancy London flat's kitchenette area, with a central island, swivel chairs and lots of shiny chrome. This was no stuffy, traditional, old winery. This was one of the many producers bringing one of history's oldest drinks glugging its way proudly into the modern age. I tried three of his wines: a young, five-month one and a couple of older ones. He taught me that if a red wine is pink and if, when you tilt the glass, the edge of the wine nearest the mouth has a bluish hint you have a young wine. I tilted and saw it to be true. If you do the same process with an older red, which will have a more firmly carmine, almost blood, colour to it, the edge will instead have an orange hue. As I was the only visitor and, I like to think, because we were getting on so well, he was happy to keep pouring us out more and more of the wines that were held back for the *degustación* sessions. As we sipped ruminating with every swallow we talked about the visitors to Zifar, my trip and life story; his plans for expansion and then about wine itself.
'Many think wine is just this. A drink in a glass. Then they open the door and, phwah! Sweet wines, Sherries, ice wines. It's a whole world!'

He was a man whose passion was infectious and it was a shame to have to say my goodbyes. As he opened the exit door he stopped and looked back in his head for some dusty book of knowledge.

'Nice to you,' he stuttered unsurely in English.

'Nice to *meet* you,' I said with a smile.

'That's it! Nice to meet you, nice to meet you.'

We shook hands and I caught my bus back to mini-Madrid comfortably light-headed as the sun had started to back down from its midday position. Despite the rocky patches Castilla y León had proven to be both a breezy walk in the park and a baptism of fire. Only thirteen more to visit.

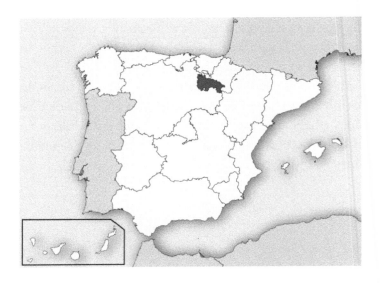

Prehistoric Viticulture

Logroño – Haro – Enciso

The following morning was cold and wet. I didn't find it annoying though. It acted as a soothing balm to my head and skin that had for days been torn at by the sun and heat. The bus from Valladolid was very comfortable but a little odd. Within minutes the driver welcomed us formally over a speaker system and then put on a film – "Interception" starring Richard Gere. There was no Spanish dubbing and the little old ladies were sharing confused glances and started clucking to each. Instead he quickly selected "Bridges of Madison Country" with Meryl Streep and Clint Eastwood, which, luckily, *was* a dubbed version. I was so pleased at the choice…

The road east out from Valladolid towards Soria trickled alongside the Duero River through scenery I had got quite used to; there was Peñafiel again with its castle sailing off in the distance. A while after that pilgrimage our bus started to leave the wine area and drifted through some strange territory. From the right side of the bus off to the river was the standard picture of green fields and trees. From the left however, the land had started to take on the aspect of the badlands of America, though smaller and greener. Most of the towns here were sweet enough, but weathered and a little malnourished. After a brief stop in the Soria bus station the road shot north and after half an hour speared into the community of La Rioja. The route from Soria took me through some of the loveliest scenery I had seen up to that point.

We first passed through a long, low and wide valley floor. Miles out in all directions were thousands of trees and masses of woodland. We passed tiny, forgotten villages that sat like small, ruddy-red islands in a vast pea-green sea. The road then coiled up into the Sierra de Cebollera, and the hills that were previously in the distance suddenly became more imminent. We snaked our way up into dark, foreboding, but gloriously pretty heights; passed enormous, sombre lakes that lapped stygianlike at atmospheric slopes; and saw tiny hamlets slotted dramatically into hillsides and deep gullies cut by small rivers. If it weren't for the little Spanish pueblos you could think you were in the Lake District. We reached an altitude where we skirted the base of grey clouds that were hanging low overhead before dropping back down towards the capital of La Rioja. We left the Sierra through a series of deep, craggy ravines and finally settled on the long, straight stretch of the N-111 that took us into Logroño.

The first three hours in the capital were plagued by the same problems that seemed to constantly torment my trip. Everything useful was shut and the looming threat of having nowhere to sleep taunted me. Logroño was certainly not unattractive but initially it was a slight disappointment after the beauty of its countryside. This negative image may have been slightly fostered by my worsening mood and the bad weather broiling in the skies. The people were also different; more rugged like the countryside, less refined, less attractive and a little stouter than their more southerly cousins. All of this, together with the slowest service I have ever received at a Spanish bar – fifteen minutes to order a drink, thirty to order food – meant that I was having a hard time liking the place. I also had had another problem with couchsurfing so I was left, sitting with a generous glass of Rioja wine, putting off having to pay at least 25 euros a night for a hostel and wondering what the hell I was going to do. In retrospect it was clear that I had yet to find my stride and was still in my petulant, naïve student-traveller mode. 'Well *why* aren't there really cheap hostels?'; '*why* isn't everything open when I want?'; '*why* is the weather being mean to me?', and other such whines.

It was the week of San Bernabé, which included two celebrations: the 'Day of La Rioja' (the day I had arrived) and the 'Fiesta de San Bernabé'. The former is to celebrate La Rioja's becoming an autonomous community in 1982. The latter is a time to celebrate the victory of a small force of resident Spanish people that held off a thirty thousand-strong invading French army under the command of Andre de Foix, Lord of Lesparre. The two days of celebration are, of course, stretched out for the whole week to make sure the people of the region can truly enjoy themselves.

All around the *casco histórico* were stalls selling food, people selling balloons, children's rides, and residents dressed in all manner of surreal medieval garb. I sat in the *plaza del aples* where the *concatedral* (co-cathedral) stands. Ornate but subtle, it was an attractive building but nothing about it made me gawp like those grand God-houses of Castilla y León. After my second glass of wine I had lost a little hope and was about to call a hostel for at least one night when Elena, still busying away back in Madrid, rang me.

'Lukey, I have some good news. There's a message from a Fernando that says his guest isn't actually coming until the 12th and if you are still interested in staying he has left his number and address.'

I slammed my glass down, nearly smashing it, and smiled the broadest smile.

'I am lucky to have you aren't I?'

'Yes, yes you are. Have fun now!'

She sent me the details and I texted Fernando. I got a response within about 15 minutes. It turned out that he was outside and actually just down the road, having a beer with a few of his friends. I texted him:

'What would you prefer I do? I don't want to bother your friends. I can wait if it is easier.'

Two seconds later he responded Spanishly:

'Come along!'

I sat at a little outdoor bar with Fernando, four of his friends and a little baby called Guillermo. They were very warm and intelligent and all in their mid-thirties. As we fought our way through the first awkward minutes – 'who is this guy? Is that a girls bag? Why is his face so red?' – I was made very welcome. One of the guys even bought me a beer. All the while the festival noised on behind us. Fernando had a roundish head with very short, receding, hair and a greying stubbly beard that gripped the lower half of his face. He was quiet, pensive and, initially, I thought, quite serious. In reality it was just that he was quicker to smile than to laugh. He talked and behaved with an easy grace that put all those around him at ease, including me.

BANG! And then trumpets and drums.

'That was a musket!' offered one of Fernando's cohort.

BANG! And then a wisp of smoke.

'You see, they are re-enacting the battle of this city when the French tried but failed to invade.'

Men were walking past us along the street in armour, with helmets, banners and spears.

'When was this battle then?' I asked.

'Pff, I don't know man. I –'

'1521,' interjected Javier.

'Right,' I said, impressed at the speed of the answer.

Good-natured conversation had awakened an inquisitive-eyed Guillermo. Mum and dad decided it was time he went back to his French-vanquishing bed and get some more consolidated rest. A conversation in Spanish with Spaniards was both never dull and never quiet so beds are important for babies. As we walked back to Fernando's flat I decided to press him for an opinion on his heritage.

'For you, what is it to live in La Rioja?'

'Nothing really. Not like if you are from The Basque Country or Cataluña. I love La Rioja; it's my home, my land. But I have lived in different places so I'm not especially tied to *this* place.'

We arrived at his flat a gentle fifteen-minute walk later. It was a straight line away from the historic centre and had a view to the river and hills. Inside were two floors, two Siamese cats and a spare room – so much for the 'couch', I thought. He gave me some clean, fluffy, towels, cooked a pasta dinner and allowed me to use his Internet. It was times like these when my faith in the goodness of people was restored. I didn't know Fernando and he didn't know me, yet I was allowed to set up shop inside his personal living space. The initially skittish cats, Bolucha and Pupilo, were slowly warming to me as the sun sank evenly over the not-too distant, wind-turbined bumps of neighbouring País Vasco. Pupilo jumped up on the sofa, covering everything in long hairs and padded over to see what I was writing in my journal. Bolucha would tip toe ever so slightly nearer, emboldened by his friend's bravery. Then I would shift my weight and he would skuttle away, slipping on the smooth wooden flooring.

I was so very lucky and as I lay my head down I wondered how much longer it would last before disaster struck in some 'it's been coming to you for a while' kind of way.

*   *   *   *

The following morning Fernando had already left for work. The early sun threw dots of yellow light through the blinds onto the wall opposite. I could have stayed in bed forever. It was one of those 50% mornings; some sun, some cloud. I have to admit that without the burden of back pain and accommodation woes, and in the morning sun, Logroño seemed far more appealing. How fickle and unsubjective I am. I strolled at leisure down to the bus station and hopped on the 10:15 to Haro. The land between the capital and its eastern neighbour is real Riojan countryside: gentle but sweeping hills all covered with violently green grape land. In the distance was the 'Cantabrian Range' of País Vasco hanging large and aggressive in the dark of cloud shadow and overlooking the placid fields of La Rioja. A guardian of grapes.

My first impression of Haro was grim. The bus didn't drop me in a bus station as I had hoped, but instead I found myself walking blind and mapless, in the rain, on the east side of town. The directions in the book were from a bus station, not from a nameless bus stop so I decided it would make sense that I followed the signs to the centre. The outer part of Haro was like all the other outer parts of all the towns in Spain that I had visited, but *more* unwelcoming. The streets were lined with ugly blocks of flats, which, in the rain, had taken on a shade of grey that I will call 'depressive' and all the shops were either weird ones selling accessories and tat or uncharacteristically gleaming hairdressers and butchers. Fortunately I soon reached the centre and the ugliness abated. Although it was still quite grey the centre had a sort of miniature nobility to it. By that I mean that it looked grand even though all the buildings were very small. In the end I found the place rather endearing. A little hub of nice smothered by a carpet of horrid. Like a reverse apple; everything you want is on the inside.

Despite my improved opinion of the place it didn't change the fact that I was still wandering around essentially lost; ever aware that I needed to find the winery I was meant to visit by 12pm. Time was ticking away but I didn't really feel confident in sticking to one direction and walking.

'What are you looking for?' said a denim-clad woman with a cigarette between her lips, noticing my confusion.

'Erm...' I scrabbled for my book 'Plaza Florentino Rodriguez, the *turismo.'*

'Ah! Carry on down this road. On your left you'll see a big staircase, it's at the bottom.'

She was right, it was. I entered, murmured *'Hola'* to the staff, and picked up a colourful paper map. I couldn't help but notice a late middle-aged English couple trying in vain to get something and to be understood.

'Carta? This is a carta?' said the English man unsteadily.

'Qué? Perdón?'

'Carta?' said the woman in full brimming English accent.

'Do you need a hand?' I offered, feeling a little sorry for both parties.

'Do you know the Spanish for map?' the gent asked conspiratorially.

'Un mapa,' I said to him.

'Mapa?'

'Yes, *un mapa.'*

The tourist office girl smiled and handed them a map and some brochures. I passed them again outside. They thanked me for my help, what little it was, and we talked for a few minutes. They were a middle class retired couple from the south of England who were camping around País Vasco. They had just come from the city of Vitoria, in the south of the Basque Country, and popped into Haro to see if there was anything to see. Easy when you have a car, I thought to myself.

Thanks to my new, very clear map I easily found my way to the *bodega* that I had arranged to visit: Lopez de Heredia (LDH) whose principal brand is the very expensive Viña Tondonia wine. That day in Haro was an example of when a day can turn from abhorrent to resplendent within minutes. I had joined the twelve o'clock Spanish tour due to time restrictions, but was glad I did. It probably added an extra hour and half onto the visit and provided a wealth of information, opinions and debate, which may not have necessarily been present, had I joined the scripted English language tour with the other tourists.

In the waiting room I saw the previous, English language, tour group relaxing in the bar. Brash, rich Germans were buying bottles and crates and postcards – generally throwing their money around – whilst the Spaniards waited their turn.
'Come on, we now go!' Barked a plump Spanish woman as she led the Germans back to their tour bus (I swear I heard sheep noises). And so we were left, about ten of us, with María José, the current owner of the winery.

After a brief history of the place we went into the fermentation and pressing room. On entering through the door from the outside one is hit by a warm blast of air that smells strongly of alcoholic wine and yeast. It was a gorgeous smell, at once winey, bready and a little Marmitey. An American couple shuffled in after a period 'sorry we're late. We're from America so it took us a little while to get here!' Unlike the shiny modern equipment at Zifar in Peñafiel, the enormous tanks in LDH were the original wood cast ones – impressive given that the *bodega* has been going since 1877. María José stressed that the whole point of LDH, the last family run bodega in Haro, is that the process is natural and that they continue the processes as they had been done for the last hundred years. After the fermentation room is the area where they made the '*barricas*', barrels. An attractive, tall room, it looked like a carpenter's workshop and was full of rusty tools, planks of wood and smelled heavily of oak and recent, warm shavings.

One character stood out during the tour. I am going to call him 'Mr jovial/bald twat'. I could never work out if he was being funny and interested or just a cocky prick. I think he was the latter. Lots of arsey questions were infiltrated, ended or interrupted with his own opinions. I got the impression that he made his own wine and thought he was God's gift to wine making, maybe even coming to the bodega with some subconscious agenda. María José valiantly answered every question and rebutted any point he was wrong on while I stood there either trying to understand the words coming out of his annoying mouth or wanting to smack him in his annoying face.

The third stage was the underground cellars. Again we were hit with a yeasty wine smell, but this time it smelled older and more ancient. We were maybe seventeen metres underground in a web of interconnecting tunnels that fanned out in different directions, some of which extend up to one hundred and thirty metres. They were dimly lit with century old lighting and there were hundreds upon hundreds of barrels full of wine, glowing like honeycomb in a dark hive. Some sat in neat clumps along the sides and some were stacked high forming long atmospheric corridors of oak. One such corridor led us into a special room lit by one old chandelier. From the bulbs cobwebs hung lifelessly, some wisping their way down to touch a dusty old table in the centre. Around us on the walls, in recesses, were shelves of bottles. Aged bottles, covered in the dust and webs of time. The room stank of mould and faintly of liquor. This was where they kept their most ancient bottles, the oldest having been bottled in 1885. Bottles there could easily fetch way up into the tens of thousands of euros but many aren't drinkable. Most from the 1940s are, but according to María José it gets flaky the further back you go from there. Corking and oxidation are both enemies of wine and after 100 years I wouldn't be surprised if something went wrong.

'If you buy one of our wines now, it'll keep for 40 years easily.'

So there's a tip. Anyone interested in prospective wealth, buy a Tondonia and in fifty years you could make some big money with LDH.

The final part of the tour was the tasting. Mr Bald Twat had finally shut up and was now Mr Jovial. Maybe I had wrongly judged him.

'This wine is great with red meats,' said María José.

'So why do we have nuts instead of steaks?' said Baldy.

Cue laughter. Cocky prick.

We sampled an eighteen-year-old white wine, a thirteen-year-old red wine and finally a nineteen-year-old *gran reserva*. All of them were extraordinary. The aromas were bodaciously fruity and dramatically deep. The tastes were complex due to their age and quality. At once I was squishing berries between my teeth whilst smoking a fine cigar. The flavours lingered on my gums and played on my tongue long after I had swallowed. I was content and stayed as long as I could, as I wanted to try and pilfer another glass of the white.

A quiet and pensive man from the País Vasco, called José Antonio, filled up his glass and then, noticing my greedy eyes, filled mine too. We talked a little about wine and about how in my country we drink a lot of it but, lamentably, don't produce much. As we were talking, mostly everyone left until it was just José Antonio, Juan (one of María José's relatives) and me in the tasting room, basically just talking about booze. María José then strode back in and finally the news was broken to her that I was English. I had shyly kept my mouth shut during the tour as I hadn't wanted to draw attention to myself and then be paranoid about getting asked a question at the one moment when I *wasn't* listening or *hadn't* understood, thus looking a fool.

'So, shall we all go to lunch then?' she said, frankly with a matter of fact smile.

'Can I?' I asked with an arched brow.

'Of course!'

'...OK then!'

This was not a trip about saying 'no' to things.

We walked out of the bodega into the overcast car park, picked up another family member, Pedro, and all five of us squeezed into a Land Rover and dropped back into the town centre. We strolled confidently into a four-star hotel called *Los Agustinos* and found a large white-clothed table. I was being 'invited' to lunch in a four-star hotel restaurant and I couldn't quite get to grips with the speed of what was happening. The *á la carte* menu was around 40€, and that was without wine. Speaking of wine, we had three bottles of the Lopez vintages. Two whites and a red, all three were glorious, tasted expensive and complemented all the food I put into my mouth.

In brief my (free) meal was:

Appetiser – selection of Spanish meats

Starter – Wild mushroom risotto

Main Course – Sirloin medallions with potato gratin, sun-dried tomatoes and a red wine reduction.

Dessert – cheese selection

Post-dessert – Coffee, chocolate and biscuits.

The group itself was an intelligent, thoughtful and romantic bunch. For four hours we talked about wine, religion, cars, what it meant to be happy, Las Vegas and Benidorm and many other things while fork-skewered bundles of food were offloaded into happy mouths. After a few glasses of wine I occasional drifted off and looked dreamily around the grand, cream-coloured building we were in. In its time *Los Agustinos* had been a convent (1373), a military garrison (1809), a military hospital (1811), a prison (1839) and ultimately a hotel (1989 to the present). It was a prestigious place in the small town. Having paid up we meandered gaily back to the car. I wasn't really in the position, or mood, to question the condition of our driver. Nevertheless María José managed to get us back to the bodega without any problems, by which I mean car crash.

María José was a philosophical and happy person (happy in the purest sense of the word). She could talk for the rest of Spain put together and had a useful and insightful opinion on almost everything. She was short with curly brown hair that was stung with grey, and had a cheeky, school-boyish face. Juan was an intelligent and sharp man who often acted as the 'interrupter' in the conversations when María José was in full swing. He had a broad forehead, receding hairline and a kind, quick demeanour. Pedro was quieter but very witty and jolly, like some content rich Roman house owner. He was slightly more portly than Juan and his face always had an aloof whimsy playing on it. All the while José Antonio, the Basque gentleman, with his white hair and stony, tight face, sat in a slow moving bubble of thought as he puffed away at a cigar. Altogether it was a joy to be in their presence and I joined in the conversation when I could or when I had something to say. More often than not I was just happy to sit and bathe in my surroundings with alcohol loosened Spanish echoing gently round the inner cloisters of the hotel. The icing on the cake was that another family member back in the bodega, called Inmaculada, lived in Logroño and was kind enough to give me a lift all the way home to right outside Fernando's flat. She was a bouncy and ebullient motherly figure who nattered away with me for the entire drive so that I really can't remember any of it.

There was no answer at the flat so I rang Fernando and found out that he was just down the street in a café with another couchsurfer called Lara. I joined them for an orange juice before we all walked back and I excitedly told them about my day.
'He's like a child come from school!' giggled my host.
They dropped me at the flat – like all good parents – and went off to fiddle with a car engine. I was left to my own devices for an hour so I wrote in my journal, sang along to my music, listened to the

cats fighting and digested the mass of fine Riojan produce sitting in the chemical soup of my stomach.

After seeing to the needs of Pupilo's eye problems the evening ended with a couple of tasty omelettes and a free show from the balcony. We watched fireworks popping and crackling and fizzing over by the co-cathedral, heralding the San Bernabé part of the celebration.

*   *   *   *

The following morning I really didn't want to get up, let alone wake up, but it was my last day in La Rioja and there was another place still to visit.

Enciso is a little village with a very specific selling point but it really wasn't the easiest place to get to and from. At the start of the day I had to take a bus from Logroño to a town about 40km away called Arnedo. From there I had to change onto another bus a few minutes later that took me to Enciso. On the return journey I sat at Enciso's lone bus stop and waited for whatever bus arrived. The bus I flagged down that *was* going the way I wanted – I had previously tried to hail a school bus – then stopped in the nearby town of Arnedillo for about 15-20 minutes before *finally* finding its way back to Arnedo. In Arnedo I then had to wait two hours for the next bus back to Logroño – a mere 45 minutes away! What the hell was in Enciso then?! Well, dinosaur footprints.

The bus left the wine fields and rose steadily through a scenic area of dramatic, emerald valleys. All through it lay little villages stuck into the hillside with the valley walls rising up and enclosing them on all sides. The towns themselves didn't look that interesting historically, monumentally, culturally or visually, but they offered a pleasant contrast to the constant sight of rugged geography. I mused about how tough and distant life could be in these tiny towns. Many people, I'm sure, wouldn't have cars – especially not the older folk. I wondered, because I couldn't logically imagine, what life would be like in those places. Surrounded by hills, in a tiny village where you know everyone, and with not much hope of seeing the rest of the world. Having since lived in Russia my thoughts on this issue with relation to scale have somewhat changed.

At Enciso – one of those tiny villages (162 inhabitants) – I followed some little green signs up small lanes towards the '*centro paleontológico*', which housed information and a museum all about the footprints and the environment that once existed there. The museum itself was rather small but was surprisingly modern and hi-tech and, importantly, factually up-to-date. I admit that I had half-expected a small museum in a small village to be covered in dust and offering scientific thinking that was at least thirty years out of date. Most of the museum logically revolved around the footprints; what conditions were like then, how they were laid, which dinosaurs made them and how they were excavated. 160 million years ago the whole area of La Rioja around where I stood was a vast marshland where toothy hunters and lumbering grazers once roamed. In the lush and bumpy valley I was having trouble imagining it so I went out to find some prehistoric help.

After getting momentarily lost I found the start of the route. The tourist office girl had given me a weighty collection of bumf that gave information on every footprint site in the whole region and a fairly vague map with a dotted route showing all the upcoming information and view points. It took me, the visitor, six km round and up some hills in a large squashed oval shape. The first stop was a collection of prints that had helped tell scientists the interesting tale of a carnivorous theropod tracking and eventually ending the life of an herbivorous beast that was plodding through the marsh minding its own Cretaceous business. The scene played out as a wooden walkway took me past a spattering of more or less foot-like indentations and two life-size models acting out a frozen final moment as toothed gums were captured raining down with the intention of sinking themselves into sweet flesh.

The road then inclined and headed up to one of the many plateaus that commanded wide-angle panoramic views of all the surrounding countryside. I tired hard to erase the humped nature of the world in front of me and envisage the marsh full of those 'terrible lizards' but it was no use on this grey day with the wind-beaten vegetation and the varied topography. I just kept thinking 'nice, this is like Wales'. Fortunately apart from the odd car and occasional small group of people I had the area almost to myself. The views were all mine to savour; the little smashed up, depopulated town of Garranzo perched on the distant valley haunches; an ancient furnace used for making tiles; dramatic hillside terraces, now vacant, that were once used for cultivation; the far off lonely music of a cow bell; the broken and buckled striated layering of rock that had burst through the green. This land felt old.

Tired and a little unstable from not eating I finally walked to the last viewpoint. More prints. Four in particular were magnificent. Four footprints of a two-legged hunter, 100 per cent perfectly captured as if they had just been made. Exhibition prints. Finally I got the feeling, the tingle I had wanted. 120 million years ago a dangerous but beautiful creature once stood right here. None of his kind remains and all he is is an impression in stone and memory. But he existed! And I was standing over his phantom feet. It made the day a success. I walked back to Enciso along the road in the loud warmth. The town appeared quickly, total, and sitting in a little lake of light amongst the dim valley walls as the afternoon attempted, in vain, to give the region some better weather. The clouds were having none of it.

It was a dull trip back to Logroño only brightened by a drunken man who was also taking the bus. First he tickled his travelling audience with the line 'ai! My grandfather, the balls', a little later he thrilled us with hiccups and a near evacuation of his stomach and finally made us chuckle with glee at the repetition of various winning lines such as: 'are we there yet?', 'if I throw up you can leave me on the street' and 'I'm sorry everyone. Live for happiness. You're all invited to a party at mine!' The more sober among us shared little private sniggers and smiles, momentarily brought together by a charming inebriate.

Fernando had organised to go out for some *tapas* that evening with Javier, who I had met the first night, and Lara from the café. We started in *'Los Rotos'* with a glass of wine and a bun that formed a pocket around a mixture of potatoes, eggs, cheese and strips of pepper. Javier was tall, had a large, square jaw and wore a large winter sports coat. He was quite a serious character, not in nature, but facially. His apparent sternness was unfounded as his softness was obvious. Lara, with her long brown hair and insatiable enthusiasm stood, hands in pockets in her long, white coat. The complete opposite, she laughed, fawned over my 'received pronunciation' accent, and generally thought everything was marvellous about everything. As we finished our first drinks we dabbed our hands with little paper tissues and moved on.

The next place, *'Charly's'* served us up more of the region's wine and a speciality of cod and pepper *croquetas* as well as a *'moro'*, a deep-fried, salty pig snout. I think Fernando was a little disappointed that I was all too eager to chomp into the crispy flap of porcine nose, let alone enjoy it. The effects of eating tapas are threefold. At least threefold. Firstly it's quite cheap so you rarely get short-changed or go home skint. Secondly it's tasty and entertaining. Obvious points, but valid. Thirdly, and most importantly, it's social. One problem I have with eating out in England is that it's often quite formal and stuffy. Sure it can be well priced and delicious, but it's not the same as a group of friends all eating communally over glasses of wine, often perched at counters. Tapas is good for the soul.

Our *tapeo* – tapas crawl – continued with the infamous Bar Soriano. It served only one thing to eat, and had therefore become famous for it: three mushrooms, simply fried with salt and their secret garlic oil formula, skewered down onto a piece of bread and topped with a prawn. One man, who was clearly suffering in silence judging from the colour of his face and the sheen on his arms and forehead, stood at a hot plate quickly flipping over all of the fungi before they burned. Not one was ever carbonised and not one was ever raw. If anything they were *too* juicy, as magma-hot garlicky mushroom juice dribbled down happy chins into tissues. The most pleasant second-degree burns you'll ever get.

Our final tapas location was more sedate. We sat down – a simple action that I was very grateful for – and the Spaniards ordered. I noticed an old Viña Tondonia advertising poster on the wall and smiled. I'm sure they would have approved of my method of *tapeo*; I greedily called for Rioja wine in every establishment. The food was *embuchado*, which were intestines all collected in a clump, pressed into a tube form, sliced, and fried with salt and garlic and served with Riojan peppers. It was a very salty and meaty taste and I loved it. I think Fernando and Lara were again secretly crushed that not only had the *guiri* wolfed down the pig's nose but he had also now gobbled up the fried intestines.

We ended up in an outdoor café, more or less protected from the new rain by umbrellas, and had coffee while a Spanish battle of the bands took place round the corner – I never thought I would hear the song 'strangers in the night' sung sounding like 'something in your eye'. The atmosphere around the tapas streets was infectious and finally I noticed all the young and attractive people that had seemingly been non-existent the previous two days. As the bars continued to spit people out into the cool night air, balancing plates of food on glasses of blood-red wine, we headed back to the flat for the last time.

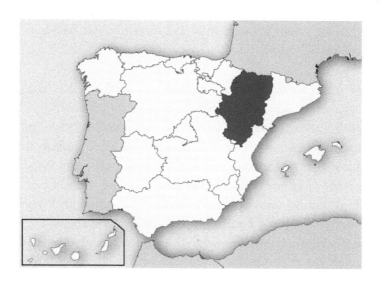

Mudéjar Spain

Zaragoza – Teruel

I slept all the way into my next autonomous community, Aragon, further east from La Rioja. I pulled into Zaragoza's huge combined bus and train station and made the long walk in the rain to my hostel. Sometimes I think the world is the most fantastic place, sparkling in its own brilliance and full of the most wonderful people and cultures. Sometimes, however, I think the world is a wanker full of wankers. I walked a sore and very wet thirty-five minutes from the station to the youth hostel – from the same website as the Salamanca one – in the south of the city. I entered, bedraggled from the rain, and was succinctly, and quite rudely, told that I couldn't stay because I didn't have a '*carnet jóven*'. I had a passport, money and the required tiredness for the service the hostel provided but I would have to look elsewhere because I was missing a flimsy €5 piece of plastic with the word *'jóven'* on it. I left on the verge of frustrated and angry tears, not because I was sad, but because I was so tired of the stupidity of things and instantly had flashbacks to my first evening in Valladolid.

Because of this situation my opinion of Zaragoza was jaded. I felt that it was a big, ugly city where the people didn't care. My thoughts unhelpfully drifted back to Fernando and the countless unrefined, but impossibly nice, people in Logroño and Haro and, in my mind, all of La Rioja. Fortunately my seething opinion only lasted until I reached the tourist office. The girl working there was beyond helpful; all smiles and light bulb ideas. She called and organised a cheap night's sleep for me, found information on the *carnet jóven* and gave me additional information about accommodation at my next stop which she then photocopied. I strode happily out into the now torrential rain and eventually, with my wilted and floppy map, found my new lodgings. It was aptly named *'El Descanso'* – the rest. I walked up the stairs and was met by a cute, but yappy little dog and a shabby old man in a white shirt who casually handed me a key after I had inspected my living space.

'How was the room?'

'Perfect. Do I pay now?'

'Yes. The owners are at a baptism at the moment. Two baptisms in fact!' he grunted with a grin.

'OK then' I passed a small bundle of euro notes into his wrinkled hand.

'If you want you can leave the big key ring here...'

'No, it's no problem.'

'But it's heavy.'

'Ah, but I'm strong,' I replied making a popeye arm.

His throaty chuckle disappeared with him into the living room and I descended the staircase to go and look around the now drier city.

Zaragoza is fairly large – the fifth largest city in the country. Thankfully my hostel was located in the historic quarter and also quite near a restaurant that the guidebook mentioned was worth visiting –*Triana*. By Spanish standards it was still quite early in the day to eat lunch but I thought I should fill up before it got too busy and I wouldn't be able to find anywhere to lay my pen and paper. The first course was fairly poor: a lukewarm plate of green bean and prawn scrambled eggs, though I think I only counted one prawn. The second course however was delicious: a *codillo* – knuckle – of pork with sweet onions and peppers. Lots of fat created a creamy and gooey sauce that made the meat glisten and the vegetables slither.

During the course of my meal I spoke briefly with the woman who had been my waitress. She saw me writing and came over to share a few words with me about what I was doing. It turned out that she was Brazilian and her son had also decided to try out publishing a book, but because it was in Portuguese he had had problems. Since then he had switched to Spanish in the hope of having more luck. I guess he was based in Spain as I couldn't imagine him having those problems in Lisbon. She never did come back to tell me whether he was successful or not and I didn't see her before I left. It bugged me because I don't like to leave establishments without thanking, or at least seeing off, the person who served me.

Although the outer parts of the city followed the same template as all the others: ugly, grey flats and seedy shops, the *casco histórico* was lovely. One area in particular – the Plaza de Pilar – was quite arresting. It is essentially a long pedestrianised oblong that lies parallel, and in between, the Rio Ebro and *'El Tubo'*, the tapas bar area. The area was dotted with sculptures, clever water features, cafés and historic buildings ranging from Mudéjar to Gothic. People were lounging happily outside, either sipping coffees or watching the world wash past; dads pushed prams as the mums walked their toddlers over to watch the pigeons bathe and splash; the ambiance was sedentary.

Mudéjar was the name given to the Moors, or Muslims, of Al-Andalus – the once great Arabic nation in the south of the country – who stayed in Spain after the *Reconquista* but were never converted to Christianity. Their architecture is a beautiful symbiosis of the understanding that results from Muslims and Christians living side by side. The dominant feature is the use of red brick and coloured tiles. The work is so unique and highly regarded that the collected buildings, the 'Mudéjar Architecture of Aragon', were made a UNESCO World Heritage Site in 1986.

All that loveliness aside, the most extraordinary part of the Plaza de Pilar was the enormous building that dominated it halfway along the riverside. The *Basílica de Nuestra Señora del Pilar*, or more simply, La Basilica as the locals know it, was one of the most imposing and striking buildings of its type I had ever seen. You will realise on further reading that I use the superlative a lot. It rises, a giant atrium, an enormous box, into the air before stopping and allowing coloured domes and its four magnificent corner towers to carry on the journey towards the heavens. Inside it is almost as beautiful. Unlike the majority of the great Spanish, religious buildings, it is big, bright and modernised with adornments. Inside is baby blue and white and well lit. It didn't feel like a 250-year-old cathedral. More like some grand government building. A walk to the bridge away from the plaza allowed me to see the basilica in its entirety as it, and the Puente de Piedra (Stone Bridge), were reflected in the near still water of the Ebro. After visiting an ancient Arab palace, the Aljafería, I walked slowly back through Zaragoza's smart streets under the soft glow of the evening sun.

In the evening England played football against the USA in the opening round of the World Cup. I could have watched it in the hostel but I thought I would go out and either find some English people to cheer with or some Yanks to have banter with. I found a very busy bar with two large televisions. Not only was the game boring and disappointing but there were also no English or Americans there. I had missed the first English goal that happened in the first six minutes and then *did* witness our goalkeeper fumble to let in a goal for the Americans thus resulting in a draw. I have rarely spent a lonelier or more underwhelming ninety minutes in my life. I only stayed the length of the match because there was nowhere else for me to go and bottles of Heineken were only one euro.

*   *   *   *

Zaragoza, in a word, was nice. Though what I really wanted to see was the small provincial capital of Teruel down in the far south of the region, or 'the backwaters' as the Rough Guide puts it. We passed through low hills shrouded in clouds and then miles after miles of green and yellow fields. In Aragon there was space, and lots of it.

I got off the bus at the little Teruel station and was irked that the pretty Italian girl I was sat opposite did not. I was then irked further when the information desk in the tourism office said that the only buses leaving for Albarracin – a mysterious old town carved into the side of a mountain and sporting a large town wall arching over the top to nowhere – was at 17:30 on Monday and returned the 47km to Teruel at 08:30 the following morning on Tuesday. I had read, and been told by residents, that public transport was bad in the region, but I wasn't expecting it to be this lacking. Maybe one there and back a day as a minimum, but only one there full stop…that's retarded, I thought! Even the man in the tourist office was shocked at the lack of buses anywhere in the paper in front of him. 'I suppose you'll have to ask at the station itself…' I was annoyed to my fullest when his suspicions were confirmed. It is the only provincial capital in Spain with no direct railway link with Madrid. It is remote.

But Teruel surprised me. For such a little, nothing 'city' it sported an absurd number of monuments and was utterly beautiful. I found the first hostel I could –the *Fonda de Tozal*. It turned out to be cheaper, more historic and more romantic than I had expected and has been receiving travellers since the sixteenth century. The bubbly and helpful owner acted as my own private tourist office and gave me some bumf and listed some of the things I could do. I didn't really know what to expect as I walked out of the front door that hot but breezy afternoon. All I knew of Teruel was its involvement in what was one of the bloodiest episodes of the Spanish Civil War. The Battle of Teruel lasted almost four months from December 1937 all the way through the harsh winter until February 1938. The two sides – Franco's Nationalists and the Republicans – lost more than 140,000 people and the city was heavily damaged by both bullets and bombs.

History hadn't been kind but a walk around the beguilingly sweet streets and snazzy, modern museum jarred with the image in my head of a knackered ruin. Feeling a bit peckish I found a place that did an appealing menu with some food typical of the area. *Jamón de Teruel*, a top class cured ham, was served with a fresh tomato salsa and bread followed by *ternasco*, grilled lamb chops with a dollop of garlic mayonnaise. It was very pleasant and I had the rest of the day and then the day after to digest both it and the town before heading back to Madrid for a couple of days to wash some clothes and get my affairs in order for the next part of my trip. Although I had only been travelling a week and was never a million miles away from the capital I did feel quite alone. When you're travelling by yourself everything feels further away and distances feel a lot vaster. A constant flood of sights, smells and knowledge wash over the senses. 'Still a lot of country ahead of me' was the thought going through my mind as I forked chunks of watermelon into my mouth and leafed through my itinerary.

The people of Spain are a people of tradition. So are the people of any country, but in Spain they really fall in line behind the set processes. A big family lunch late in the day; going for early evening *paseos* afterwards in groups, even if it's raining; closing or shutting down for the afternoon even if it isn't hot and it *is* busy. Experimentation, be it altering the usual timetable or even just trying new things didn't seem to be in the Spanish mindset. Of course this is not a rule to be applied to everyone – Fernando was a good example of someone who wasn't afraid to expand his horizons – but it was something I had noticed. My housemate Elena is the same. If I cooked something that wasn't instantly recognizable as Spanish she would put her hands over her nose and mouth, or just look at it with a face full of concerned disgust and say something along the lines of 'What the hell is that?!' She would never ask to try it. If I could manage to force her to try a little I usually received an 'Actually, that's quite nice!' And then she would tuck into her lone slices of cured sausage and munch breadsticks.

I personally find that this world is not as fun if you don't play with it and I worry about people who trundle along in it not enjoying new experiences. There is a book (and a later a film) called 'Yes Man' about a man who changed his life around by deciding to say yes to everything for one year. Now, I am not suggesting you do this. You can imagine the problems that could arise in areas of drug dealing and prostitution. But do it more. It was something I had tried to get through to Elena, but the girl, God love her, is stuck in her ways, like many Spaniards.

They are stuck in more than just their ways. Spain, like Italy and other Mediterranean countries and cultures, is a very familial country. Family is the most important thing. This isn't to say it's not in the UK, but we use it differently. I feel that in Britain the family is there to support, train, form and set free the children. In Spain it seemed to be more to support, train, cushion and keep. It's not uncommon for offspring to stay in the family until well into their thirties. In Britain we are 'taught' that the best thing you can do is to go out, get a job, and land on your own two feet. To be independent. It's not really the same in Spain. When I told my more culturally unaware Spanish friends about this they took it as a sign that there is less love in the British family. There isn't. It's just a more pragmatic approach to raising children. Again, this isn't to say the Spanish system doesn't work, it does, and I do love the big family atmosphere they have. The scene with the large unit gathered around the table outside, dishing out food and wine, is commonplace. When the young of the family go to university it is often the one closest to their home and when they finish they tend to stay in the family house until they are fully financially capable of leaving. In Britain it's more common for young people to get out as soon as possible, preferring to eek out a living, just paying the bills but 'living my own life'.

Unable to reach a conclusion on which was the superior system for parenting I thought it best to walk off the food and wine I had just consumed. I also didn't want to go and see all of the monuments, as I was saving them for the following day, so I chose a direction and walked away from the centre, over a sculpted sixteenth century viaduct and in an upward direction away from the town. I found an epic set of stairs that led up to an eagle's nest type of building. I'd get a good view from there, I thought to myself. After startling a tailless cat and occasionally peeping round at the ever-changing view I reached the top of the unmanned outpost and took stock of my surroundings. The positive was that all of Teruel could be seen along with the surrounding, shrouded Sierra de Albarracín. The negative, however, was that due to the town's inevitable development it was only the tops of the monuments that I could see peeping up among the surrounding buildings. I spied a path and more distant climes.

It tore up through some small bare trees, past scurrying red squirrels, and towards an area of electricity substations. The sky was menacing with marbled blacks and bruised purples but I decided to press on taking myself uphill and along a muddy red track. Within minutes I was walking through woodland that skirted a small, but dramatic clay ravine. It started raining. The path kept going up through the hills and sometimes got quite sketchy. There were no nannyish health and safety signs here. As it continued to rise it put more and more distance between the town and me. I was walking a large perimeter route around the capital. Teruel itself was never more than a couple of kilometres away and was usually constantly visible, but then at some point I lost it all together. I lost the bloody town.

The rain got heavier and the air was fresh and smelled of wet trees and pinecones. A runner wheezed past me; a little muddy pond sat neglected between high walls of earth; a natural cave protected a couple of dirty mattresses; and a breeze had managed to find its way to me. The path then descended abruptly as the sun finally flung off its cloudy shackles and the landscape changed as if Mother Nature had flipped a coin. Lowland fields of wheat, bobbles of bright purples, reds and yellows glowed as the spring flowers showed off and the Sierra de Albarracín now shone proudly, warming its body. After clambering through mud – with constant shoe cleaning via the old tried and tested method of picking-with-stone – walking through an under-road overflow tunnel and climbing up the last steep road back to town, I finally returned to my hostel and my bed just before the heavens opened for an encore. I shoved some towelling into the crevices as the windows frame started to leak. It was six o'clock in the evening. I closed my eyes and accidentally slept for thirteen and a half hours.

*   *   *   *

Rested more than I had ever been I awoke very early with the sun and the subdued hum of *Turolense* life rising up around me. After lounging a bit and showering, where I exhausted the hostel's hot water, I slowly padded out into the Teruel morning. I walked through the small, but stately, Plaza del Torico, at its centre a column topped with a little bronze bull. Soft pastel pink, blue and yellow walls welcomed the morning light with small-town grace. Waiters were setting out tables and shops were pulling up their shutters. I popped to the post office to buy some stamps – I had decided to send a postcard from every region to my grandma and my great aunt and uncle – and then continued to the end of the road where I encountered both the impressive San Martín Mudéjar style tower and the imposing baby blue seminary that sat opposite it.

The picture-postcard Plaza de la Catedral sat slotted in the area between the tower and the Plaza del Torico. A large, yellow town hall directed the gaze towards the bulky and surprisingly well-hidden cathedral. It looked like a mess of Mudéjar; in fact one of the Mudéjar towers was stuck on the side of it with Arabic red bricks, arches and coloured ceramic tiles all greens and whites. I went in through the main entrance. On reading the book again I found out I was supposed to have entered through another door and paid a few euros. It was lofty and interesting inside, but nothing really extraordinary. It seemed more functional; some old men were kneeling and sending prayers up to some private higher being. Breakfasting at a little café called, as translated, 'Eve's Original Sin', I continued to ponder Teruel as it buzzed now more fervently into life. Crunch went the toast and squish went the strawberry jam.

The tallest, most ornate and most accessible of the 'City of Towers" towers was the Torre de Salvador. I climbed four floors of tight, lit staircases, occasionally punctured by a central information room, to a height of 40 metres. The view was wide reaching and refreshing, although not well 'designed'. As with the hill views of the previous day all the historic buildings could be seen…but only the tops.

There were enough of them to make you look but their full beauty was always tantalisingly out of reach. Continuing down the same road as the tower and away from the centre I was carried on cobblestones to the Escalinata neo-Mudéjar – a grand-staircase from the 1920s built in the Mudéjar style. Even though it wasn't of any historical importance it was, if nothing else, a pretty smashing way to enter a city.

I continued my Teruel relaxation and recuperation regime by having a tasty potato lunch at Bar Gregory, opposite the staircase. With my dish I ordered a *caña* – a small glass of beer. It was so often my default drink. I wondered about Spain's relationship with alcohol. It is clearly a far healthier one than the binge-madness in the UK and in a country where my beer or glass of wine costs less than a coffee or fresh orange juice, it struck me as a little surprising. Despite the prevalence and cheapness of alcohol in Spain I never saw it as a negatively affecting factor. It is probably Spain's blasé attitude to alcohol – it is what it is, a product, and not just a means to a drunken end – that has caused this. That and they are a 'producer country' so they have a long history of having it at hand and having it woven into – or should that be filtered into – their society. After paying I decided, just to fully complete the poor town, to do a walk, in the rain, around the outside.

The perimeter walk didn't reveal anything new or exciting apart from a good view to the hills where I had walked the day before. I crossed the viaduct; almost slipped over at a zebra crossing, whence I shared a whimsical and knowing glance with the waiting car; bought some fruit at the LIDL; and ran through the increasingly heavy rain to the hotel Mudayyan. Of course I wasn't staying at this hotel, but my friend Imogen told me of an interesting piece of quirkiness that lurked downstairs underground and usually reserved itself for the eyes of guests. There was only a bored-looking girl working the coffee bar inside, the owners were probably off on lunch, but she said that I could go on down. I descended two flights of stairs, unlocked a glass door and entered a little stone walled room where a couple of torches and hard hats sat in a cubbyhole. Under the hotel was a network of tunnels – kilometres of them – some of which were once used by priests to travel to and from the sacristy in secret during the Spanish Civil War. According to an urban legend one could get to any part of the *casco antiguo* using these tunnels. The hotel proudly presented a small section of one of them.

I passed through a little doorway and down a small and narrow staircase bathing in the light of tiny lanterns under a low, pebbled ceiling. 'No way!' I said under my breath. The lamps then stopped so I activated my phone light to take me right down into the pure, low, pitch-black tunnel for another few metres. As I stooped and shuffled through I chuckled to myself, 'you've got to be kidding me'. I was in a hotel with underground tunnels, in a small city called Teruel, in a near forgotten part of Spain in the south of Aragon – I literally wouldn't have thought of ending up there.

My room provided shelter for a couple of hours while the rain tried to drown the streets. If it was any other room in any other town I might have been annoyed, but I felt at ease in my sixteenth century quarters. Night swiftly drew a dark curtain over the sky and the electric orbs of Teruel came on. The Mudéjar structures threw striking shadows on themselves as light and dark played together. Buildings were lit up, roads were lined with ground level lamps, everything shone wet and the main square sparkled as if light were bouncing off smashed glass. All over the Plaza del Torico's surface were thin rectangular lamps embedded at various angles. When turned on the effect was mesmerising. I honestly didn't expect the mix of so very old and so very contemporary in such a place. This may have been due slightly in part to Teruel's modest period of regeneration. It has tried to, indeed has had to, fling itself further into the public eye. When one thinks of Spain one usually doesn't think of Aragon – unless you are a history buff like my mother. And if and when you do think of Aragon you may not initially give much attention to Teruel. For this reason a campaign group was founded in 1999 with the slogan *Teruel existe* – Teruel exists. Unfortunately this prompted smartarses, like Elena, and everyone else not from Teruel, to start mock-responding '*Teruel no existe*'.

I am glad I did go though. It was, well, still is, a thoroughly endearing little place to unwind for a couple of days. The only negative point was the five hours it took to return to Madrid – via the impressively fortified town of Molina de Aragon, a fifteen-minute wait in a smoky bar full of truckers and the sweeping Maranchón wind farm in La Mancha community.

Capital Language...

I returned to Madrid for a couple of nights, as most of my clothing needed what a parent might call a 'decent wash'. 2010's World Cup had started proper and the day before I headed off again Spain were up against Switzerland in their first match of the competition.

Football fans are interesting. For the majority of the life I've existed enjoying this world, I've spent near to none of it watching football. When I was younger I supported Arsenal with my friend Ollie, who still supports the Gunners to this day. We went to the Highbury stadium together, I had a team scarf, knew all the players, had my favourites and knew most of their upcoming matches and current league position – mostly thanks to Ollie though. When I was about 11, and within a couple of seasons, I became disheartened with the game and finally lost interest as almost all of my favourite players were either transferred away or retired. I was never a particularly fervent supporter anyway. Sure it was fun, and it was nice to say 'This is *my* team', but I would never, could never trade blows or even kill for it. Despite the passion, the old adage holds: 'It's just a game'.

But the World Cup and European Football Championship are different animals. OK, so I could be from London but support Liverpool, great. Maybe that northern team loses and I dab my teary southern face. That's one thing. But when it's my entire country at stake I get into it. Then I catch the fever. I 'Ooh' and I 'Aah'. I call the referee a wanker and I sporadically call 'Offside!' I instantly think football is the greatest social glue ever invented. I love the passion of football fans, not the aggressive or the violent ones. Leave that at home. I love the shared emotion. The 'we-are-all-in-this-together' feeling. Like when you watch fireworks and everybody gasps at the same time at the big rocket and then giggles because everybody gasped at the same time at the big rocket. I love the playful swearing of the football fans, especially in Spain. They share the same creativity, or obscenity, as the Brits.

A couple of teachers and I went to a little bar to catch the second half of the Spain-Switzerland game. Naturally we were joined by many Spaniards in red shirts and with desperate faces. I have rarely seen so many unsuccessful shots and opportunities at the goal for one team than from Spain in that match. One guy, sporting the Spanish team strip and with a flag around his neck as a cape, was becoming more and more incredulous as every shot went wide, landed straight into the Swiss goalie's hands or bounced off the posts. With his rising desperation his verbal frustration became more and more amusing. It started off with the customary '*No me jodas!*, 'You're shitting me!'. It's quite a casual term with the young of the country. This then elevated to *'Me cago en la leche!'*, a rather obscure frustration expression along a similar vein but translating literally as 'I shit in the milk!'. This was proceeded by *'Me cago en la madre!'*, 'I shit on the mother!' and was ended by the funniest variation I had ever heard, *'Me cago en Dios!'*, 'I shit on God!'. Each one accompanied by both hands cradling his agape mouth or his entire head depending on the nearness of the goal. Spain lost that game. I felt for the guy. I then hung around in pub territory for the rest of the evening and savoured the brief moments with my friends. The following day I was back on the road.

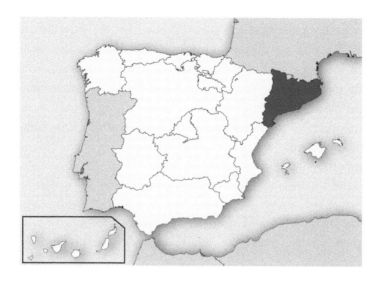

From Sea to Sky

Barcelona – Montserrat – Sitges - Girona

This next stage of my trip didn't start particularly well. My original plan of waking up at 5:30 in the morning in order to catch the super-swift (and super-expensive) 7:30 AVE train to Barcelona in the community of Cataluña, was affected as I had absentmindedly spent longer than I should have the evening before trying in vain to woo a French girl in a Madrid bar. As a result I gave myself another couple of hours sleep. I would get the 9:30 instead. I woke fine, packed up my trusty blue bag and took the metro once again to the Chamartín station in the north of the city. Perfect timing. I walked confidently into the ticket office and took out my wallet.

'One AVE ticket to Barcelona please.'

'The AVE goes from Atocha.'

'Atocha?' I pressed.

'Yes.'

'Right.'

Atocha is the station in the *south* of the city. So I'd take the 10:30 then, I thought to myself. I ground my teeth, exhaled violently through my nose and caught a local *cercanias* train down to Atocha, took my ticket, waited for my number to be called and again walked up to the desk.

'Hello. Give me a ticket for the 10:30 AVE to Barcelona please.'

'OK, one moment.'

'Thank you.'

The snappily dressed man tapped away at his keyboard, his eyes flitting over the screen.

'OK, the 10:30 is full so I can offer you the 11:30.'

'Fine; perfect!' I said with a smile through clenched teeth.

One hundred and fourteen euros later I was sitting on the high-speed train. A group of American girls were eating fruit and vegetables and were offering 'chocolate cookies' to little Spanish kids. Some people were running for the train while others calmly scrunched their dying cigarette ends into the platform and wandered on with an 'I've done this before' air about them. I felt excited. I know it was only a train, but it was a *high-speed* one. By standard rail the trip would have lasted more than eight hours, while by the AVE it bulleted me there in about three. It was a modern, clean vehicle with big, comfy seats, wood panelling, arty lighting and whose trajectories shot out from the capital in various directions. The Madrid-Barcelona route was inaugurated in 2008. It certainly had more atmosphere than the First Great Western regional trains back in the UK.

Within the first ten minutes we were flying through Spain at speeds of up to 300km/h. I had never travelled that fast on land, despite my father occasionally trying to on the motorway. With thirty minutes left the sea finally muscled its way into view in a very blue manner. I suppose you could say that it seemed very azure of itself. There, there's a pun. You can keep that one. It was the first time I had seen the sea for at least a year and it was clear from the first glance that it hadn't lost any of its beauty. Well done sea, I thought. The train darted in and out of tunnels a lot of the time along the route, so the views acted their lives like in some grand, Victorian zoetrope. It was also only in the tunnels that you could hear the speed, the roar of the train, the deafening boom of 300km/h. Leaving the last tunnel a more urban environment of industry and residential areas started to spring up around the tracks. We had arrived in Barcelona.

After following some cryptic instructions to get the key from the flat where I would be staying – 'Go to the Europcar office and ask for Tony…' – and after a period of blindly walking around the absurdly complicated road system by the station, after actually *finding* the flat where I would be staying, after de-bagging and changing clothes I was finally able to take stock and relax. I looked out of my hosts' living room window. They had a balcony and a view. I didn't have that in Madrid and was secretly jealous.

My hosts weren't there on arrival and I was keen to see them. I had visited Barcelona before, and had stayed with the same people, although in a different flat. Like many of us I often get urges to help people. It can be a special report about Africa on the BBC, some documentary program or just a charity telethon that sets me off. In 2006 I decided that saying 'Oh, I wish I could help' wasn't good enough. There is only so much good that can come from giving money in a plastic bag. Through a friend of my mother's I managed to get in contact with a missionary couple that were living in a small town in Guatemala doing work in the poorer areas. I thought that this would be the perfect opportunity, so I emailed them and quickly got a response. I ended up spending one month with them building staircases, repairing walls and roofs, creating drainage facilities and various other practical tasks in order to improve the lives of people who hadn't the money to do it themselves.

In Houston airport on my way to Guatemala I made friends with a guy called Ken; a bubbly, extroverted and entrepreneurial man from the United States, who was raised in Italy and is of Costa Rican descent. It turned out he was going to be doing some work setting up computers in a small village on the shore of Lake Atitlán. During my stay the family were kind enough to take me on little weekend tours, one of which took me to this lake. On the way there I established mobile contact with Ken, and we actually managed to meet up by some old boats bobbing in the water. As if old friends we embraced and joked and jibed. We shared our very different experiences of the country and then, lamentably, parted ways.

In 2008 I was living in Alicante, in Spain, as part of my Erasmus year. One day, out of the blue while I was shopping, I received an international text message from Ken along the lines 'Well howdy! Listen my man I'm gonna be in Barcelona this November and it would be just peachy if you were able to come'. I responded 'tell me more'. And he rang me, from America. As lucky coincidences would have it two of my acquaintances at the time were driving there for a romantic weekend away so I cheekily hitched a lift. In Barcelona, Ken introduced me to his friends Caroline and Ben who were gracious enough to let us stay with them for free. As payment Ken prepared some fried chicken and I offered some gargantuan pasta salad. The buoyant American and I parted once again but my lines of communication with him, Caroline and Ben stayed open due to the wonders of the Internet. In 2010 I re-established contact with the pair and they were more than happy to have me back a second time.

As they weren't in when I entered the flat I was left on my own. I dunked Anna's trusty blue backpack on the sofa, had a drink and some cereal, admired the view from their balcony one last time and headed out. My first stop was the Ramblas.

Anyone who has visited Barcelona will probably have started here. It's the most famous street and it splits the old town areas in half. The poet/hero Federico García Lorca once said of the Ramblas that it was 'The only street in the world which I wish would never end'. In reality, especially coming from Madrid, it didn't produce the same effect. As a walkway it was pleasant enough; however, it was so drowning in kitsch tourism that it was more of a farce. There were entire sections devoted to stalls selling crappy t-shirts, books and postcards; sections for buying obscure artwork or having caricatures drawn; and areas with dozens of street-performers, mostly living statues – these I quite liked. The shameless and cheap tourist feeling also stretched a little into La Boqueria, Barcelona's, and some say Spain's, greatest food market.

I barely heard any Spanish spoken there. The majority were young couples or groups of young American, English or French girls out to do some 'culture' before hitting the beaches. The entrance was wrought iron and arching with its official name, Mercat St. Josép La Boqueria. Stained glass, painted fish and foodstuffs adorned it. Inside my senses took a wonderful beating. I never thought I would be blinded by fruit and vegetables. Colours. So many colours. Perfectly presented masses of the most vibrant, high-definition foods. When my eyes settled on the mountains of photogenic comestibles I noticed the quality. It was top quality. Whole flanks of stalls were devoted to artisan chocolates and edible rainbows of sweets. Then came the musty smell of red and brown cured hams and legs hanging meatily next to a range of cheeses. A little further in and the sea hit me. Fish. Armies of dead marine life – crustaceans and molluscs - lay in coffins of ice waiting to be dropped in the pot. If I had money I would have bought the lot. I would have asked if La Boqueria was for sale, before nonchalantly tossing a disgusting handful of notes at a man cutting some Serrano ham and proclaiming victoriously 'I'll take it!' Instead I opted to buy some cheese in order to thank my hosts, who I had yet to see.

'*Hola*, how can I help?'

'I'm looking for some cheese, from Cataluña. I want it strong.'

'Strong?'

'Mm, strong strong, like Manchego.'

'These six are from different provinces of Cataluña. These three are strong, and this one is the strongest of them all.'

'Give me 150g of that then!'

I smiled smugly and felt safe in my ivory tower as the American tourists behind me discussed the possibility of *trying* to buy something. I could have helped, I suppose. It was simple moments, like buying cheese in a market with no problems, that made me feel grateful to every languages teacher I had ever had.

I continued down the Ramblas to its end at the refreshing and airy Port Guell area. Part functional port, part marina and part leisure area. A long boulevard with cyclists and rollerbladers skirted the waterline and allowed an expansive area to sit and relax away from the roads. A fancy walkway cut through the boated waters of the marina and led to an area called Port Vell where cinemas, rides, restaurants and bars ruled the roost. I sat in the shade of a palm tree with an ice-lolly and watched the world unravel itself around me. A family perched by a mooring bollard, legs dangling, tossing crumbs to fishes; large gulls wheeled in the air and cawed at the cyan water; locals and tourists sailed past on the red and white hire bikes; and the mournful bellow of a ship's horn crumbled through the wet sea air that stuck to my nostrils. It was lovely. For a moment I wondered if I shouldn't just put an end to this silly trip and instead spend long, sunny days doing nothing by the water. I am not a beach bum by any means and I don't care for sunbathing much but I find that water, especially the sea, has a most powerful pacifying effect on me.

I was careful not to lose the day though. I finished my lolly, licked clean my sugar-stickied fingers and went into the Barii Gotic. This was the heart of the old town. A twisted jumble of old, dark streets and high walls, pockmarked here and there with small squares, little specialist boutiques and small, aging and unchanged cafés and restaurants. Fewer tourists pervaded deep into the Gothic Quarter's web compared to the Ramblas but they were still there. I heard throaty French echoing down shaded alleyways and the intolerable bark of 'and I was like oh my god!' from herds of Americans. It was an atmospheric area, though, and classically Spanish. I walked north and finally bumped into a metro station. I had more than enough time to have a look at the Sagrada Familia, a building that has been under construction since 1882 and is a UNESCO World Heritage Site despite not being finished.

I boarded the horrendously full train and went to see the beast. Depending on your point of view the Sagrada Familia is either outstandingly ugly or remarkably beautiful. I thought it a mixture. Architecturally I thought it was a work of art and showed how the imagination could play with buildings. The towers and turrets and gaping archways littered with statues and images were a phenomenal shrine to the power of human creativity. Just don't look near the base, I thought to myself, or all you'll see is tourists. It was originally just a church but as its importance and position grew it was consecrated and proclaimed a minor basilica in November 2010. Its life has been a divisive one: will it overshadow the city's cathedral? Has Gaudi's original vision been disregarded since his death? Would the new AVE line damage the building? Is the architecture a visual blessing or blight? Whatever has happened, is happening, or will happen, one fact shines through all the mess: Antoni Gaudi's mark is permanent.

He was the man behind so much of the city's architecture and the effects of his crazy modernism are scattered over the city. He has even earned himself a UNESCO protective charter for his works.

The downside with the Sagrada Familia, however, is that the building is constantly, and famously, covered in scaffolding. This time was worse than when I had visited two years before. Cranes rose with the decorated towers and a whole side was masked with netting. Caroline told me that if it were publicly funded it could be finished in a few years. Instead it is privately funded and as a result progress is slow. Now, with Spain's economy flirting with 'junk' status, and construction being one of the more heavily affected sectors, the pace is geologic.

I took the metro back to the flat and noticed, just out of interest, three main differences with Madrid's underground:

1. Madrid was a little more clearly signposted down in the tunnels
2. The trains were a lot wider in Barcelona
3. In the Madrid metro I would hear *'próxima estación'* - next station - in a man's voice and then the following station's name in a woman's voice. In Barcelona it was the reverse with the woman setting up for the man's finish.

Interesting for me anyway...

When in the evening Caroline finally arrived we went to a shop where food was bought to make dinner. I paid. It was only fair, and they didn't complain. It then materialised that Ben had been there all along, all day, sleeping in his room. We played the 'catch up and questions' game and then quickly reverted to the 'banter like old friends' game. Caroline is an attractive woman with an enormous smile that ignites as easily as tinder. Ben is a German who sounds like a Londoner. He has a punishing sense of sarcasm and is controversial enough to spice up conversation but not offend anyone. The three of us sat on the balcony with the view of window-lit apartments and the distant glowing ochre spires of the MNAC (Museu Nacional d'Art de Catalunya) unknowingly polishing off three bottles of Catalonian cava.

*   *   *   *

The following day I went to a magical place a little way west of Barcelona called Montserrat, a Catalan name that translates as 'Serrated Mountain'. The train passed through more of the industrial land that helped make Cataluña, along with its powerful partner País Vasco, the dominant force it was and still is in the Spanish economy. Of the region's GDP the secondary sector comprises around 37%, compared with, say, Andalucía, where it is around 9%. Before, during, and really since the time of Franco Spain has never been considered much of an 'industrial nation'. Its main sectors are primary: fishing, agriculture, mining, and tertiary: tourism and real estate being the most prominent. Having said this the automotive industry in Spain is still one of the big guns, generating 3.5% of the country's entire GDP and managing to subsist with only one real seller, SEAT. For this reason I was a little taken aback, and even a little unhappy, when I noted the heavier handed architecture of the plants and factories.

The first view of the mountain of Montserrat was extraordinary: a sheer mass of rock and earth just sat, seemingly alone and swallowing the vista. A little yellow cable car whisked me up the grey walls of stone and deposited me in the Benedictine monastery complex that was perched in a small bowl protected on one side by higher peaks and on the other by a 550m-drop to the bottom. I entered the basilica, as it was the only free of charge area. I wasn't disappointed by it but neither was I blown away. Two things did set it apart though: firstly was the absurd number of happy snappers. Walk in, use eyes, small digital camera, take photos which will probably never be seen again, sporadic flashes and onto the next photo box that needs to be ticked. I took photos too, so, I suppose I shouldn't complain. But, I don't know, it just seemed different. I take a photo if my subject is beautiful and not just because it is there. The second was the long lines of people that studded various sections – for example, in the basilica to touch the 'Black Virgin' (or Black Madonna – a statue of Mary in which she is depicted with dark or black skin). The legend of this Black Madonna, or, *la Moreneta* – 'The little dark-skinned one' – goes that the Benedictine monks were not able to move the statue to construct their monastery, so instead they just built around it. This could, I suppose, account for the monastery's extreme location.

I wanted to get higher and away from the sheep. Fighting the urge to go 'baa', I left and took one of the funicular trains up from San Juan inferior (the monastery base) up to San Juan superior, where the views lived. From the station fanned out a variety of scenic walks that led the visitor, usually, to little monasteries and hermitages scattered around the peaks. There was a big, white sign that displayed the rough outline of each walk as well as a projected duration and level of difficulty.

Either there was a large Russian population in Barcelona or I had coincided with a bus trip or Montserrat is just randomly popular with Slavs, because there were a lot of Ruskies there. I was chuffed though. That both my languages splashed together and sharing an impossibly beautiful place with me was quite a treat. I went to a vending machine in order to buy some M'n'Ms that would constitute a healthy lunch. A Russian man was there at a neighbouring unit. He was a young, blockish man, with three kids, and he fawned over their every move and comment. The machine swallowed my money greedily and his machine was obstinate that it would not be giving him his coffee. He looked at me and my testy 'vending' machine.
'No work?' he asked in English.
'*Nyet, nye rabotayet*', no it doesn't work.
I was proud of myself at having initiated some Russian. He then, presumably thinking I was a kinsman, started firing off Russian at an unintelligible rate. I suppose about the state of the machines in front of us. I then froze like some woodland creature in headlights. I couldn't summon up the knowledge or courage to continue what I had started. Concentrating on my machine, I muttered to myself in

my most English English 'God...bloody thing...great!' and tutting in the hope he would just think I was what I was. We parted after he banged his machine, which then finally choked out a syrupy brown mulch that was his caffeine kick.

Before the funicular made its last descent of the day I managed to do two of the three walks. The first led me along a ridge that had walls of stone on my right and wide arching arms sloping down to the valley floor on my left. The path then rose up to a tiny little chapel that sat alone, surveying the opening up of the lands of Cataluña. From there it rose again to a very strange 'feature'; a tight passage made of bricks that hugged the side of a sheer wall. It bent round with the curvature and became the width of only one person. It must have been the narrowest monastery in history. After breathing out there was a crumbling stone staircase that led upwards into its own disintegration and downwards to rejoin the original path. I could then choose to walk back to the sentinel chapel or rather to the funicular base. The whole walk itself was a gentle forty minutes and pretty enough for anyone.

The next walk was the longest, hardest and most enchantingly dramatic that Montserrat had to offer. In retrospect flip-flops were a bad choice. I left the station round the back and within minutes was slapped in the face by the beauty of the mountain. Reaching a little path with a barrier my gaze was drawn down through the slopes to the monastery area flanked by the now small-looking walls of San Juan inferior. I curled around further until the plains, monastery, and valley floor of that side of the mountain were hidden from view and I was left walking round the rim of a giant bowl. In this area there was a superlative view of the fantastical rock formations that wouldn't have looked out of place in 'Conan the Barbarian' or some other swords and sorcery adventure film. Grey rock figures stood out amongst vibrant green undergrowth; large shark fins; giant dinosaur teeth; knobbly fingers; sharp daggers; bulbous mushrooms were all present in massive sizes as the environment unfurled. The views just kept getting bigger and more awe-inspiring. Life was abundant on Montserrat. Life and nature was everywhere. Purple flowers had their nectar drunk by strange bee/moth creatures that looked more like tiny birds, a herd of goats humped and sparred with each other, and butterflies and flying beetles went crazy in the air as mating season kicked in.

Unbelievably the path continued up, this time to the monastery of Sant Jeroni – another sweet and isolated chapel. In time honoured tradition the best was saved until last. I climbed steeply to the Sant Jeroni peak, which was no mean feat in sandals. At 1236m I was rewarded with a view that genuinely did take away the air in my lungs. I swore under my breath as the vista engulfed everything in front of me. In one direction was the entire mountain jaggedly rolling away like a mystical ECG and in the other, the largest amount of space I have ever seen in one view. It looked like a shot from a plane window. I couldn't take it all in. My eyes darted round hyperactively as I tried desperately to drink it all up. I couldn't. I took fifteen photos of the same view in the hope of capturing it. I couldn't. I could only gawp. If I were drunk I might have cried a little. I hated the fact that I would have to leave it.

Restarting the long route back to the funicular I startled a couple of goats with the incessant 'ferrrlip, ferrrlop' of my feet. They ran onto the path, bent their heads round, stared at me suspiciously and then tanked off down the mountainside. Dirty, painful and with quivering muscles I finally reached the railway and dropped back down to the monastery. There was one more walk I had wanted to do but wasn't able to due to the lower funicular having already closed. I decided to call the day over and take my cable car back down, passing on the first one because there were too many people and I really wanted to stand by a window. I sat; finally resting my filthy and cut up feet and waited a few minutes for the next one. Hearing approaching voices I childishly darted to the cable car bay door so that I would be the first one on. A family of Americans entered.

'Excuse me, do you know when the next cable car is?'

'I'm afraid I don't. But I presume that it's on its way up.'

It was. However, when it arrived and emptied its paltry late-in-the-day selection of visitors it just hung there, closed, and inactive. The friendly mother of the family turned to me with large doe eyes.

'We have seven minutes to catch the next train to Barcelona. Do you think we'll make it?'

'Possibly,' I responded optimistically.

We didn't.

I ended up hanging around with and talking to the family until the next one arrived. They were on a cruise holiday and were passing through Barcelona for a couple of days. Dan, the boyfriend of the attractive daughter Sophie, was an intelligent and easily likeable guy of 21. He loved England and was a big fan of English telly such as 'The Office' and 'The Inbetweeners'. The family (mum, dad and Sophie) and Dan all hailed from the town of Fargo in North Dakota, the same place as features in the famous Coen brothers' film of the same name. According to Dan and Sophie it is a tiny and boring place, though mum and dad didn't complain. We caught the train together back to Barcelona and completely ignored the scenery. On the train we inherited, via the approachable nature of the Americans, an Indian girl who was confused about how to get back to the centre. We talked about travelling, sport, struggled in vain to teach the Americans the rules of cricket, and discussed the beauty of language for an hour until the Barcelona-Sants station appeared. Coincidence had it that we were taking the same metro line, with the same changes, to almost the same stop – one away from each other. Our momentary friendship burst as I bid them all farewell and we shared the customary 'Lovely meeting you' and 'Enjoy your trip' niceties.

I carried on, grubby, sweaty and fatigued, to a bar opposite the Barceloneta beach where I met Caroline. We watched the appalling England vs Algeria football match, complete with myriad beers, a saucy Bristolian waitress, gobby fans, desperate faces, and constructive criticism such as 'You fucking wanker!' and 'You are shit!' directed at the floundering English side. Nil-nil and 94 minutes of my life wasted with fellow countrymen. I felt disgusting but I finally got a shower back at the flat and, after another couple of shared bottles of bubbly cava, collapsed on my bed.

*   *   *   *

The next day, a Saturday, didn't really go to plan either. But this time it was a good thing. I *was* going to explore Barcelona a little before meeting some Dutch people for their football match at 13:30. It was a plan I was basically OK with but OK in a sort of begrudging way. I then changed my plan and decided to take the morning slowly and go around Barcelona after the game instead. At 14:00, slightly confused, I knocked on Caroline's door. 'One minute!'

A minute later she burst into the living room, phone to her ear and wrapped in a pink towel, 'OK see you shortly'. She turned to me, 'New plan. We are going to the beach'. Within an hour our train was sliding into the beach town of Sitges a little south of Barcelona. She apologised to me about changing all the plans. I was over the moon. I told her how this was what I wanted. To be shown things, experience things I wouldn't normally have thought of. She kept sending texts and coordinating with the people we were to meet at our destination. Fingers firing over plastic buttons.

Caroline, in her own words, had become more Spanish after her 4 years there. Plans don't mean much to Spanish people. If you invite them to a party at the weekend they will say yes regardless of whether they already had plans. They will then proceed to work on a subconscious and non-malicious 'best offer' system, often making last minute or spontaneous decisions. This time the method worked a charm. Sitges is a beach town famed for hosting the most lavish gay *carnaval* in the country and it hummed with energy. It was a clever place that delicately interlaced pretty, historic lanes with more modern beach flats and shops. It was handsome, rarely ugly and very relaxed. We arrived at one of beach sections – we being me, Caroline, a vivacious Londoner called Debbie, her Spanish boyfriend Jesús and her cheerful friend Kim who was on holiday – and set up shop in the usual beach fashion; towel down, cream on and burn.

It was a fantastic location. Turn one way and the visitor was looking at a palm-treed promenade that sat between the sand and a line of pleasant beach flats, culminating in a beautiful cream-coloured church. When one turned the other way there were leagues of glittering sea. Glittering as long as the sun was out, which it wasn't, much. It kept dipping behind clouds for long periods. We didn't get much tanning done so instead we played a numbers game called Rummikub on our towels. We were irked as the wind picked up and disturbed the sand and discussed backup plans should we have to vacate our seaside location. Discussion over, we all gawped at some fantastic exposed breasts and joked about going over and congratulating the girl. After only an hour and a bit it had become sufficiently nippy that almost everyone on the beach was putting their clothes back on and leaving. We glanced over the azure once more as the sun made a final dazzling appearance and went in search of some food.

We found a gay little crossroads square; gay because of the organised rainbow gay excursion sat at a café on one corner of the pedestrianised area. It really had to be there where we stopped. This was like so totally Sitges. We sat down, ordered some tapas and got the ubiquitous *patatas bravas*, olives and a couple of typically Catalonian foods: *fuet*, which was similar to spiced salami, and the very typical *'pa amb tomaquet'* – bread rubbed with garlic and fresh tomato. The triumvirate combination of Kim, Debbie and Caroline was a winning one. The air was loud with crackling laughter and innuendos as we drifted in and out of Spanish for the benefit of Jesus.

'Are you from Barcelona, Jesús?' I asked, and giggled when I thought of him answering 'No…from Nazareth.'

'Yes, but my parents are from different regions.'

'Do you consider yourself Catalan?'

'Depends on the moment. I am not like these crazy nationalists though.'

'I've read that Catalans are a very proud people.'

'Yes. The ones that are firmly Catalan and are against unity usually haven't really seen the rest of Spain, you know?'

'Do you speak Catalan then?'

'Of course!' he said with a broad, toothy smile.

Despite having been part of Spain, as it is now known, for 500 years the heart that beats inside the community is not Spanish. You take public transport, go into a shop or just walk around town and the first language you see, and often hear, is Catalan. It sounds like a bashed up cocktail of Italian, Spanish, and French with an occasionally Russian accent, and on paper looks a little Portuguese. It is also not some endearing dialect that occasionally pops up on signs or is spoken by a few folk in the villages. It is a fully blown language spoken, considering all linguistic regions, by somewhere between nine and nine and a half million people. That's about the same number of people that live in Mongolia, Slovenia and Ireland combined.

One night I asked Ben to describe the Catalans in three words.

'Stingy, closed…and something else.'

They were identifiably Mediterranean but the more restrained manner, paler skin and different features made them seem foreign in their own country. Being English, I didn't find them particularly closed, but they clearly were not fiery Andalucians or 'here's the shirt off my back' Riojans. We did get a glimpse of the famous stinginess on the train back from Sitges. We all had zone-1 cards that had taken us through the gates and into the beach town with no problems. On the return journey a man came round doing the checks accompanied by an unnecessary pair of skinny, scruffy security guards that looked about eighteen years old. Apparently our cards didn't actually permit us to travel to Sitges. We spoke in English.

'But it let us through the machine,' we protested acidly.

'Ah, but the machine doesn't know where you are going,' he replied with a seemingly practised cockiness.

We had to pay for the fare, plus a few euros fine on top. Angry at this blatant example of daylight robbery we resisted the urge to speak Spanish and maintained the 'but we are just dumb tourists' routine in the hope we would receive some pity. We initially felt victimised but then it happened to a group of young Spanish people who were sat opposite us. This was clearly a clever tactic to catch people travelling back to Barcelona who had made this mistake. Our conversation, full of venom, turned to speed cameras and the general injustice of the world. In the evening we all consoled ourselves with healthy quantities of cava and spurious conversation.

*   *   *   *

The next morning I screwed up twice. It was becoming a 'thing' I did. I had planned to get the 9:46 train to Girona but, with a head that smacked of alcohol abuse, I instead gave myself another hour in bed. I would get the 10:46. Nobody was there to wake me or disturb my morning. Caroline and Ben were still very much asleep. I then underestimated the delay caused by a train station that lacked clarity. This fact together with the many, many people using the station made it tricky to know where I had to go. I was no longer in some Castillian town with its three or four platform affair. Walking around like some parentless child in a supermarket, the 10:46 train came and went. I returned to the flat, waited, feeling like an idiot for a while, and then finally trudged *again* to the station and caught the 11:46.

Girona is a classy and photogenic place. It was like the walls themselves knew they were pretty. I swear I saw a little church pouting as I focussed my camera. Girona has been likened to Venice for the sheer-sided flats that stand directly on the water's edge, no banks. And, with the absence of Venice on the 'places I have visited' list, I found it a fine thing to behold. The slim Onyar River splits the town in two, while down both sides of the watery corridor pastel-coloured flats of different colours rise up and follow the current until the end of the built-up area. Soft reds, yellows, pinks and blues glowed gently as the sun warmed them, throwing reflections onto the water. I crossed the broad, cream-coloured main square, traversed a very slender bridge and slinked through a doorway, which looked more like an entrance to a big, coloured burrow built by so many furry, bipedal rabbits.

Walking around Girona I almost never saw a street that didn't capture some internal sense of romance. Some were stony, cobbled and impossibly narrow; some looked like a black and white artist had just discovered what colour was; some were full of arches and tunnelled promenades; and some just looped around corners, up and down and around like those Escher staircases, here and there exposing some tiny, forgotten medieval building or rustic little café. It was an enchanting place and, fortunately for me, most of the tourists stayed around the main square or the area around the cathedral and the magnificent stone staircase that led up to its door.

There was a complex of tiny gardens with some little steps. These steps were surprising as they trailed up and down and along a vast path system, which I later found out was the old Roman wall that had long since been absorbed into the city. It tapered up to elevated views of the cathedral and ruins before rising quickly and delivering me to a tower that offered an amazing vista of the entire town from the terracotta-tile Spanish roofs out to the Catalonian Pyrenees brooding on the horizon. I walked along a long spine of wall to another tower and tried to imagine what it would have been like running up and down the wall, 20m up, in full armour and in the heat of the Spanish sun. It was a wall that had been put to good use. Girona, by the eighteenth century, had been besieged twenty-one times. In the nineteenth century it earned the nickname 'Immortal' by surviving separate five attacks from French forces. 'L'immortale'.

Sheathing my imaginary sword I initiated my favourite activity of the trip – finding somewhere to eat. That something to eat was annoyingly elusive until I came across a small alleyway-cum-courtyard where there were a few restaurants all competing on price. I chose the most endearing looking one and had myself a selection of typical Catalan dishes. I started with *patatas de Olot*, small potato parcels stuffed with spiced meat, and followed it up with *botifarra catalan*, which was basically as close as I have seen to a real, English-style sausage, flavoured with herbs. Surrounded by stone walls, I could have sat in my wicker chair all afternoon but I was soon brought back into the land of living by some new customers wanting hamburgers.

I walked away feeling both sated and superior. The town's clientele didn't improve much and I soon despaired again when I heard a group of German boys asking some passer-by where they could find a place that served pizza. I wanted to shout at them and ruffle their styled hair. Why travel all the way to another country only to eat pizza? Unless it's Italy, in which case fair enough. There were lots of young Germans there that day. It looked like some end of term school trip. The boys were boisterous and vying for the attentions of the girls, who sat pretending not to notice. They annoyed me profusely. But, all being said, I was thoroughly happy with the day I spent there, and could one day see myself retiring there with Emilia, my still beautiful future Spanish wife. Just as long as there are no German kids.

For my last evening Caroline, buzzing around the living room thinking of what we could do, settled on the idea to take me up to the 'magic fountain'. From the viewpoint by the MNAC, and after negotiating both the hundreds of people and the random and loud Harley Davidson convention, we were treated to a free show. A massive fountain sprayed and jetted water into the air, as different coloured lights somehow seemed to change the hue of every drop. Music played in the background so sometimes the water was dancing to classical music and sometimes to pop. We showed up for the evening's final performance – movie themes. I recognised a sprinkling of 'Titanic' and a dash of 'E.T.'. At times the fountain appeared like some decorated, multicoloured trifle and at others a broiling, steamy, blood-coloured cloud. It was a startling spectacle and I was impressed and gladdened that it was free. It was heart-warming to see families, couples, friends and tourists all enjoying it together. More than just some gimmick it was, like most things in Spain, utterly unpretentious. Honest.

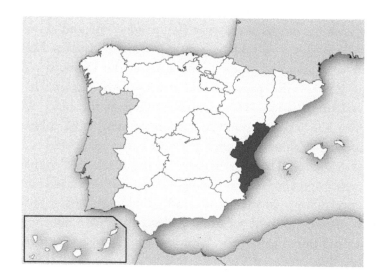

Pyromania and Rice

Valencia – La Albufera – El Palmar – Denia - Alicante

The train to Valencia took almost five hours and for the most part was unremarkable. The first hour and a half, down through Cataluña and into the Comunidad Valenciana, was appealing – little beach towns, with holiday looking flats, affronted by the impossibly bluey blueness of the sea. Beaches drifted in and out of view as we sailed past. Here and there were little coves or old naked men bronzing their bits. However, the remaining landscape down to Valencia was unfortunately dull and I had to spend a large part of it sat near an extraordinarily fat man snoring away like it was about to go out of fashion. His walrus-like body heaved and keeled like some beached sea-mammal. His lips often flapped and his uvula trembled and spluttered.

Once in Valencia I met with Nicola, a girl I knew from a European cinema course unit we had shared at university. She happened to be staying with my contacts and was free to meet me and show me the way to their flat. I would be staying with my friends Malou and Imogen who also had studied languages at the University of Bath. Walking through the quite familiar streets of the city centre – I had holidayed there twice – I was able to look at the place with new eyes; eyes that had set upon the corners of many other places in the same country. Valencia is a city of wildly extravagant streets and vast areas of grandeur. The most lavish was the Plaza del Ayuntamiento, which was originally built in the classic Spanish neo-baroque style to house prestigious finance and trade buildings. They stood and loomed proudly around a central pedestrian square adorned with a fountain and bursting flowers. This was the template for most of the large area that is central Valencia. It was a far cry from the medieval excesses of Castilla y León or the quiet Mudéjar of Aragon.

At a little café we ordered a couple of beers and some *sobresada y miel*: a chorizo meat paste on bread, drizzled with honey. It was a funky place called Los Escalones de la Lonja. Personal, and not like the soulless franchises that abound on the thoroughfares, it sat in a nook between two high-walled buildings and was hidden from most human traffic. The front of the menu was covered with cartoons of people saying various things directed at some character called Frank in the middle. One character was a woman with a nose stud and sleek brown hair.

'I bet that's our waitress,' said Nicola looking up from the menu as a girl holding coffees walked past us.

As the waitress headed back to the café I caught her eye.

'Excuse me, are these cartoons of the people who work here?'

'Yep, and there's me there!' the waitress prodded the stud-nosed character on the menu with pride.

It appeared Nicola was right.

When my hosts finally arrived we expressed our pleasure via the medium of hugging and the old 'Soooo, how have you been' pitter patter. Imogen is a creature of such bubbling happiness and enthusiasm for life that it could verge on the annoying. It never does though, because she's more honest than anyone and lives with a free whimsy I could only aspire too. Covered in freckles and with luscious brown hair kissed with auburn, she seems to float through life on a zephyr of innocence. Malou is an intensely attractive girl with features that are the slightest bit mousy. More than her physical attributes I had a mad crush on her at university for her keen wit and sarcasm. She is quick to laugh and faster to retort. As a pair they are annoyingly well-dressed and insufferably fun.

In the evening I helped Imogen prepare a whopping great roast chicken dinner for her friends who were coming round. If foreigners were coming, Imogen, or Immy, loved taking it upon herself to dispel any notion that in Britain the food is terrible. In the end we had Ida and Tor from Norway, Cristina from Germany, and Rohun from the UK. After some butcher-like carving from yours truly we sampled our British feast. For some it was their first roast, for the rest of us it was a long needed taste of home. Months of tapas had led me to forget the sweet, familiar taste of an oven-cooked chicken, served with spongy vegetables and crispy potatoes, swimming in a placid lake of rich gravy.

After dinner and some glasses of red, Malou showed me her 'walk in wardrobe'. Because I am really mature I decided it would be most amusing to lock her in. Maybe not a move expected of someone my age, but it *was* amusing. The situation however became gradually more worrying as I couldn't seem to unlock the door. Malou started calling from inside – 'Ok, funny guys, come on now, let me out' – and people started to trickle out of the living room to see what all the fuss was about. I unfortunately timed my stupid act the same night that Malou and Imogen's housemate, Elias, had invited a small army of Americans back for burritos. As a result there were twenty people wondering why some chubby, red-faced, prat had just locked some innocent girl in a cupboard. It soon became evident that there was some problem with the lock. Fretting occurred. Rohun, the excitable Londoner was going crazy:

'Oh my God, she's gonna die!'

'Keep it down, the neighbours!' said Elias.

'How long can you survive in a closet?!'

'Keep the noise down!' he hissed, emphasizing the word down.

'Is there enough oxygen??'

'*Rohun!!*' he snarled.

'How hard can it be to get out of a closet?!' added some unknown voice from across the pond.

'Well it took me 20 years!' barked Rohun, his hand covering his face in concern.

He later admitted that he had been very camp about it all and joked happily when the video of the ordeal was later uploaded onto Facebook. Eventually Elias, having stood with his hand on his chin for a while, upped the tension and brought out his big plastic case of power tools. He took out the electric screwdriver and removed the handle on the closet door. Standing up and breathing deeply, he thought for a moment and said:

'Right, everyone, just stand back. And can you close that window.'

'You're not going to kick it are you?' peeped an American guy.

'Can you warn her?' said a girl.

'Shh, shh, everyone just be quiet please.'

Fortunately, before our inmate had to break the door down from inside he tried the Switzerland approach one last time.

'Malou, can you just push the door a little?'

And as if by some cruel streak of luck the door opened easily and Malou emerged like a slightly bemused rabbit from a hole, greeted by a crowd of onlookers.

'I was alright in there actually,' she beamed.

*   *   *   *

I woke up at 9 o'clock to an empty room. Malou had already gone to work. I rolled off my camp bed and breakfasted with Immy. Within the hour we were taking a tram to the beach. The public transport within Valencia is a bit of a joke in Spain, with local buses being the only useful option. The metro is state-of-the-art but goes nowhere needed and completely avoids the centre, whereas the flashy tram route only really services some university students and beach goers. Happily this morning Imogen and I *were* beach goers and it was a sleek and seamless trip through town and out to the Malvarossa beach. We set ourselves down under the sun about 10m from the water and cooked ourselves.

A quick thing about sand: love and hate have never been so well melded together as in these microscopic silica-based granules. As you lie there on your towel it's deeply relaxing to run your hands and feet through the sand. Digging deeper you mix hot sand with cool and temperatures trickle over you. However, the moment, the very second, you apply sun cream or have a quick dip in the water sand becomes a miniature plague of irritation. Every crack, crevice and surface with even the smallest levels of cohesive prowess gets coated with the little ochre buggers. You can't wipe it away because it's on your hands, you can't add more cream because it's all over your legs. You have two options:

1. Take the high road, as adopted and suggested by Imogen, and just ignore it and enjoy the fact that you are on a beach in Spain.
2. Or do what I do – bitch and moan, 'Bloody sand', 'Everywhere!', and eventually run into the sea as a feeble sign of protest before repeating the procedure again.

Imogen had a class in the afternoon so I tore myself away from the long arm of yellow sand and the legions of attractive, half-naked bodies and joined her, ice-cream in hand, on the tram back to the city. Having separated from her I enjoyed a drink with Malou for a while in a chic little café in some light-filled back street as we waited for Immy to finish her class. When she finally materialised, rosy-cheeked and smiling like a toddler, we all went to one of Valencia's free art galleries, the Muvim, to see an exhibition by the Cádiz born artist Fernando Medina called *'Nevando Tinta'* – 'Snowing Ink'. After our fill of paper-based emblematic art it was then Malou's turn to go and teach a class so I was once again left alone with the bubble of life that is Imogen. I felt like a child being passed between two loving, but separated, parents.

'Why don't we hire a bike?' I offered.

'OK!' she said without more than a second's thought.

Easy.

It's nice to know that in this hectic world of emails, agendas, Blackberrys and meetings there is still place – a little adventurous place – for a thing called spontaneity. We found a tiny bike shop and there Immy sweet-talked the owner to give us two hours with two city bikes for only €10. So charming is she that she can negotiate in a shop – a shop with a fixed rate. After adjusting our seats a bit we were off, slightly wobbly and scared of going out onto the roads. In England I love cycling and I have no problem taking the road. But there was something about Spain – where liberal horn use and over enthusiastic application of the accelerator and brake pedals were par for the course – that made me really not want to get off the pavement. Some minutes and a few startled Spaniards later, we managed to decant ourselves into the *Jardín del Turia* park and begin our ride in earnest.

Valencia is a bit of a town planner's/architect's wet dream. Not only for the neo-baroque excesses and the ultra-modern, otherworldly Ciudad de Artes y Ciencia, but also for what they did to the river Turia. In 1957 Valencia was struck by a catastrophic flood and, to prevent further devastation, the waterway was diverted southwards onto a new course that instead skirts the south side of the city. The result for Valencia was a lush, sunken park that follows the course of what was once the riverbed. It is stuffed with lawns, shimmering ponds, tinkling fountains, paths, spectral flowers, sports pitches, cafés, sculptures, exercise areas and even zen gardens. The traffic leaves it untouched and instead passes over on the now obscure looking bridges that loom strangely as if somebody had left them there forgetting to add the water.

We flew past groups of friends playing football, kicking up dust clouds; past the bridges and fountains; past families with dogs strolling or picnicking amongst the trees. It was a moment to feel truly alive. Cycling through a beautiful, safe and unknown area is refreshing. We left the park and weaved in and around the turquoise pools and ivory-coloured curves, wings and bulges of the science and arts complex. The heat was intense and the city's location meant that it was humid. We kept on cycling. To stop was to suffer. After trying, somewhat in vain, to reach the port and dockyards area we slowly wheeled back to the bike shop.

That evening we met up with a fairly large group of people and went for some tapas. Seldom in Spain did one have a 'sit down meal' in the evening, let alone in high summer. It was the usual selection of cheese, dried meats, tomato and bread, along with more fancy nibbles: pâté with olives, curried turkey on spinach, grilled chicken with fig sauce and various other clever treats. After the food we had another drink in a bar with plastic, painted show-girl legs sticking out of the walls, but, bludgeoned sleepy by the heat and the day's exercise, we called that our last drink and returned to the flat. I was finding it difficult to make it through the days in the coastal part of my trip. The crippling humidity combined with the ferociousness of the sun, hanging like some cruel lamp in the blue sky, meant that by the time the evening had arrived all I wanted to do was sleep, preferably next to a fan.

*   *   *   *

In the morning, before I split from Imogen, we went into the enormous Mercado Central. It is one of the biggest indoor markets in Europe, dwarfing its more celebrated Barcelona-based cousin both in terms of grandeur and aesthetics. I bought fancy pâtés as a gift for my upcoming hosts in Denia: pigeon with armagnac and pheasant with red wine. The market itself was an astounding example of the *modernista* style of building. Inside it looked like a cross between the skeleton of a whale viewed from the belly up into the ribcage and an empty, metal church. As the market stalls themselves were only a couple of metres high the overall effect was an abundance of space. Imogen fluttered away to another lesson and I visited the Mercado Colón; another modernist market, which is now a collection of swanky shops. It was big, red and hollow. A shell, essentially. It felt like Paddington in London, but miniature, and with no trains, and…Spanish. So, not a lot like it really, but it did…feel like Paddington.

At 12:54 on the dot I, slightly ashamedly, caught the tourist bus – one of those long, red, LOOK AT ME I'M A TOURIST ones – to La Albufera, a large, freshwater lagoon about 11km from the city. The bus was almost empty as I only shared it with two old Spanish ladies nattering to each other and a middle-aged German man who sat legs crossed, a leather satchel round his neck, looking thoughtfully out of the window. Escaping the madness of the city we glided quickly into the lands that sprawl out from the lake. Endless broad views of rice paddies and sunken grass; millions of little green shoots submerged in flooded, nutrient rich fields created a strange, foreign landscape.

These tiny, inconspicuous plants form a cornerstone of both regional and national economy and are a powerhouse of Spanish cuisine. Paella isn't just another thing to eat; it's deeply woven into the culture, geography and social traditions of the region. It's a way of life.

The evening before, I had managed to speak with three of Imogen's students after their class.

'For you guys, what is it to be Valencian?' I asked.

'It's to be the best, for sure! But seriously, it's my home, my life, you know? I *am* Valencian,' said a lively woman with frizzy blonde hair.

'It's where you come from, it's your heritage,' added another.

'If I talk to a foreigner, of course, I'm Spanish. But if I am in Spain I am Valencian first and Spanish second.'

Then there was some debate about this hierarchy between the students themselves. They squabbled, using their hands as emphatic props. I also added, just to spice it up, that many Catalans are Catalans full stop. One student said that the Comnidad Valenciana is different to a lot of other regions, citing Andalucía in particular.

'For example we have no thick history of traditional dance or music. We are not quite like the south.'

I then finally pressed an issue that had been bugging me for years.

'And…why paella? I mean don't get me wrong, I like it, but it's not…incredible…'

'Oh it is! Paella's the best!'

'What are you saying, paella is fantastic!'

Having calmed down, one of the girls helped me understand.

'Paella, well, rice, is our life, our tradition. It's from our land. On Saturdays, for example, it is very common to get together round a huge paella, all the family, or friends, and eat and talk.'

It wasn't just the regional tradition but also a social glue. Whether it was the most exciting taste or not was beside the point….or not even the point…or barely close to being the slightest bit pointy. It was their version of a British Sunday roast. It was a dish to bring them together. It wasn't about the merits or defects of the food itself but just the fact that paella, like food should, keeps people together. And I, loving my food, had to respect that.

The lake slid into view and my intrepid crowd of four arrived at the tiny town of El Palmar. We were immediately taken away from the bus stop and to a jetty where a powerful and dark man was waiting for us by a wooden engine-powered gondola. It was one of the boats the locals used for fishing out in the waters. Due to the depth of the lake, large bowed or heavy boats would have been all but useless. The gondolas were able to skim over the surface. Our pilot, shining in a red shirt, used a large pole to push us out a little and then pulled a cord, causing the little motor to splutter into life. The Albufera was a placid, serene, if not overly beautiful, place. Green reed banks and tufts of thicket formed arms that prodded out into the water while small, narrow channels curved away out of view. Our boat washed in and out of them. We buzzed out a little way into the lake itself but never to the centre. It was of course, at 2,800 hectares, quite a large body of water.

The Albufera is also a haven for migrating birds, though where we were you wouldn't have known it. As a result of its importance for these winged travellers the area was placed on the Special Protection Areas list in 1991. There were some herons, ducks, small white storks and terns using the vegetation and air as both battlefield and playground but the main bulk of them were probably far away from the towns that dot the area. In the distance Valencia could be seen, in a heat-haze, flexing its muscles against the horizon. We 'put-put-putted' around for maybe half an hour before the small jetty came back into view. The driver turned the engine off and instantly we were coated with silence. It was palpable; I could feel it in my ears and in my head. The pulse of blood. Nobody spoke. The only sound was the wind tickling the reeds and some far-off bird chatter. I smiled and closed my eyes. I hadn't experienced such quiet in so long. It was comforting to see the old ladies, the German fellow and the boatman himself doing the same thing.

I had paid the bus driver a few extra euros so that I could be picked up later. I talked with the sweet old girls – who were fascinated by both my nationality and my mission – up until the bus stop but then said farewell. They were off back to the city whereas I about turned and marched off into El Palmar in search of their famous paella. The town was neither beautiful nor pretty. It wasn't ugly though, just small and normal. It did, however, have a unique atmosphere. It was almost entirely devoted to the production, cooking, selling and eating of paella. In El Palmar they lived and breathed rice. Every other building seemed to be a restaurant or café offering all the variations of the dish. I finally, given that there was a case of much of a muchness going on, settled on a place on little street, Plaza de la Sequita, which was lined with eateries. I decided to sit down inside as the humidity had been rising the further south along the coastline I went and it was really rather uncomfortable. I was also ever paranoid about how sweaty I may or may not look. I suppose the enormous wetland didn't help matters.

As I read the menu I was brought a beer, some bread and a few slices of very fresh tomato liberally drowned in olive oil and salt. I ordered two Valencian specialities: *all i pebre* – eels in a piquant sauce – and a classic seafood paella. The eels, wriggly bastards, showed me for the foreigner I was as I keenly tucked into the fish wondering if I was supposed to be crunching up the little eel spines. I decided I wasn't supposed to because if that was the intended method, it was crap. Flaking the flesh off the bones changed my opinion in an instant. The sauce was oil, garlic and paprika, which formed a small lake in which potatoes and creamy eel meat writhed. I continued writing in my journal and could sense an interest, or concern, from my waiter. He was one of the restaurant's head honchos and in the reflection in a shiny marble pillar I saw him and another waiter talking to each other under their breath and looking in my direction. At one point he walked past and practically peered over my shoulder at what I was writing. He then came out with a little dish for me.

'It is the same eel dish, but this time with onion. It's even nicer I think.'

It was a sample dish and was the same as before but enhanced by the sweetness of the onions. I probably wouldn't have been given it were I alone and not writing in a black leather notebook. Letting my belly relax for a while, I pondered the amusing reactions of the waiter. 'How were the tomatoes?', 'was that all alright for you?'. He really wanted me to be happy. I decided against spilling the beans that I was really just a tourist and not someone important.

As I was writing a big, straight-backed man in a white polo shirt and chinos, who was there with a group of four adults and some children, came over. He had rosy cheeks, lifted by the wine, and a big, grey, bushy moustache.

'Excuse me. I am sorry to interrupt, but I was curious as to what you were writing.'

I explained my intentions.

'Ah. May I sit?' he said steadily and with a practised courtesy.

'Of course.'

He bowed his head, carefully placed his glass of red wine down on the table and took a seat.

'So where have you been already?'

We talked a while about the different places I had seen and where I had yet to go. He was a *madrileño* who had lived many years in Italy before finally resting in Valencia. His name was Antonio Ribas Jiménez and he was a captain of the Valencian Navy. Years of military service and travel had led him to Valencia, with its easy atmosphere, Mediterranean way of life and good weather. He had some Italians visiting and wanted them to taste the best paella around, thus their presence at the table opposite me.

At some point during our conversation my two-person paella (because traditional paella can't, or won't, be served for one) arrived and was placed in front of me. Given the dish's fame paella can be found on almost every *menu del día* or in every Spanish café and bar. All too often, though, it is either reheated from frozen or just not nice. Paella pans are large and so don't often come in a size that will be acceptable for one person. So, in a typical *menu del día* it arrives as a dollop on a white plate. A lot of restaurants, like the El Palmar one, insist on two-person paellas as a minimum. Despite it being annoying if you are alone, it ensures that it has been prepared fresh, and it comes out sizzling in the big, black pan it was cooked in.

'A two-person one?' he enquired in his steady measured tone, lightly touched with surprise.

It was at this point that one of his friends, a jolly Italian woman, came over to see for what reason her host had left.

'A two-person one?' she enquired before even introducing herself.

'Yes, I'm English, it's fine.'

Antonio emitted a small laugh, his moustache bristled.

'Well, we will leave you to eat your paella and continue writing.'

Paella still, even after El Palmar, isn't my favourite dish. Having said that, the paella in El Palmar was still easily the best one I had tasted. Gently tangy fish, citrus and saffron flavours sat, scattered like cushions on a velvety bed of rice, upon which a few baked prawns and mussels lounged in a dead, marine way. I couldn't finish it all, though I managed an impressive, or gross, three quarters. It was a sad day for sea-life but a felicitous one for my insides. When I had finished, clearly beaten by the food, Antonio approached again, 'would you like to join us for coffee?'. I said I would. More than coffee they also gave me some shots of a digestif liqueur into which we dunked some chubby wedges of *bizcocho* (a sort of sponge cake). We talked for another twenty minutes or so about Spain, England and Italy and their differences before settling our respective bills. Mine was about 10 euros more than I had hoped to pay. I consoled my now thinner wallet with the fact that I had had a wonderful time. Outside in the wet heat Antonio, now with even ruddier cheeks and a further away look in his eyes, seized and shook my hand, gave me his contact details and got out his keys.

'Well, this is my car. Send me an email when you have finished your book so I can read it!'

He left El Palmar and I chose to go for a walk in order to get some views of the lake from the banks. Strolling all the way out of the

107

village, I passed wide, irrigated rice fields, small El Palmar houses with their thatched roofs (*barracas*), and gardens rich with lemon trees and bulging green tomatoes slowly ripening red in the sun. The sun was hot and the air was thick in my nostrils. Somewhere I couldn't see, I could hear what sounded like countless thousands of birds making very bird-like noises. Like a BBC documentary soundtrack. Soothing Attenborough voice. Hushed. 'And here we don't see the INSERT ANIMAL'. Recession TV. Budget nature. 'The Power of the Planet: a crisis edition'. I never got that postcard view of the lake I had seen on the tourism bumf, but I got some glimpses. Walking back to the village I noticed the conspicuous tourist bus bombing down the road. He then noticed me, stopped, incurred some angry honks from the one car behind him, and let me jump on.

In the evening I overcame an eating-based nausea just in time to attend the San Juan celebrations. This is the Spanish name for a celebration the likes of which is common to many cultures, mostly European – the arrival of the Summer Solstice. The UK has Midsummer, the Germans call it Sommer-Sonnenwende, Norway celebrates Sankthansaften, the Estonian name is Jaaniõhtu, while the Russians have fun on Ivan Kupala Day. All involve that time-honoured combination of nature, alcohol and fire.

The festivities started with a walk to the beach from a bar located near the coastline. The absurd scene that then rolled itself out in front of us was one of thousands of people on the shore. Some were huddled around bonfires, some around BBQs or just collected in clumps around piles of food and drink. I could barely see the sand for all the bodies there. It was strange because it still didn't really look that busy. Oddly for Spanish people it seemed that the conventions of personal space were finally being upheld. Not like in the Madrid metro on a workday where it was perfectly fine, and common, to have your face pressed deep into the moist armpit of some glistening forehead in a suit on his way to some important sweaty business.

We marched out a little way towards the water – about halfway between the promenade and the sea – laid down various blankets, jumpers and plastic bags to sit on and officially launched our San Juan celebration with a toast. Smoke filled the black sky, glowing orange with streetlamps and fires. Our eyes stung but it was fine. The smell of burning wood and salty air was thick and perforated the entire area, clogging nostrils. Some groups near us were playing music and dancing, while at the far end of the beach a large stage, complete with a light show, blasted out some indecipherable tunes that too quickly were lost in the hubbub. Most people were in swimming costumes, bikinis, or shorts but out of my group I was surprised to find that I was the only one to wear apt clothing.

I decided to make the most of this fact, as I had never swum in the sea at night. Squeezing past huddles of people, dodging discarded beer cans and making sure I didn't place my feet firmly in someone's fire, I finally broke through the line and met the water. There were people in the surf as well as people on the sand but there was a strange division. Like when you have a massive crowd, then a gap, then a police line. I was in the police line, but wetter and noticeably more naked. I waded out. The sea was black as oil. Black water against a black sky. The waves were almost indistinguishable from the nothingness above them. Soggy phantoms lifted me up and down or smashed into my face. I treaded water and turned 180° to view the beach. It was also a little eerie. Individual people and their features were hard to pick out. Blurry human shapes. It was just a long, black, heaving line of person-like silhouettes forming an endless barrier along the coast as the space above their heads illuminated orange.

I rejoined my group and stood drying myself next to our neighbour's fire. One of the traditions of San Juan was that at midnight one had to jump over waves and/or a fire seven times. Lacking our own flaming pit Rohun, Imogen and I took to hopping over the waves along with hundreds of others. We carried on along the shore towards the end of the beach with the stage but never got to the thing itself as our attention was distracted by a small, lonely fire looking a little sorry for itself. We couldn't resist the temptation to do our seven jumps, take some photos and give the little pit of flames one last hurrah before he died.

As a group we all decided to leave our initial place and see where we drifted. We tidied up our area and, like the responsible lot we were, took away the rubbish and wedged it into overfilling bins. We ended up back on the promenade, where we stayed, standing for what felt like an age. The girls had set off searching for meat, as the stalls around us all seemed to only sell grilled corn on the cob. A sea-air fuelled hunger. They came back, unsuccessful, after about fifteen minutes and then tried another direction. The rest of us stood, clutching plastic bags and towels, twiddling our thumbs. After another disappointed return I stepped into the fray, now hungry, and left with them in search of dead, cooking animals and, following our senses, found a couple of stands a few metres from us. Microwaved hamburgers and hotdogs, three euros each. We queued and got our money ready; greed driving us to buy awful, awful food. Imogen and Malou rolled their eyes and folded their arms. Someone then pushed in. A thing that doesn't best please an Englishman.
'Um, there's a queue,' I offered as sarcastically as I could.
The girl doing the food then gave a knowing smile to me but then inexplicably went on to serve them before us – the same 'us', who had been talking with her for the few minutes up until that point. Immediately wishing she would microwave her own stupid face we left to a nearby, well-timed and well-placed BBQ with five fat kebabs sizzling on it. We bought them instead.

I spent some time trying to find my flip-flops. It turned out that nobody wanted my high-end camera, mobile phone or money.

Instead some four-letter word had stolen my bloody footwear! At the peak of my confused wrath a Finnish guy and two attractive Swedish girls showed up and started talking to the Norwegians. I was dizzied by so much Scandinavia. Half an hour after *that* episode we found a dying fire and thought it deserved to be resurrected. With a combination of about twenty newspapers and two massive hunks of wood – neither of which mix together well for a steady burn – the little fire crackled back to life. A young urchin-like boy on the beach then brought us small bits of wood, giving our fire an extra half an hour of life. Cold, bored and maintaining what was essentially a pile of burning paper we realised we weren't going to see the sunrise. We begrudgingly called it quits at around 5:00am. I walked back through Valencia in my bare feet on the cool pavements. Imogen removed her shoes and did too, just so I didn't feel too bad. She's sweet like that.

*   *   *   *

The following morning, too early to get more than a sleepy goodbye and a floppy, sleeping cat hug from the girls, I caught the bus to Denia. I had family friends there who said I was more than welcome to drop in and stay for a night. Far be it from me to pass up an opportunity to revisit where they live.

Patricia and Enrique Farne, originally from South America, came and built a home for themselves in the large Valencian town of Denia after reading an advert in a 1999 copy of the Sunday Telegraph that read "Build your house in the Costa Blanca". It invited prospective buyers to visit the town, which he did. Falling in love with the area the family then bought a plot and built a property. The architects and builders, however, had different ideas and ballsed up the project, not completing the house according to Enrique's original plans; the whole building was seven metres out of place and the views that he had wanted were affected. They later sold this house and moved to another property where they still reside today.

'Why did you move there then, to Denia?'

'I had decided to move here since my roots and character is very Latin. Patricia comes from Colombia and I come from Chile, so we did not have the same origin and so we did not consider to go back to one or the other Latin country. They are very different, and culturally they are very different too. Chile has a more European influence while Colombia is more North American. Besides, with two children born in the UK, South America was considered to be far away. Spain seemed a good compromise, close to our kids and offering language and cultural similarities with Latin America.'

Enrique and Patricia are fresh faced, happy people who go about their business with a relaxed demeanour granted after years of earning their position. Enrique glides around in shorts and chinos, looking, facially, ever so slightly like a Latino Woody Allen while Patricia is shorthaired, energetic and has a voice that sails away languorously. Their house looked like it had been cut out of a 'rich list' California magazine and glued into one about Spanish coastal settlements. A beautiful white house with cream finishes stood opulently on an incline with a broad view of Denia and the sea to the east and the rising hulk of the Montgó mountain instantly to the west. Two and a bit storeys of elegantly furnished rooms with various antiques and porcelains added a touch of irresistible class to an environment that had no desire to shy away from home comforts: TVs, family photos and comfy sofas. Outside a cyan swimming pool wallowed and waited for bodies to cool while walls with bright purple flowers and little lemon trees lent a colourful backbone to the enclosure. The main attraction in my eyes was the little building that was separate from the house at the far end of the swimming pool. Enrique is what one would call a film buff. I am a film buff. Enrique is the film buff to beat all film buffs. He built himself a personal cinema with a 3x2.5m screen with six Lazyboy armchairs and even a little bar by the entrance. I looked forward to seeing it again as the palm trees and small, coastal towns flitted by.

I got off the bus and scanned for my ride. Blasted by the heat the world seemed hazy for a moment. It was like some shimmering scene from an Egyptian transport hub. A bus pulled out of the little station and revealed Enrique sitting in an open top BMW car wearing a fine, cream, Panama hat, waving to me with a large smile. We zoomed up away from the centre towards the breezy Montgó area and left the standard beach town to be pounded by the sun.

At the house I presented my tiny excuse for a present – the pâtés – and was rewarded with an exquisite welcome feast: cool, fresh melon wrapped lovingly in tangy Serrano ham followed by some perfectly cooked steaks. After the richness of lunch Enrique and I then retired, in a very manly way, to watch something, anything, on his cinema screen. We chose to watch Slovakia destroy the previous World Champions Italy in one of the most surprising World Cup upsets ever, interspersed with occasional snippets from Isner vs Mahut playing their first round Wimbledon tennis match, which turned out to be the longest ever tennis match in recorded history. It finally ended after eleven hours and five minutes. Tired of sport we started watching the James Bond film: Quantum of Solace. Ok, so I wasn't spending these couple of hours pouring insight into my ever-filling flask of experience, but it was hot outside, and the man had his own cinema.

Patricia had invited me to a local art exhibition in the evening so before leaving I chose to first enjoy the soothing waters of their pool, and then try and make myself look vaguely presentable. I had – dare I say it for fear of sounding sexist – a 'girl' moment. What should I wear? When packing for the pan-Iberia trip I hadn't prepared for much soirée-based activity. Sure I had some jeans but the thought of entombing my poor puppy-eyed, fearful legs in denim was entirely unattractive. I opted for a blue polo shirt and my white shorts. We got in the open-top and flew down the hill back into the town. Once or twice I clutched the seat. Enrique knew these roads, but I didn't. 'This is much quicker than a bus!' I yelled over the howling buffeting of the wind. I was glad my shout was met by contented laughs.

After slotting the car into a parking bay we entered the UNG, a sort of Spanish Open University, and went upstairs to where the noise was hiding. A couple of kids, laughing like mad things, ran down the stairs past me and a reverberating hum of conversation approached. Patricia had been taking part in an art class and tonight was the opening night exhibiting some of the students' work. As far as I could tell it was one piece per student. Dodging more crazed kids we swerved into a large room full of people staring noisily at paintings dotted around on the walls and on two central standalone partitions. Far from pretentious art critics, the space was bursting with family members and friends proudly enjoying the work of their loved ones. It was also an excuse to have a good, loud, Spanish chit-chat. The few Germans there (for Denia has a selection of expanding ex-pat communities) were almost imperceptible amongst that most wonderfully cacophonous machine that is the Spanish voice. Patricia's effort was a fine one; a landscape of snow-topped green mountains leading down to water. What I found most charming about the exhibition was how these art students, mostly just 'normal' people with a hobby, had experimented with so many different artistic styles to provide often wonderful and occasionally dazzling results. Autumnal scenes, still lifes, flowers, abstracts, 3D images and portraits all hung proudly.

'Oh, that's María's' and 'Aw, it's so beautiful'. The evening gave me a little window that allowed me to see what art was all about. That little bit of feeling in whatever nuance it comes to. If you look at a painting or listen to a song and you feel nothing, you are bored, and the art has failed. Maybe not for everyone, but for you. I, for example, loathe religious art and Holbein style portraits. I respect the talent behind it but I find it mostly dull and repetitive. Throw a Turner, Kandinsky, Dali, Van Gogh or Banksy in front of me and my heart beats faster. The Louvre has its Mona Lisa, the Reina Sofia its Guernica, and the National Gallery has its Bathers at Asnieres. The most famous, and indeed revered, painting in the Prado, in Madrid, is '*Las Meninas*' by the enviably talented Spanish painter Velazquez. I used to think it was rubbish until I went round the museum with my Irish friend Anna who chided me and spoke so emphatically about it that I upgraded my opinion from 'it's rubbish' to 'it's not bad'. But I'd still rather look at a Rorschach test paper if I am totally honest.

Before you think I'm a hater, I want to state that this is one of the things I love about art. There truly is something for everyone. Some people like beautifully crafted art, realism or the Renaissance style and some prefer the wackier stuff like cubism, abstract and surrealism. Some like pop-art. Some like awful cough-damianhirsttraceyemin-cough art. I dislike it, and that's my right. I distrust that kind of non-art. Some say, and it really pisses me off when they do, 'you just don't under*stand* it'. Some say that if those people love art so much they would allow a semi-cubist sculpture of an angry carrot to feel right at home wedged up their backsides. I don't want to understand it. I shouldn't need to understand it. I want to look at it and say 'yes, I like that, that's good'.

I think my scepticism of art made its first appearance on a school trip to the Tate Modern in London when I was maybe ten years old. I don't remember much, but I remember one painting in particular that really dug deep and annoyed me. It was a blue square; nothing more. Just a blue square. There was a little information panel beside it giving the unfortunate viewer a pretentious name followed by an even more pretentious explanation. That was the moment. When I was ten! How's that art, I thought. And that was it.
'*Tres, dos, uno!*'
And there was the photo of all the art students.

After the exhibition we took a stroll up to the compact old quarter, which was classically Spanish but only comprised a couple of streets, and then down to the port where we enjoyed an enormous frozen yoghurt that was, according to Patricia, healthier than ice cream.

'If you were here a couple of weeks earlier you would have seen the bulls running into the sea,' said Enrique, prodding his ice-cream substitute with a plastic spoon.

'I'm sorry?'

Bous a la Mar is a festival in Denia that has been denoted, like *San Fermín* and *Las Fallas*, a festival of National Tourist Interest. It is celebrated between the 5th and 13th of July and, like all bull-related celebrations, is a little controversial. The highlight of the weeklong party is the spectacle of the bulls running down the main street towards a makeshift bullring on the shore. The aim is then to attempt to chase or goad the bull into the sea, hence the name *Bous a la Mar* – Bulls to the Sea. Some brave, or idiotic, people will then jump in with them and swim alongside. It is this goading and bloodless baiting that makes the celebration ruffle the animal activists' feathers. However, unlike bullfighting, the bulls don't seem to suffer and tend to swim away unharmed. And, as with *San Fermín*, it is usually only the drunk or stupid that get injured.

Dinner was bread with sliced tomatoes and Serrano ham served with a crisp white wine. The view was fairy lights and far off ships. The next word was bed.

*   *   *   *

In the morning the energetic Patricia had agreed to take me up the Montgó Mountain. We couldn't walk to the summit as it was an 8km route and there wasn't enough time. Instead we headed half way up to a cave with a natural pool inside it. The sun was devastating. Either it felt like it had to remind the world what it was after all its recent absences or it just really wanted to see me burn. Enrique gave us a lift up to the beginning of the Parque Natural de Montgó and we set off.

A zig-zag led quite steeply up a hot stone path towards the splintering off point of different walking routes. The air fizzed with heat and the sound of crickets. It was thick but carried a helpful breeze. We ascended a steeper path towards the cave and my brow became wet. The last part of the walk skirted us round and eventually into the raised cliff face. The smell of flowers took itself onto the high zephyrs.

'Those are the fragrant virgin's bower flowers, they're typical of this area.'

Small creamy white drops of flora with even smaller red mites scurrying over the petals signposted the final stage of our ascension. A roman staircase and inscription ushered us up. The text was a snapshot of history that related to us the existence of a military detachment, *vexillatio*, which once was based there, keeping watch over the coast and protecting Roman Denia (*Dianum*) from the enemies of Emperor Maximus.

I noticed a hole in the grey cliff-face and childishly hopped and bounced up towards it. Realising how my enthusiasm must have appeared, I turned.

'I'm certainly still quite immature.'

'That's good though!' Patricia returned.

Smiled we headed into the un-signposted black little cave. To guide us we had Patricia's handheld torch and my surprisingly more powerful phone light. It was deadly silent and felt ancient. Low-walls and everything were covered with an eerie yellow dust. It felt like some prehistoric tomb. I ventured in as far as I could, navigating jutting out hunks of wall and ducking under ceilings that seemed to yearn to reconnect with the ground. At the end of the tunnel I felt truly inside the mountain. Still. Nothing. Nothing but for a tiny moth dancing euphorically in the cloud of illumination emanating from my phone. A beaming saviour in the pitch black. We scrambled out into the breathing world and climbed a little further to get to the cave we had actually come to see. Some crumbling doorway pulled us into a nondescript square chamber with a dark corridor leading off somewhere unseen. We activated our lights again and went down it, being careful to step on the little stones that poked their heads out offering us dry passage through the puddle that had settled from the recent rains. At the very end a large, squashed hole sat gloomily in the inner wall. I swung my light through it. A deathly placid, cold, freshwater pool sat unattended. It was the fullest that Patricia had seen it. It snaked round to God knows where and I wished I had my swimming trunks on.

'Taste it, it's beautiful,' she said.

It was as close as I have tasted to the 'perfect' water. It was like drinking the most refreshing, tasteless fruit juice. So quenching that it didn't need to bother your palate with flavour. Reluctantly I pulled myself away from that place and sweated my way back down the mountainside.

The Montgó site doesn't receive so many foreign tourists. It is a more private place for locals, people in the know and school trips. However, this may be on the verge of changing due to Denia's flashy, new tourist office complete with the same external touch screen panel I had seen in Valladolid. I secretly hoped that it didn't. Walking down in the buzzing heat we talked about food culture and different types of tourists, which included a brief foray into the nature of the ex-pat.

'To our surprise when we first moved to our property in Spain (the house we built and later on sold at a loss) we ended upon a hill with maybe fifty properties, all of them occupied by either Germans or German speaking Swiss nationals and despite that they had been living for years in Spain they did not speak Spanish nor English.'

After a swim, a shower, and a spectacular jambalaya style Chilean rice dish I was driven down to the bus station and seen off on the 17:30 to Alicante, a city where I had lived and studied for my Erasmus year at university.

The only thing that aroused a sentiment from me on the road to Alicante was the bus' pit stop in Benidorm. It was the second time I had entered into its vile grasp. The first time was when I had just finished my time in Alicante. A small group of us had wanted to see a bit of the coast so we took the small FGV tram northwards. Having heard of the famous town for so long we decided we had to see it for ourselves. Benidorm is one of a collection of blisters that blights the Eastern arse of Spain. I'm sure you already know the public image of the place: impossibly ugly tower blocks that provide holiday space for impossibly shambolic people; fine beaches laid to waste by fat bellies and chalk-white bodies crackling red in the Costa Blanca sun; shops that offer more faux-British food than Spanish and a big, fat invisible sticker on everything that says 'PACKAGE TOURISM HERE!'

We walked into a sweet shop and were immediately offered assistance in English by the attentive Spanish lady working there. I was slightly taken aback what with being Spanish students living in Alicante where, thankfully, the *lingua franca* is still Español. We answered her in Spanish and she seemed equally taken aback, but then smiled gratefully. We were a little disgusted by the situation and felt quite sorry for her, the fact that she, in her own country, had to start her day with a foreign language. The onus, we thought, should be on the tourist to at least make an effort. We managed to stay in Benidorm maybe two hours before feeling sick and high-tailing it further north to the deliriously pretty, white-walled town of Altea, a mere twenty minutes up the coast.

Before returning that second time I had read about how Benidorm was essentially a massive success story for Spain with regards to tourism and so I started thinking maybe I had previously been a little hard on the place. Seeing it for a second time I once again wrestled with my middle-class nature and had to remember how lucky I had been in my upbringing. Thanks to my parents, I was treated to a variety of fascinating and mind-broadening holidays to places like America, Oman and Hong Kong. My parents are not beach-folk so there was never a sniff of coastal resort in the planning stages. Also, again with my lucky position in life, we had enough to splash out and not look at package holiday deals. I dwelled on this as we crawled through the place. These were just normal people having a cheap and cheerful vacation as they could afford it. I'm sure that venturing into Thai monasteries and scaling Icelandic glaciers isn't everyone's idea of fun. Some just genuinely enjoyed the Benidorm experience, who was I too judge?

I started to feel a little ashamed of my haughty nose-up views but then I saw some bald men sporting outstanding bellies that crept out under the bottom of their England football shirts. I instantly wanted to run out of the bus, grab them and shake them screaming 'WHY ARE YOU HERE?!' Then I would find all the beleaguered Spanish people I could and apologise: 'some of us *are* interested in the Spanish side of Spain. We aren't all just paying for an England with a hotter sun and a whiter beach'. I still don't know if I'll ever make my peace with Benidorm or package tourism in general. I suppose I'm guilty of a kind of class snobbery that I am unable to shift.

When we reached Alicante, about forty-five minutes later, I felt a very tangible sense of nostalgia. My heart beat faster and I looked around like an excited puppy trying to take stock of everything its eyes laid upon. 'There's the X where I used to Y', 'Ah, there's where W and X Z-ed ', 'Haha, and remember when J drank X beers and P-ed all over B', and so forth. My mind was a flood.

Alicante will never win an award for being a beautiful place for it has, like many *costa* towns, suffered a little at the hands of change. However, it has a small, but charming, historic quarter – locally called 'El Barrio' – and an impressive castle that stands proudly over the whole city. I found that from almost anywhere of note in the town it can be seen popping up into view on its own private hill, Mount Benacantil.

The poor little fortress changed hands a lot of times during its long life. Its origins date way back to the 9th century when the Muslims controlled the majority of the Iberian Peninsula. Three hundred years later, in 1248, Alfonso X's Castilian forces swept into the area and captured it. The Castilians, however, only managed to hold on to it for a mere 48 years when, in 1296 it was conquered by James II's Aragonese forces. After this the castle experienced a calm four hundred-year siesta until 1691 when a French squadron bombed the living daylights out of it and it was seized by Napoleonic troops. The castle then had to endure the War of Spanish Succession, spending years under siege from a combined force of English and Dutch. In 1706 it spent three years under English control until Bourbon supporters packed the building's base with explosives and all but blew it up. After the end of the conflict the value of the beleaguered fort began to decline, as it was no longer of any great strategic importance. For a while it was a prison, for a shorter while became a place to house cholera victims and beggars and finally, in the 1960s, it became the tourist attraction it is today.

I waited at a little outside café for my host, Rodrigo, to arrive. I had lived with him for the six months I had spent in Alicante and then had met up with him and his girlfriend almost exactly two years prior to my return to the city - he had been staying for a couple of months in Didcot, a southern English town known for its power station, and was using his dad's house. I was really rather excited to see him again and stretched my one beer out to last three quarters of an hour while I waited. He was late. I paid up and leant against a familiar wall until my mobile phone beeped. I finally found him at the end of the main drag called La Rambla. He walked up to me with a big 'there he is' smile and gave me a warm, tight hug. It was truly great to see him again. As with the last time I had forgotten how athletic, tall and tanned he was. We exchanged brief pleasantries and then he introduced me to his friend Leon, who was sat, a vision of Mediterranean chic, on a classic white Vespa in shorts, a colourful t-shirt and Raybans. Rodrigo had his little, more sporty, scooter waiting dormant behind. It was certainly an improvement on his last bike; a little old banger that had once struggled to take us up the castle hill.

'Right Lucas, you're with Leon!'

Still bearing my weighty bag on my back I crammed on the little helmet and balanced myself on the rear of the Italian bike, joining my hands round Leon's front. A biological seatbelt. I knew the reason for the rush. At 20:30 was the Spain game against their Latino counterparts Chile and the watches were currently telling us that it was 20:15. Apparently we still had to buy some supplies. The two bikes buzzed up La Rambla toward Mercadona, a middle-range supermarket, a Spanish Sainsbury's. I lingered in the entrance. An obvious tourist with my big rucksack and rouged skin, I tried looking native by casually wielding my helmet.

20:20, running out of time.

Rodrigo and Leon were in a queue of a million other people buying snacks and alcohol for the game their country was about to play in. Everyone was checking their wrists. I mused that if England were playing the fans would have been prepared for it far in advance. But hey, this was Spain, lateness was in their blood. After a problem with change in the tills we bagged up the shopping and screamed off north through the city.

20:26.

We flew past old sights that were once part of what I called 'home': the market, the bullring, the fountain on the outside of the centre. If we had continued along that road I would have ended up at the university where I studied. Instead we veered off left and towards an area of clean but politely nondescript flats.

20:32.

'Joder, corre, ha empezado!', 'shit, leg it, it's already started!'
Three pairs of flip-flops ran across the road from the car park, into
a building, into a lift and then into a flat.
20:37, we hadn't missed anything.

I happily dumped my rucksack, prepared myself for introductions
and then entered the madhouse. Five guys, excluding us three, sat
gesticulating and talking loudly at the football and at each other.
Abel, Diego, Manolo and two others whose names I never
remembered greeted me immediately and politely and then returned
to giving helpful advice to the Spanish players, seeing how many
crisps they could fit into their mouths in one go and drifting in and
out of the banter that helps form any friendship – that mixture of
idle chat, personal insults, jokes and secrets. After a quick argument
about some missing items from the shopping selection it was back
to business.

I tried, over the noise, to strike up some form of conversation with
my old friend.
'Rodri, where's Marina? Are we going to visit her?'
'We're no longer together. We broke up. But we'll still see her.'
'Ah.'
A great start I thought. I tried a different tack.
'So how about that little pet dog you were telling me about. Is he
with Marina then?'
'No, he died.'
'Right.'
The other guys laughed jocularly at my unfortunate question
choices.
'Don't worry man, it's no big deal,' he said with a wink.
A great start indeed.

Spain scored two goals that match. Each was accompanied by
shouts, hugging and running outside onto the balcony to loudly

profess national greatness. I, of course, supported Spain. I had even brought a little Spanish flag with me. But even so, my status as a foreigner disallowed me, at my own internal request, from joining in fully with the celebration. Who was I, some random Brit, to join in the post-goal ecstasy of a country I didn't even belong to? They may not have minded, but I wasn't sure. Some of my friends and I had sometimes cruelly expressed annoyance at Americans in Madrid hanging around with Spaniards, vocally supporting a team they knew nothing about or had no link with. So it seemed. I suppose if you support someone, you support someone. Full stop. Despite this I held back and just commented, in a pleased way, on the goals, clapping with meaning. The game finished and Spain had won. Good, I thought to myself, now we can go back to Rodrigo's and relax. Leon stood up and puffed out his chest.

'Right boys, are we going out then?'

We piled into cars and onto bikes and headed back into the centre of town. I don't know if I would ever own one but there is a strong and very base thrill to be had zooming down a road on the back of a scooter. This time my bag was in a car so I could move more easily to enjoy the views without thinking 'if I shift left too much with this bulk on my back we are going to end up making very swift and bloody friends with the hot tarmac'. The wind made my eyes water but I could still make out the lit-up muscular castle, bright and golden-whisky coloured on its stony pedestal.

Two horn sounds.

'Alright gay boys!' they cheered.

It was our contingent in the car. I responded jovially with a double thrust of the two-fingered salute as we pulled away from the lights.

Rodrigo lived in a small flat in the heart of the *barrio*. Besides being a typically Spanish jumble of atmospheric streets, this area is the beating heart of the city's social scene. Almost every doorway – and there were seemingly hundreds of them – was either a bar or a club. Some were tiny and had just one room. Some had three floors and took up a whole stretch of buildings along a small street. During my six months there I used to spend at least two nights a week in the *barrio*. Guacamole nights at Austins, a boogie at Carpe Diem, the balcony at Hanoi, were all part of everyday conversation for us students. Alicante had, and still has, a very lively and active Erasmus community. Walking the streets around the warren-like centre or the larger, glitzier places in and around the port, you could hear all the familiar tongues of Europe mingling with the more obvious English speaking ones. The overall effect is jolly and non-aggressive.

We spruced up back at Rodrigo's and then walked down to the Playa Postiguet or, as I called it, the beach, as it sits right inside the city. A gentle, yellow curve of sand 667m long that had the warm Mediterranean Sea gently lapping at its shores. Tonight the beach was crammed. We had turned up for the final ten minutes of Alicante's firework competition – held at midnight at the end of the San Juan festival. Onslaughts of rainbow coloured explosions; chemical flowers that floridly smashed into life and rippled outwards to burn through the spectrum; and sequences of flashes, sparkles, whizzy things and poppy things of all different colours but emanating from one single rocket, were shown to us. And Alicante responded with cheers and applause. To signal the end of the show, firecrackers, held along a banner from one end of the beach promenade to the other, were set off to cries of delight. The last few didn't go off until about a minute later when they scared the socks off some bystanders.

The boys were not the usual kind of guys I would socialise with. Away from the football and security of home they changed into what the Spanish would call *chulos* (we would probably use the adjective 'cocky'). They were out to get girls. There were five of us: Leon, Diego, Rodrigo, Abel and myself and within five minutes of the firework show having ended I knew I was out of my depth with them. Rodrigo bumped into a pretty German girl he had met on a course once and introduced her to us. She turned to Abel and asked:

'What's you name?'

'You can call me darling,' he responded, clutching his heart.

I couldn't have said that.

'Where are you lot going tonight?'

'I'm going wherever you're going,' he said with dreamy eyes.

Again, unbelievable.

Even some of the other guys were astounded at his *cojones* despite it not working, at all. We then embarked on a ridiculous 35-minute hunt for alcohol that ended up at a 24-hour shop. I sensed that, although being a Spaniard, Leon was, like me, getting impatient with the walking speed of his fellow countrymen. Frequent 'Jesus, come on' comments backed up my hypothesis.

Liquored up, we made a home, and bar, for ourselves on the beach near a group of girls who were out on a hen-night. Soon, forming a triangle around us, two more groups of the far fairer sex arrived. Astoundingly the two new groups were also hen-nights. All Spanish. Sat there with my merry band of *chulos* I knew it wouldn't be long before we made some contact with them, but it was a wandering, drunk old guitar player and his drum-banging friend who acted as the catalysts. He sat down by my brigade and creaked out a tune that we flamenco-clapped along to. Naturally this caught the attention of the satellites around us. Finishing his song with an 'ole!' he moved onto the group of girls behind us – a collection of maybe nine ladies all dressed in black and sporting cat ears. We made sure they knew we were watching them. He then strummed a final chord and went and sat by the next lot. The drummer had wandered off by that point and the guitarist had ceased to play. We turned back to our conversation. Ten minutes later the black cats came over to us.

'Ok, so we are going to play a game. Do you know password?' trilled a pretty girl, clearly the bride-to-be, what with the addition of a red flower to her costume.

Password is a very popular television quiz show in Spain. The contestant has a word he/she must guess and the host feeds clues in

the form of single words. The contestant has to keep guessing until the correct answer is reached. For example, say the word was 'lake', the password round might go like this.
Host: water
Player: river
Host: big
Player: ocean
Host: inland
Player: lake
Host: correct! You win a family holiday and this lovely Daihatsu!

The cats wanted us to be the players and the wife-to-be would be the host. Of course, being a hen-night, it was maturely themed around sex. Diego, Abel and Rodri both had their turns – I forget their words – and performed fairly well guessing within a few clues. The wife-to-be then turned to me.
'Careful with him, he's English,' said Leon sniggering.
'Do you understand the game?' she asked playfully.
'Yeah, I think so.'
'Let's play then!'
Cue chants of LUCAS! LUCAS! LUCAS! from the boys.
She began.
'Sex.'
'Love.'
'Number.'
'69.'
'Correct!!'
Cue shouts and applause.
'*Joder*, how fast man!'
'Haha, *la hostia*, that was so quick!'
Cue me feeling very smug but managing not to show it. I heard an aside between two girls 'shows the difference between Spanish and English men, doesn't it. You say 'sex' he says 'love''. The girls, done with us, diffused back to their belongings and sat down.

The boys were expressing their interest in talking to the other group of girls now that the guitarist had vanished. Another catalyst arrived and I was beckoned over by the group of cats. Leaving my macho unit, I sat down and played entertaining foreigner for a while.

'Teach us English, we need to learn!'

I stayed with them maybe a quarter of an hour before they announced their desire to go to a bar or club. I stupidly decided to stay with my host and his friends. I sat down and said my goodbyes and maybe-see-you-later's to the feline band as they prowled away and looking at my new surroundings, performed a mental forehead slap. Two girls were talking conspiratorially to each other while another chatted to Rodrigo; Diego was flirting with some blonde bimbo; Abel was giving a hand massage to another and Leon was brushing the cheek of the most beautiful member, the wife-to-be. I was so far out of my depth with these lads that I wouldn't have touched the bottom even if I had dived down. When the group finally decided to move on I made an excuse and went back to the flat to sleep.

Not only was the heat crippling the further you strayed from the beach; the day's travelling had knocked me for six. A few dazzled moments before I fell asleep on Rodrigo's couch the boys burst into the flat needing trousers and shoes. Belts were jingling. Spray, spray, cologne. Squirt, slick hair. 'Sleep in the bed man, screw the sofa!'. Slam went the door.

*   *   *   *

The following morning I woke up, showered as quietly as I could and left Leon and Abel sleeping. It turned out that Rodrigo and Diego had slept, and in their eyes annoyingly *only* slept, at the flat of one of the girls after going back for a small house party.

I didn't really know what to *do* in Alicante. I had already lived there so I wasn't just a tourist ticking boxes. I decided to embark on a little nostalgia tour and walked around the barrio, up to the large, white bullring, into the modernist central market, down along the road to where my little former flat stood – wedged in between buildings far bigger than it – and finally up to Alcampo, an enormous supermarket where I bought food for the evening dinner I was planning.

I returned to my now awoken Spaniards. Antitheses of when I had left them. Jumping around, listening to music. As soon as I arrived we hopped back on the scooters and once again mosquito-noised our way to Mercadona. Food needed to be bought for lunch. There was something I had wanted to do, wanted to cook, for all the months I lived in Alicante but never did, and now was my chance. On the road up from the supermarket was the horsemeat shop called '*José y Ana*'. We entered into a small, white wall-tiled shop, with a mass of bright red meat placed on the counter and an equine calendar on the wall.

'What part of the horse is that?!' I asked in awe.

'The top half of the back leg.'

Pure muscle, pure meat.

The jolly lady sliced us seven plate-sized steaks off the mountain of flesh and placed them in white paper on some scales. During the weighing a breathless lady walked in wanting some chicken breasts.

'Do I know you?' asked Rodrigo tentatively.

He did. She was one of the dinner ladies at the Alicante university caféteria and despite being in a rush was more than happy to warble. We surreally descended into an out-of-nowhere discussion about how the university called her a thief if and when she gave too healthily sized portions of food to the students. We reacted with concerned faces and murmurs of agreement. She finished her rant with a kind of 'oh well!' shrug, kissed us all on our faces, squeaked 'I've got boys your age!', swiped her bag of poultry off the side and left. I turned to Rodrigo, 'only in Spain man…only in Spain…'

Marina, Rodrigo's ex-girlfriend joined us for lunch. She has long black hair, a beautiful, olive-skinned face and an intense enthusiasm for so many things. She reminded me in many ways of Imogen. After a large pasta dish cooked by the boys we talked about photography and how our lives had changed. Then everyone quietened and lay down wherever there was space.

'Oh no…' I said to Rodrigo jovially.

Instead of joining my Spanish friends in their perfecting the art of mid-afternoon sleeping, I decided to be stubborn and go for another walk. The air was moist, smelling of hot walls, and the sky was roasting proudly. I visited an event that was being held in the centre of the *barrio*. It was called '*Alicante Medieval*' and was a similar event to the fiestas of San Bernabé in Logroño. Coloured banners were strung up over the alleyways, some shadowing entire squares, and along all the streets were arts and crafts stalls and food stands. Hot grills smoked with steaks and blackening pork chops; a huge pan bubbled with an octopus in it; costumed artisans flogged carpentry, embroidered goods, sweets, breads and all manner of non-typical items. The air thickened and the noise increased.

Outside the Concatedral de San Nicolas a classic, sea-blue, open-top VW Beetle sat with white ribbons leading from the front of the bonnet to the top of the windows. I had never been in that building. I quietly pushed open the door and went inside. A wedding was in progress. The priest was talking into a microphone and a large camera, the style a television crew might have, was pointed at the couple, panning at the appropriate moments. I took a quick snap with my camera but thought I had best not hang around even if it was a public event. The heat and humidity were becoming unbearable so I finally gave up and fled back to the flat – not that it was much cooler there.

In the evening we once again took the two-wheeled wonders to Manolo's flat in the north of the city. It was time for me to prepare my feast. My *chulo* banquet. I went into my cooking mode burying myself in the work. An army of helpers cut and peeled a whole bag of potatoes for me. The horse steaks were seasoned and stacked on a plate ready for the hot oil. So bloody and red. Two packs of oven-ready, pre-cooked *patatas bravas* sat in foil tubs waiting for instructions to be followed. I boiled the potatoes and, with the help of Diego, used a handheld blender to create a smooth mash. Two packets of blue cheese were melted together with a carton of cream, then seasoned and put to one side. I lay the steaks in the pan – one minute of oily cremation on either side. There was still the question of what to do with those miserable instant *bravas* potatoes. I scratched my chin as Diego looked on expectantly. It was strange to see him sedate and not dancing. I added the meat juices from the resting plate back into the pan and threw them in. A healthy splash of some Spanish red wine, a little sauce combining the *bravas* sauce and some mayonnaise later and we were ready to go. The table was laid and the boys were getting the knives and forks together.

'Lucas, first you must make a toast,' said Manolo, head of the house. '*Hurry the hell up Leon!*'

'This is my gift to you, the greatest hosts I've ever had,' I said succinctly.

There were big cheers and compliments that made me blush followed by the sounds of cutlery and gnashing teeth beginning to wage war against the spread before them. The meal was a hit.

Finishing my slab of horse and mountain of potato I lent back, breathed out, and patted myself on the stomach. I didn't need that meal and, in the heat, probably a soup would have been better. But it was a nice way to end the evening.

'We going out then?' asked one.

'Hands up who's aiming to *fuck* tonight?' added another.

Chulotastic, I thought miserably.

Reaching Rodrigo's flat again I managed to fight off the 'come on's' and 'it'll be fun's' and was able to secure a quiet bed for the night. I had to catch an early train back to Madrid and just couldn't function in the clogging humidity. I was a little disappointed with myself and must have appeared a killjoy, but it was too hot and I was too tired.

*   *   *   *

Rodrigo appeared in the morning with some gorgeous, busty Spanish girl in tow and a glint in his eye. I surveyed her through heavy eyelids and was quietly impressed. I showered and packed and said goodbye to my drowsy friend who had, as soon as I had freed up the bed, collapsed into a heat-fuelled reverie with the girl on his shoulder.

'Until whenever the next time is, I guess,' I said quietly.

I still loved the guy but it was certainly a different side to the 'boyfriend' steady-man character I was used to.

Capital Flying...

I walked straight back into the hot, dry wall of heat that had seeped down from the sun to fill the streets of Madrid like some boiling gas. The wind from the nearby Sierra de Guadarrama was failing to enter the streets. I surprised Elena, who had forgotten my return date, and began packing my bag for a brief sojourn to England to celebrate my grandmother's birthday.

A monumental spanking from the German team 4-1, forcing England's exit from the World Cup, was the only moment I had to share with my friends before I had to take my evening flight back to

133

the UK. I left the capital with my English tail between my legs and was the butt of many jokes from my Spaniards.

Madrid airport. Easyjet evening flight, annoyingly but unsurprisingly delayed. An LG promotional TV had been set to *telecinco* in order to show the evening's Spain vs Portugal game.
Madrid airport. Easyjet evening flight's customers gather in a jovial bunch around the screen. Airport workers watch the game with the passengers and occasionally shuffle back over the buffed floors to their desks where a phone is ringing with an echo. The passengers giggle.
Madrid airport. Easyjet flight B4012. Fleshy humanoids gasp and cry and put off getting onto the plane until the last minute. A cheer and applause signal that Spain are through and a line of smiles disappears into a metal tube with wings.
Madrid airport. Easyjet flight finally takes me home. Late but I wouldn't have traded the experience for anything.

An afternoon BBQ with my friends, a posh lunch for my dear grandma's 85th and a visit to my friend Victoria in the sprawling tangle of Camden in London and home was done.

Spain at the turn of the month into July really knocked the thermostat. The hot, dry wall had become suffocating, brutally crushing any hope of even an idea of a breeze. Cruising into the mid-thirties and above would be the norm for the next two months and to be honest it scared me. I hate intense heat. I don't cope well. I sweat and dehydrate and ruin T-shirts and generally just look like a misplaced, shaven polar bear with ruddy cheeks and more freckles.

Lingering in my dinky flat had become an abuse. I shared one electric fan with Elena. She slept with Carlos. I didn't envy that bed. To touch another hot body on such a night would be abysmal. But then I didn't have a body to touch. Maybe I should have been jealous. The streets warped and waved in the day as the imaginary sounds of scrubland crickets filled my ears between horns. Were I to return I would invest in air conditioning.

With the sweltering air wrapping their fat, hot hands around anything and everything, I did, finally, build up the courage to leave my flat and its fan and restart my tour. My first stop was Pamplona and the Fiestas de San Fermín.

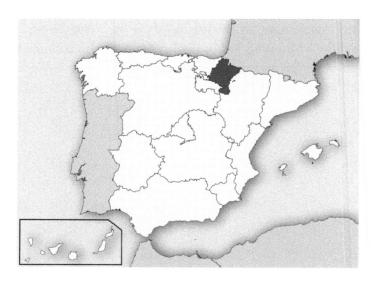

Running with the Bulls

Pamplona - Olite

Due to the sheer number of people going to the Navarran capital of Pamplona my ticket office lady, in Madrid's swampy Avenida de América transport hub, had to give me a route that would take me to the north via Zaragoza. I suffered for four long hours in that bus. I always seemed to choose the side of the vehicle to sit on where the sun was entering through the windows. I kept playing an open/close, open/close game with the little blue curtain, as I really wanted to see the view, but also didn't want to completely soak my t-shirt before I got there. It was clammy, the air conditioning was weak and my clothes were sweaty.

It was the day of Spain's semi-final match against Germany and it was much hyped as the Deutsche had been playing strongly all tournament. The bus driver put the commentary on the radio for us, just loud enough that it would disintegrate our cochlea and frazzle our eardrums. The radio commentator was ridiculous. Firstly, for the speed at which he spoke: fully automatic assault mouth. Secondly, for the theatrical flourishes he added to the proceedings. Faster and rising in pitch as the players neared the goal and lazy deflations when something went awry.

I sat on the other side of the aisle from two girls who were also sniggering at the football. I made contact with them right before we had even set off when I heard one of them saying in English how she couldn't find a bin. I then, in a gentlemanly, not creepy way, butted in and mentioned that there was a receptacle behind their chairs. Noticing the shared laughter at the football I steeled myself to butt in again just before we got to the Pamplona bus station.

'Are you guys going to San Fermín?' stupid question I thought.

'Yes.'

'Are you going to run?'

'No.'

'Where are you from?'

'I'm Italian and she's from Pamplona. We both came here from Brussels,' said a girl with a peaceful face, a mole on her lip and a small ring in her right nostril.

'Are you going to run?' asked her friend, whose small, brown eyes nooked into an approachable face while some black glasses balanced on a petite nose.

'No. I'll take some photos. I have my white shirt and my towel to sleep on. So, if you know a good park that'd be great.'

'You are alone?!'

'Yes,' I explained my situation.

As the bus doors opened and people started to disembark, the Italiana shared a private word with the Pamplonesa. I secretly crossed my fingers.

'Give us your number. We will go out later – you can join us if you like.'

'That'd be great! Thank you.'

'My names Elena, by the way,' said the Italian.

'And I'm Itziar,' smiled the other girl.

'Well, see you,' Elena trilled.

Spirits lifted, I left the bus station and ventured into Pamplona.

I had walked about five minutes before feeling like a bit of a dolt. The whole city was crawling with people wearing the typical San Fermín outfit. Traditionally it is a white shirt and white trousers with red sash and a red neck-scarf. And there I was in my green beach-flavoured t-shirt. Turning back sheepishly, ever more conscious of how much I stuck out, I bought a scarf and belt, donned my friend Nick's white shirt – perilously on loan – and re-entered the madness.

Like basically every Spanish settlement Pamplona is split into the historic quarter and the 'new bit'. I thought just the centre would be busy but certainly wasn't prepared for the actual number of people that seethed, stumbled, danced and bumbled in, over, around and often under every part of the city. Impossible hordes of red and white San Ferminers clogged everything. As I walked further into the historic part there was an almighty roar. Thousands of cheers erupted all over the city. Spain had scored against Germany, 1-0 in the semi-final. Bodies spilled into and out of bars. The roads were full. Cars were useless.

I had never seen so much drunkenness and debauchery in my life. It's not the kind of thing that usually affects me, but even I was a little taken a-back. Legions of pissed Australians is my most stark memory on arrival. Many of them were shirtless but the majority were covered in muted, tie-dye, bullet wounds as sangria and other assorted drinks were given a taste of what flying felt like before the inevitable absorption into fabric. The odour of the city was potent.

The overriding scent was that of urine, lots of it, mingled with booze and the odd stench of frying meats. It was heady in an unpleasant way.

I walked down a long promenade, the paseo sarasate, and arrived at the plaza del Castillo where a giant TV screen had been set up in order to show the football. The thousands of people had set up shop long before I had got there. I waded in as far as I could but then got cold feet when I noticed that I was surrounded by many different 'foreigners-on-tour' groups with buckets of alcohol and once-white shirts dripping with red booze. Fearing the fate of my friend's shirt and knowing I had no secure shower for the following morning – the guidebook erroneously said there were showers in the bus station – I retreated to the back streets just before the final whistle sounded. Spain garnered their place in the World Cup final and splashy, alcoholic fireworks were shaken up and sprayed into the air. Nick's shirt was safe.

Round some other interesting medieval corner I was met with a marching band celebrating San Fermín. People at the front waved large banners and were followed by trumpeters, horn players and drummers. They in turn were followed by lots of good-timers jumping and bouncing to the music. At 11 o'clock, coincidentally the time I happened to be going back to the station to use the facilities, a firework competition, akin to the one in Alicante, kicked off. The scattergun colours and super-hot, iridescent plumes and explosions were served up with the typical vocal appreciations they deserved. My favourite exaltation was after an onslaught of eye watering flashes and bangs when a tipsy Aussie slurred 'well that was fucking bright'. I snorted along with some others and then headed back to the centre where a beautiful girl in a waistcoat was already selling tomorrow's paper.

'Extra! Extra! The Navarran daily is already on the streets! Extra! Extra!'

Around the time that Itziar and Elena said they would contact me I decided to go and rest a while, wait, and let San Fermín flow past me. It was dizzyingly hot – like a sauna. Claustrophobic. Wave after wave of dual-coloured partygoers washed past. It was delirious: many zigzagging creatures, clumsily holding big plastic cups that were slowly losing their contents with every jerk; the occasional smash of something glassy; a shout trying to locate another group member; a song; a firecracker. There were many sounds looking after me as I waited sleepily. My head started to bob as the warm air drifted into my skull and tried to pull my eyelids down. After a long while I thought to myself, 'screw it', and gave in to sleep. As if sensing the submission my leg vibrated. It was Itziar and Elena. They were in a bar and they were telling me to come along.

With the help of a map and some elbows I managed to fight my way to the Irrintzi pub. I was introduced to a group of six girls in a deafeningly loud and volcanically hot bar. It was a little awkward. For the sake of our sweat glands we migrated outside and found a location in the air. Outside I found introductions a lot easier. It was a big group of Pamplonan girls, one Italian and one wilting Englishman that would constantly grow, shrink, split and reform over the course of the next six hours. Elena was working for Amnesty International and Itziar was promoting Navarran interests in the EU, so I felt that I was in good hands. The rest of the ladies were just as charming. Utterly insane, but charming. Fun and ballsy were traits I noticed more with the northerly Spanish. The southerners tended to be more flamboyant and humble. Once we got over the introductions and my being English, it was business as usual. Business during San Fermín meant only one thing: party, party, party.

You could say that San Fermín is all about the historic tradition that is woven so tightly with the fate of the bulls, but in reality it's just a massive piss-up. I'm not usually one for oversized booze-guzzling parties but, as with San Juan, Spain had got it right again. Despite the brash Aussies, and occasional shirtless English brute wobbling down the street with a bloody cheek, it was a very good-natured event. We spent most of the night outside talking, meeting people, throwing crisps in each others big and very alcoholic drinks, eating (well I did) and occasionally diving into one of the musical saunas for a quick jump up and down before running outside as our bodies reminded us that oxygen was necessary if we wanted kids in the future.

There were grills set up with burgers and, my personal favourite, *chistorra*: a sort of spiced red sausage with a smoky bacon flavour. The girls all protested as I waltzed over, saying I shouldn't eat it unless I wanted the contents of my bowels to ask my body impolitely if they could please leave. I batted their advice away with my hand.

'*Tengo una constitución fuerte!*' I garbled.

It was gloriously tasty. It had 'guilty pleasure' and 'probable diarrhoea' written all over it. I swear the swarthy looking cook had an evil grin when he slid it in a bun for me. I didn't suffer any problems, only moreishness, fishing around in my wallet for notes, or coins, or anything resembling currency.

'One's enough Luke. You don't want to risk it,' laughed a Pamplonan.

'How would you describe the people from Navarra?' I asked Itziar.

'We *navarros* are very noble. We are a people of the earth and are very loyal to our friends. It's an effort because we aren't especially open, but once you make a Navarran friend, you've made a friend for life.'

*   *   *   *

Around 6:30 in the morning the black of the night sky melted away to wispy duck egg blue. The bars swept out embarrassing heaps of plastic cups onto the streets and the crowds started to dissipate. We sat for a while on Calle Santo Domingo waiting for the start of the bull run.

The running of the bulls is a tradition that dates definitely back to the fourteenth century, but maybe has its roots in the thirteenth, and evolved at the same time as the country's more prominent bullfighting traditions – matadors, suits of lights, swords and suchlike. The first 'official' celebration of the modern day representation of the San Fermines was in 1591, though it was a far more low-key affair in comparison with its current version. Historically it was just two days, a procession, some music, a bullfight and some general merriment. As the years passed fireworks, dancing and more days were added until the seventeenth and eighteenth centuries when foreigners took notice – due to the new adornment of bull running – and started visiting. With regards to their effect on the levels of debauchery, it seems nothing has changed, with one clergyman of the time fretting about 'the abuse of drink and the permissiveness of young men and women'. It seems that over the centuries the original religious meaning of the day – celebrating San Fermín – has been lost.

At 7:30 we walked down the road used for the bull run, passing drowsy drunks and bug-eyed tourists. Itziar knew someone with a flat on the street where one could get a great view of the proceedings. We clambered down through the audience to the wooden barriers erected for directing the beasts and preventing bystanders from being gored. On the road were all the brave/drunk/adventurous runners waiting for hundreds of pounds of bovine flesh to charge at them. The girls, my guides, had gone through the barrier but I was a little behind them due to the number of spectators. I was stopped at the barrier by the police.
'He's with the two girls,' said one.
'I can't let you through with your bag.'
'But I'm not going to run!'
'No. I can't let you through.'

And that was it. Because of one arsehole policeman on a power trip I was left alone and with a tiny view of the tops of the runners wedged in between various backs and buttocks. When the bulls finally did rumble through I didn't really see anything and it was all over in a second.

'And that's it everyone,' said one drunk with a wry smile and outstretched arms.

I was crushed and angry. Angry at Itziar and Elena for not coming back for me, angry at myself for relying too heavily on strangers and angry at that arsehole policeman for being an arsehole and near ruining my San Fermín experience. I had really wanted a photo of the bulls rushing past and a shot showing the fear and excitement on the faces of the runners. My disappointment was exacerbated when Elena later showed me the video she was able to take. Their view was perfect. I walked with them in a private grump until our paths parted. They were going home to Itziar's family house and I was off in search of a shower as I felt like hell, sweaty hell. I had to keep reminding myself that my night was amazing even if I hadn't seen the bulls – my main reason for coming. It wasn't *really* the girls' fault. They didn't even need to spend the evening with me but they did. All my anger was curdled with gratitude. At least I had one more chance the following morning.

After showering at a well-run public bathroom complex – where the queue of partygoers and homeless people left the building and wandered outside – I returned to my most favourite bus station and bought a ticket to the town of Olite, 42km south of seething Pamplona.

I was uncomfortably hot and my eyes and head stung with tiredness but Olite was striking and pretty enough to overcome my constant battle against the heat. It was all sculpted stone and chocolate brown walls and it almost looked like a model village set up by some giant to amuse his overblown kids. Entering the baking main square I smiled as Olite showed me the ace up its sleeve. It could have been enough just being pretty but then to go and have a fairytale palace in the heart of it made it quite a special place indeed. The building had been the seat of the Court of Navarre until its union with Castille in 1512. It was also, at that time anyway, one of the most luxurious medieval castles on the continent.

'Surely there is no king with a more beautiful castle or palace and with so many gilded rooms,' wrote one twelfth century German traveller. It rose up and dominated the town with eight or so large Disneyesque turrets. The palace was the same colour as the rest of the town, golden ochre. Dulux: Spanish Honey. But it was the grey-blue turrets that defined it. After a small entrance fee I passed through some chilly, dark, and atmospheric halls that demonstrated the building's architecture. It was then a case of taking my own route up and around. The walkways led past skeletal, window-lit rooms; past tiny verdant gardens, sparkling green; and then up to the lofty heights where the towers held vigil over the town.

The signposts cleverly took the visitor higher and higher each time. Looking one way from the highest point I could see a Navarran bodega – creating wine that is becoming more and more well-regarded in Spain – and the fuzzy bumps of the Navarran Pyrenees off to the North. Turning east and the hills were closer and more modest; Olite sat, going about its business; storks clicked and a tractor ploughed a far off field. The last turn and the palace heights and its breadth and body were all on show for me. It was quite a sight. One I enjoyed for as a long I could while the hangover-curing wind whipped around me and tried to buffet me off the tower top.

Finding something both regional and cheap to eat in Olite proved a mission that basically bested me. All the places down the old stony back streets, away from the view of the palace or churches, were either too expensive or didn't offer anything 'Navarran'. In the end, thinking about the costly nature of San Fermín, I caved and headed to a little café where I had a red pepper omelette sandwich (as peppers were fairly typical of the region) and a glass of Navarran rosé wine – rosé being the regions speciality. Sharp and tangy, it refreshed but didn't inspire. It was horrendously cheap though so, sat in the shade and disgusted with the amount my skin was leaking, I considered getting blind drunk to take my mind off how grotesque I felt, but instead paid up and sat in a breezy little tunnel until it was time to get the bus to Pamplona.

Almost every seat on the bus was filled with young San Ferminers from some previous town on their way to the party to belittle all parties. At the next town we opened the doors to an odd pair: a loud chanting drunk and a little old lady. She came on first, a fuzz of grey hair, and fiddled with coins from her purse. The chants from the drunk behind her enticed sung retorts from the large group of boys near the back of the bus. He then shouted louder. The silver hair, still buying her ticket, told him to shut up or wait for the next bus. He sang louder and his dark olive skin glistened. She finished paying and came and sat next to me. The drunk staggered down the aisle. As he passed us she slapped him on the arm as if he were her grandson. He sat at the back with the boys who adulated him as he plonked into a seat. The next forty minutes were equal parts silence and normality, and mad, alcoholically concocted choral compositions; alliterately speaking. When the girls at our end of the bus sang a song about Alicante and the city's football team, Hercules, which had recently been promoted to a better league, the old lady smiled. I think it was the only the yob she had a problem with, not the jovial banter. I like to think she was just one more chant away from joining in herself.

With a free afternoon I spent some hours walking around Pamplona. Every morning, after the clean-up crews had been at work, the town reverted to its original state for a while. A sense of relative calm had taken over the city when I got back and many people were sleeping off what could very fairly be called alcohol abuse – either in homes, in fields or in hedges. I walked to the northern tip of the old quarter. A promenade stretched along the city wall, where a staircase and fancy lift were there for use if I wanted to descend into the new town. Peering over, I spied the river Arga sliding past grubby flats and a typically dodgy looking funfair. The path offered a broad view to the north of Pamplona and its hills but it was almost too hot to give a damn. It was 37° C and had the same humidity as a swimming pool. It was horrid and I hadn't brought enough clothing. All my shirts stank.

I ventured back into town past the parque de la Taconera with its low, sunken gardens and birds and deer. A red and white market, stalls selling fried food, little gardens and families out strolling before the chaos restarted, all helped to rest the mind before the definite and fast-approaching madness. I showered again and eventually ended up at what then felt like home, base camp, my free hotel, the bus station. It was 20:30 and I had yet to sleep since leaving Madrid for Navarra. I lay down and had a fitful 45 minutes on the slippery concrete floor in the central concourse. It was far cooler there but much less comfortable than the grassy park upstairs.

A text stirred me from my 'slumber'. Itziar and Elena were outside in the bus station park waiting to watch the fireworks and wondered if I was interested. I was and found them, fresh faced and clean, sat on a bank on the side of the road. It was good to see them again. We swapped our very differing day experiences and then pushed deeper into the park as the crowds began to coalesce. We made a space for ourselves and watched another spectacular show. It looked like the Castellón firework team had got their inspiration from the Harry Potter films. With the sheer amount of colours and explosive trickery it looked too clever to be just fireworks.

The group I was with – a group that had slept by the way – decided, after the last bang, to go and drink in some bars. I finally gave in to my eyelids and told them that I really needed to get some rest, at least a few hours, before the next morning blistered into town with its bull run. Itziar and Elena told me, with concerned faces, where I could go if I really was going to sleep outside. I said my goodbyes and walked for about fifteen minutes, found a tree in an area of park that was populated, but not too well-lit and lay down. I neither wanted to be invisible nor obvious. I wanted people to think, 'There's a guy, he might be sleeping, or relaxing, or waiting for friends', then hopefully adding 'so let's not steal, murder or rape him'. It was with a little trepidation that finally, fully clothed, I lay down under a tree.

Apart from a gypsy woman offering me a ring – some twisted marriage proposal perhaps – no one ever came near me. The world was loud with crickets and groups of friends slowly winding down their evening fun. I stretched out on my towel, my satchel underneath acting as an awful pillow, and closed my eyes. The grass was a little scratchy and the breeze wasn't as forthcoming as I had hoped. I drifted in and out of sleep. One minute I was lost in the warm, familiar darkness of dreams, the next I was listening to the accidental comedy of a group using the path behind me:
'Hold on a minute guys!'
'Why?'
'BLEEERRRRGGGGGGG' – 'splash'
'Hahahahahaha!'
I smiled, shifted my neck on my bag and tried to find sleep again, managing about three hours before a combination of lowering temperatures and paranoia that I was being bitten by things with proboscises drove me to scoop up my belongings and leave.

At the bus station I sat down and tried to summon up some energy. It wasn't long until I had to leave for the bull run. It was 4:30 in the morning, still dark and I was drunk on sleep deprivation. People were stumbling around like zombies, the whole area reeked of urine and a young guy, with curly blond hair and a eyebrow piercing, was going from person to person looking for some form of help, blubbing weepily. The first time he approached me I didn't understand him. He threw a 'forget about it' hand, walked away and theatrically shouted 'Why, why, WHY?' as he banged his head on a wall.

Approaching me again he exhaled and sat down speaking in some of the worst drunken, broken English I had ever heard. I could see him trying really hard to come up with the language. As I figured it, at 4:30 in the morning surrounded by hot piss-scented air and feeling more than ever in need of a bed, I had three options:

1. Play dumb and leave
2. Find out what was going on in Spanish
3. Find out what was going on in English

When he said 'can you take me to a salvation?' I reckoned it might be fairly serious so 'option 1' was out of the window. I didn't want him to start pouring his heart out and weep all over me so I was going to help him but we were going to do it my way, 'option 3'. Instead of bleating incessantly as before he focussed himself in order to come up with the correct English so that I would understand. I occasionally chipped in with Spanish just so I could clarify that I had actually understood but he never grasped that I actually spoke his language.

The dilemma was a little trivial in the end, and I should have predicted it. He couldn't find or contact his friends and was convinced that they had abandoned him in some twisted act of cruelty. He wept on my shoulder for a few seconds before pulling himself together and sniffing moistly. I patted him on the back: 'just try your friends again'. That was my Trisha/Jeremy Kyle/Jerry Springer, genius, agony-aunt, life-altering advice. Eventually, after a few minutes he got through to them with a warped smile. He came back over to me, sniffed again, wiped his hand on his trousers, invited me to come with them and then shook my hand. I politely declined as I had my own plans.

*   *   *   *

Failing to re-establish with the girls I walked groggily down towards the road where the bulls would be hurtling along a couple of hours later. It wasn't yet busy. In fact it was so early that some burly men were still setting up parts of the course while the drinkers petered out. I was on the front line, right near the start, where the bulls fly out of the *encierro* – pen – and use the road like a runway to bash the newspaper-wielding runners; it is tradition to smack the rear of the bull with a rolled up newspaper, spurring it on and proving one's manliness. With so much time to spare I chose a spot with a good view and sat with my head in my hands.

At 7:30, and with the crowds really starting to build up, I got to my feet, rubbed my eyes, stretched my back out, and waited for the horns that signified the start. The police were busy removing the last of the drunks they deemed too inebriated to run – both for their own and everyone else's safety. One man caught their attention as he had been drunkenly entertaining the crowds for quite a while. I suspect the police had let him stay for that time because he was keeping up spirits, but then when the more serious side arrived they really had to remove him. He had quite a reputation and wasn't going to let being on the other side of a thick, wooden barrier get in his way. He strayed left and right on the verge of falling over but never quite did. The crowds shouted their appreciation for his lack of balance and he in turn performed for us. Some antics caused the police officer to approach him again, whereupon our drunken clown tried to give him a big kiss. This produced an enormous cheer from the audience and chants of '*torero, torero*'. The people down in the street had no idea what was happening. Our man was led away a little and released. The drunk seemingly dispatched, the officer got back to the business of doing some final checks before the run.

The clown wasn't finished though and set about proving he was 'sober' by skipping over some bollards and sitting on one. He promptly fell off that bollard spilling most of his beer, chucked the can away, picked up his little red scarf and opened it out to form a mini bullfighter's cape. He trotted wonkily back to the barrier. The now thoroughly unimpressed policeman walked up telling him to leave. Our man dodged left and dodged right, as if he were facing a real bull, jumped over his cape using it as a skipping rope and was finally led away, all the way this time, by the arm. He left waving his scarf to cheers from his fans.

The air was fairly cool still and with fifteen minutes left some TV crews were finishing up their interviews with the more presentable runners; participants on the streets were energizing each other with slaps on the backs and manly shoulder grasp hugs and shakes; and the people watching the madness started to take out their cameras. At 7:55 there was a bizarre ceremony that was repeated three times. The rolled up newspapers were held aloft as all the runners faced the wall below where I stood. There was a chant whose words I couldn't discern but ended with a rousing 'SAN FERMÍN!!' In the crowds there was a more playful song filling the area:
Uno de enero, dos de febrero,
Tres de marzo, cuatro de abril,
Cinco de mayo, seis de Junio,
Siete de Julio, SAN FERMÍN!'

At 8:00 there was a loud noise as the bulls left their pens and then another rocket bang to signal that they had been fully released onto the streets. From my vantage point I could see the eight beasts galloping along the road to meet the crowd. Faces of stern concentration; of fear; of unfocussed, glassy drunkenness; of naïve excitement, all splashed together as thousands of pounds of angry mammal rushed towards the twitching runners. Some people ran at the bulls, sidestepping them and slapping their hinds at the last moment. Some instantly jumped to the side to try and flatten themselves against the wall or vault over the barrier. And some attempted to run alongside, or in front of, the animals. I imagine it was the latter bunch where the injuries, deaths and broken or wrongly positioned bones occur. It was all over in an instant. Bang, bull, cheers. That was it. But what a thrill it was. A split-second barrage of flesh and muscle and then quiet. A second group of more sedate bulls was then released to clean up the stragglers and with that the *encierro* was finished. For visitors it was then either home, hospital, park, or day-trip. Lots of choice. For me it was time to leave the unrestrained, unapologetic and pleasantly unpoliced madness of San Fermín and return to my capital.

In the fetid depths of the station there was a brief confusion as to which bus I needed to take. San Fermín and its legions of different travelling groups from so many different places had basically screwed up the system. It was 9:35 but the boards were showing 'next departures' at 9:00; the boards down by the buses were saying that said bus was going one way when in fact it wasn't – the number of people who asked for San Sebastián when I was going to Olite was just silly; and in general the sheer number of people meant that many were simply leaving late. We had some tardy and confused Australians on our Madrid-bound coach.

I got talking to a woman next to me who I initially presumed was Spanish but actually was an affable middle-aged American called Mary Ellen Fox. She was visiting her daughter and grandchildren in Madrid and had just finished visiting friends in Logroño. She lived – at one time – for fourteen years in Spain and currently was living in Dublin. She was a fascinating person, and we talked the whole way back discussing family, Russia and Spain, and our respective countries. She told me tales about a Spain I only knew through study.

In the early 1950s, right in the heart of the Franco era, Mary visited Spain luxuriously with a friend and, despite finding the country beautiful, was shocked by the comparatively absolute poverty. She thought for a moment, searching back for a memory she wanted, no doubt buried deep in a universe.

'In those days chocolates always came wrapped up individually in foil. I remember one day when my friend and I ate a whole bunch and then left the house. When we returned later the maid had collected all the screwed up wrappers, opened them all out flat, stacked them in a neat pile and tied them delicately together with a ribbon. She thought they were so valuable'

As well as being enlightening, talking to Mary confirmed yet again the fleeting and miniscule nature of my task. Here I was next to a woman who had lived in the country for fourteen years and had experienced a time I couldn't imagine. And then there I was thinking I could get to grips with the nature of country simply by visiting its component parts. I faltered a little inside and wondered what I was actually learning besides just seeing beautiful places. Maybe nothing. Maybe more than I knew. It was a shame that, on parting with Mary in Madrid, we didn't swap contact details.

Capital Winning...

On Sunday the 11th of July history was made. Spain won the World Cup.

I spent the match wedged between some of my English friends and a whole load of Spanish people in a bar near the Plaza Mayor. The heat was at once incredible, comical and hideous. Before the game had even begun people were fanning themselves, wiping their brows and doing that t-shirt ventilation technique where you pull it to and from your chest in the hope of enticing up a wind. I had given up my preoccupation with my personal image and was only worried that the body-paint Spanish flags on my arm and cheek would melt away.

For the first ninety minutes nothing happened. So many chances but no goal. Everybody escaped outside to grasp a few breaths before the compulsory thirty minutes of extra time. The heat was rising with the tension and I had lost my flags to the rivers that were running over my skin. Everyone felt disgusting but we were way past caring. The match was like some sick, ticking time bomb that you passed round a group. Something had to give. Nobody wanted penalties. The tension was electric and heart failure was a possibility. The atmosphere in the bar was too tense. A man from the press with a big video camera was standing by to capture whatever version of aftermath lay before him. With only four minutes to go a Spanish footballer called Andrés Iniesta fired the ball into the back of the net.

The reaction was cataclysmic. The roar, the scream, vocal chords shredded to pieces, sweating bodies hugged and kissed and jumped on whichever other slithery, happy body was closest. No one was quiet those last four minutes. Euphoria was sloshing around the bar like some water pistol fight at a kids' party. Today was a good day to be in Spain. Some people hushed and were cautionary.
'It hasn't finished yet guys!'
But no one listened.

The final whistle, the ceremony, and captain Iker Casillas raises the Golden Trophy. The noise was impossible. The cameraman caught the madness; I am now on some strip of film somewhere. We took to the streets where the insanity raged on. More singing. Cars drove past with flags dancing in the wind and with the typical sports horn beat – 1, 2; 1, 2, 3; 1, 2, 3, 4; 5, 5. Every car, bike, local bus and even recycling truck was honking his or her country's victory. Fans were throwing fireworks, people were banging bins and dancing on the roads and red and yellow was *everywhere*.

The Puerta del Sol – the central square of the city – was teeming with life. People had climbed up onto anything climbable. This included the massive statue of Carlos III in the centre. Safe it was not, but on the eve of the country's, arguably greatest, sporting victory, the police sure weren't going to stop them. In fact, if anything, they seemed to be enjoying themselves too. Standing, arms folded, in lightweight uniforms, and laughing to themselves.

I left my friends and walked all along the centre of Gran Vía with hundreds of Spanish people. The few cars that had decided to brave the crowds and drive, beeped the fans joyously and the fans shouted back. Some people had large flags and would allow cars to pass through them like bulls. And so up to Plaza de España, which was also coated with a thick layer of people. Residents were honking plastic horns out of their flat windows and waving their arms. As I neared *my* area of Madrid, Argüelles, the incredible noise and energy all but vanished. Soft whispers of far off mayhem were all I could hear before the silence of my sauna-like flat.
It was a good day to be in Spain.

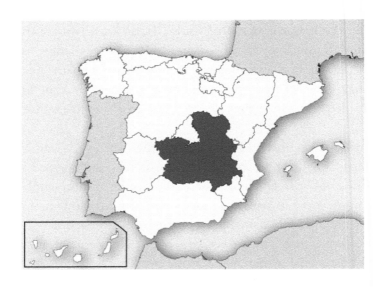

Quixote

Segóbriga – Uclés – Villanueva de Alcardete

Living in Madrid, Castilla La Mancha was a community into which I had dipped my toes quite often – see appendix. Due to time constraints I could only dedicate one day to the region on this trip. But it was a hell of a day.

During the end of my time at my academy I used my students' knowledge and probed them about the places I wished to visit. The Spanish, like any other nation, are more than happy to offer up reasons to visit various places in the country they call home.
'Don't go to Valdepeñas,' said Alfonso one day; 'My family has a *bodega*. Let me know when you go and I'll take you.'

Fast forward a month and a half and I was greeting Alfonso and his friend Alfredo on a hot morning in the La Latina district of Madrid. We were going to 'do' La Mancha in a day. I saw a side of the region that would have been essentially inaccessible to me had I been relying on only my wits, guidebook and public transport. Alfonso and Afredo were quite similar: middle-aged, comfortably stocky, quick to laugh and with keen senses of humour. They wore loose fitting shirts with dark sunglasses and ushered me into the air-conditioned vehicle.

The road out of Madrid headed southeast into real La Mancha country. Some arching hills lumped around before sliding gracefully down into the expansive plains that are so characteristic of the area. A place where horizons look too far off. The colours were distinctly manchegan; rough muted hues of yellow, brown and green. Alfonso was from La Mancha and was in his element, smiling with a longing look in his eyes as he lightly clutched the steering wheel:
'This is what makes me feel relaxed. The sense of space that La Mancha gives. If I go to the hills of the north it can feel claustrophobic for me.' Something caught his eye off to the right on a hillock, 'Ah, there is one of Don Quixote's windmills!'

The rain in Spain doesn't fall mainly on the plain, but the wind does. As in Navarra, La Mancha is an area where this element is king and scattered over the region are vast wind farms. In terms of capacity Castilla La Mancha is just behind Castilla y León and produces around 3,700 MW each year. Cervantes might have been surprised at their new form and Quixote might have been a bit put off for the traditional windmill of La Mancha is a squat, white cyclinder with four brown, even sails. The new ones are those tall, ivory spears that stand in long files and inspire such polarised opinions.

'Is there a strong regional identity in La Mancha?' I asked.
'No, not really. Due to our location we are sort of the 'that bit around Madrid' area. We don't have the traditional culture of

Andalucía or the intricate history of some of the other regions. Historically, during the time of conquest and reconquest, La Mancha acted as a kind of large defensive, or offensive, buffer zone.'

'How would you describe the manchegan people then?'

'Open, like La Mancha,' said Alfonso matter-of-factly.

'But open also in terms of progressing,' added Alfredo, 'It is every little village's dream to one day have a Corte Ingles.'

'As a *guiri*, for me La Mancha is cheese and Don Quixote,' I offered.

'Oh God yes, the number of small places claiming it's their town that was mentioned in the novel is stupid! But the cheese, that's good.'

Our first stop was the ruined Roman town of Segóbriga, a once important urban and commercial centre that sat on the route between Zaragoza and Mérida.

'When I was little they were beginning to excavate it. Before they came, people who lived in the area would just show up and take things. I would drive up on my scooter and root around. If I saw something interesting I'd take it home. I now have loads of Roman ceramics, pieces of bowls etc.'

Segóbriga is buried within the heartland of La Mancha, a stony scratch in the middle of space. It started to decline when the Roman Empire came to an end. Internal communications between Empire settlements decreased and the city became less important and more cut off. Adding to its decline was its main industry – the mining of *lapis specularis*, a selenic gypsum that was used as windowpanes for rich families. Everything was going well until it was figured out how to make glass in sheets. All of a sudden nobody in the Empire wanted *lapis*. Glass was simply the better material for the job. Then with the abusive arrival of the Visigoths and, later, Muslims Segóbriga's fate was sealed.

A near complete amphitheatre with a capacity of over 5000, a battered bath house complex, and a near complete Roman theatre were the main sights at the ruin. The hills were studded with history. I loved it for two reasons. First of all was the impressive quantity of Romanware that had been preserved for so many hundreds of years. Yes the area had lost most of its decoration, and whatever statues remained *were* lacking hands and heads, but it was still an area of surprising survival. Secondly, there was enough greying rock to really build a mental image of what the place must have looked like. This meant one didn't have to rely on just the imagination.

The heat was rising but it was windy enough to feel comfortable and even pleasant. We passed through the little museum without really bothering to read all the details and while I bought some obscure postcards – Segóbriga only sold postcards with pictures of items excavated from the site, but not of the site itself – Alfonso tapped into some information being given to a tour group.
'Did you enjoy it?' Alfonso asked me with a hopeful expression.
'Of course! It was very fine.'
'Then Mérida is going to give you a shock,' Mérida is Segóbriga's big brother and is over in the Western community of Extremadura, 'The whole place is full of this stuff.'

On the road to Segóbriga I had cooed at an enormous building off in the distance. It was a minor detour and Alfonso said it was definitely worth seeing. After our fill of ex-Empire rubble we backtracked along the *autovía* and arrived at the tiny village of Uclés. Before entering proper we stopped at a viewpoint. At the base of a small hill the modern pop strains of Lady Gaga blasted out of a speaker system as dozens of children ran back and forth across a concrete school sports court. It was the time of the year when the *campamentos de verano* – summer camps – were in full swing. These camps offer adventure activities, mountain biking, quad biking, team sports, creative activities, English learning, and freedom from parents. They also offer the opportunity for parents to have a break from their children.

'As we have no music of La Mancha this is what you get!' laughed Alfonso.

Perched overtly on the top of the hill was the mighty and rather ostentatious Uclés monastery. Coaxing the car up a steep road we parked by a grand seventeenth century façade. The sublime inner courtyard was all custard coloured walls and cloisters forming a square not unlike that at the University of Salamanca. On the left side a flat-topped tower rose up and on the right a more traditional spire spiked. Both were clean, proud and ornate. It surprised me that it didn't get even a mention in the guidebook. Uclés was now also used as a school and a base for the summer camps. The *comedor* – dining room – was full of tables and chairs and children's artwork and posters mixed casually with the ancient, wooden ceiling and the old, carved engravings of faces and shields. In the arched cloisters outside, the shaded colonnades were surreally lined with table football and table tennis tables. Children's voices echoed somewhere in some corridor.

The monastery's chapel was simple and voluminous. A tall, light-grey chamber was adorned with banners and flags with the cross of Santiago and crosses of the Calatrava. Santiago is the male patron saint of Spain and whose nickname '*matamoros*' – Moor-slayer – is now considered not politically correct. Tradition has it that he miraculously appeared to fight for the vastly outnumbered Christian army during the battle of Clavijo. He is reputed to have blasted in on a white horse in order to aid Ramiro I of Asturias against the Emir of Córdoba. No doubt a load of old hogwash, it is nonetheless very romantic and has provided a lot of opportunity over the years for grand works of art.

A few simple chapels housing artworks and manuscripts lead down the wall towards the altar. There a large golden reredos rises to the pale cupola 25m up. Right in its centre surrounded by shiny brilliance was Santiago himself, sword held aloft, sitting proudly on

160

some muscular steed. For me Uclés was a stark reminder that you can only do so much with just a guidebook. I wondered how many tourists had taken a bus along that same *autovía* and had also thought 'that looks interesting. I wish I could...' but never would visit it.

It was times like that when I was glad I had tapped into a bit of *enchufe*. Its basic translation would be 'networking' or more importantly using said network for personal progression. *Enchufe* is a fairly easy thing to use in Spain, as on the whole Spanish people are almost all disconcertingly open and giving. This was a trait, maybe stereotype, that I would find strengthened as we finished at the monastery.

Leaving the clandestine grandeur of Uclés, we drove to Alfonso's hometown, Villanueva de Alcardete. Although La Rioja is the most famous region for Spanish wine production, La Mancha is actually by far the largest. For miles into the horizon, and in La Mancha that's a lot of distance, field upon field of vines rolled out. It just so happened that Alfonso's town was right in the middle it.

A large black gate opened for us and we entered a wide, open area that affronted a broad, chalk-white house with a shady porch by the front door. It looked like something out of a turn of the century film about life in provincial Spain. According to my guide for the day, it was a typical Manchegan style house. In the courtyard stood a woman, beaming, waving with one hand and shading her eyes with the other. She wore a full-length floral dress and welcomed us with open arms, dust circling her feet. It was Alfonso's mother, Encarnita. We then crossed the courtyard to where a low, wooden shelter stood in the shade of some trees next to a beckoning swimming pool. In the doorway of the little building was an old gent sporting a pale blue linen shirt and a smile. It was Alfonso's father, Emilio. As we greeted the parents another car crunched into the drive. It was Alfonso's bubbly sister Piluca and her fairly serious French boyfriend Laurent.

We all entered the wooden hut where Emilio had returned to battling with his Freeview box, trying to get the TV channels in their right places. Various family members were struggling to help him. Alfonso took the remote and fiddled.

'I don't want *La Sexta* there! It's all red propaganda,' he barked.

Alfonso had warned me lightly that his father had been a pro-Franco, pro-Fascist character. But apart from a few weary *'please dad!'* comments from his children, to me he just seemed to be your classic old person; a little bit racist, very bad with technology but exceedingly polite and well-mannered. What he also was, was Spanish, and that meant he was generous. Before I was shown the family *bodega* or even the house we had a cold beer, cuts of ham, and a choice of two Manchego cheeses laid out for us. One was soft and near white, *manchego fresco* – aged for only two weeks; the other, and far more my kind of cheese, was a hard, classically yellow *manchego curado* – aged for between three and six months. This one was preserved in olive oil and had a nutty, salty taste that tickled my tongue and slapped the roof of my mouth.

The family's now dormant *bodega* had produced wine for over a hundred years but ceased to function in 1985. We climbed inside through the same space where the trucks bearing grapes would once have docked and dropped their loads into the churning blades that went on to produce the *mosto*, the blended up fruit mulch of what is essentially freshly pressed grape juice, that goes on to ferment in the large tanks. He flicked on a couple of lights and the aforementioned tanks were gloomily revealed. Their shape was unlike those in La Rioja or in Ribera del Duero. Instead of tall, metal cylinders or large wooden casks they were vast, clay amphoras.

'The original manchegan tanks were in this Roman style,' he said as his voice echoed round their bases.

In the room next door there were another thirty tanks made of cement that were a more recognizable cylinder shape. The atmosphere was musty and smelled of dust and forgotten industry, rust and wooden beams.

'My brother and I would love to get it working again. If not there is talk of setting up a *museo de vino* in the town, so maybe we could refurbish our *bodega* as a place to educate people about the wine industry.'

I walked up a crumbling staircase to where I could shuffle between the open mouths at the tops of the fermentation tanks and peer into their depths. Over me, the low beams of the Manchegan roof flexed their ancient fibres as they held up the ceiling. Light drifted in heavily from a small round window and glowing shards slid in through little cracks in the roof.

'We leave little gaps so the built up gas produced during the process can escape…isn't it wonderful.'

Alfonso was clearly very proud of his bodega and often wanted to make sure I liked it. He would check and sometimes double check with me that I found it interesting or that I was enjoying myself. I said yes every time. He *should* be proud, and with plans in the pipeline I hoped to one day return and try some of his wine.

The house also held some surprises. Inside, ornate, blue and white speckled tiles formed bands around the predominantly white-walled rooms. The rooms themselves were full. Every table, shelf, mantelpiece or flat surface was covered in history. Books, collected items, keys, trinkets, boxes, papers, all arranged as if they were in some glassless display cabinets. The walls were also busy, especially in the front living room. Every space was filled with a decorative hanging plate from different places all over the world. The overall effect was a little disarming. I felt that I couldn't really sit down, even if I had wanted to, through fear of disturbing some minute equilibrium; a rusty key conked out of line or a sheet of paper lifted out of place by the slightest zephyr from under a cushion as I moved.

While the table was being set up for lunch our group was joined by Alfonso's brother, Emilio (junior), his wife, Isabel, and their daughter, Isabel (junior). We sat around the TV in the little wooden hut as the channels were finally sorted out. With a wet pop and that unbeatable 'glug, glug' sound we were served an aperitif of a locally produced rosé wine. It was a necessary coolant for a body whose temperature had been rising as the sun reached its zenith.

'Come on!'

Encarnita was calling us to eat. Another wet pop and another glug as a local red wine produced by Alfonso's brother-in-law was divvied up to the troops. It was cooled in the Spanish way, in the fridge, so that it felt less like a mulled wine and more like a grape juice. First off we had *gazpacho*, the ubiquitous tomato soup. Summer in a bowl. Even though it was out of a carton everyone around the table still hummed over its tangy loveliness in much the same way as one might have had it been prepared fresh in the morning.

While Laurent was using the loo, Emilio (junior) took the piss out of Piluca for having a French boyfriend, much to the mirth of everybody else around the table, except Isabel who slapped her father on the shoulders. Siblings are siblings no matter what the age. Young Isabel fawned over his accent and when he got back the whole family started to discuss the way he spoke and lament the difficulties of French pronunciation. The Spanish, keen though they may be, are not the best at *not* sounding Spanish.

'*Boisson* is drink and *poisson* is fish,' said Laurent steadily.

'Buessin.'

'No, *boisson*,' he repeated patiently.

'And that's fish?'

'No, that's *poisson*. This is *boisson*.'

And so it continued for a period of time that was far longer than it should have been.

The seventeen year old dog, Daffy, with his weak hind legs, shuffled past us as the main course was brought to the table; a regional dish of stewed chicken with chunks of Iberian ham. The vegetables were potatoes, well, crisps. I declined the crisps and took bread instead. At pudding time fruit, ice cream and three bottles of wine were brought out. They were sparkling wines but because they were from Villanueva de Alcardete and not Cataluña or France, they couldn't be called cava or champagne. So instead we had three thick green bottles of *vino espumoso*. After a couple of exciting cork pops we were all commenting about the wines as if we were uppity connoisseurs. I have noticed that with the Spanish there is less faffing about when talking about wine, and food in general. It is a trait that has warmed me to them more than the French or Italians.

'The L'etué is better. The Alcardet tastes of vinegar,' and that was that. Review over. There were no hollyhocks to be found in a Spaniard's wine critique.

It was with great regret that I had to tear myself away from this gigantic region. As with every Spaniard I had met on my trip I was offered a home from home if I ever needed it. 'Social *enchufe*' I'll call it.

'You always have a family here,' said Encarnita as she kissed me on both cheeks.

Driving out of Villanueva de Alcardete we lost ourselves again in the endless wine fields of La Mancha.

'Stop the car here for a moment,' said Alfonso.

Alfredo pushed the car into a pile of dirt and we got out and looked at Don Quixote's land one final time. Alfonso exhaled with a faraway look in his eyes.

'The space,' he whispered to no one in particular.

Featureless though the land was between the grape fields and the capital, two interesting and arresting oddities pop up as the road slowly draws the driver back into the concrete jungle.

Seseña is a municipality located in the north of Castilla La Mancha just before the road meets the border with the Madrid province. It contains a ghost town that remains as a quiet reminder of Spain's economic woes during the 'noughties'. During the construction boom of the 2000s an idea was hatched by developer Francisco Hernando to create a huge residential development that would provide 13,500 residential units and would cost over 9 billion euros. The scale of the project, however, didn't hold true to the original proposition – for example water and gas lines weren't included in the plans so that the completed units were essentially uninhabitable. Due to the Spanish property bubbles of 2008-2009, the developer ran into some problems sustaining and financing the massive project. By mid-February in 2008 fewer than three thousand of the finished apartments had been sold and less than a third of those were occupied. It later materialised that the reason the project was green-lit so unusually quickly was that authorities had in fact been bribed. The results were twofold: the local mayor was arrested and northern La Mancha was left with a barren, cold, soulless place.

Ten minutes further north in Getafe, a chalk white monument spears into the big sky. Cerro de los Ángeles is a hill. It is, however, a very special hill. It is the geographic centre of the Iberian Peninsula. On the top of it there is a fourteenth century monastery – Nuestra Señora de los Ángeles – as well as the Monumento al Sagrado Corazón, a chalk-white, 26m pillar topped by an 11.5m Jesus with outstretched arms. It was built in 1919 as a dedication to the country and was inaugurated by the then king, Alfonso XIII. Much of the original monument was obliterated by the Civil War and to this day bullet marks can be glimpsed on the walls of the various buildings. This car window view served as a mood-lifter after the grimness at Seseña.

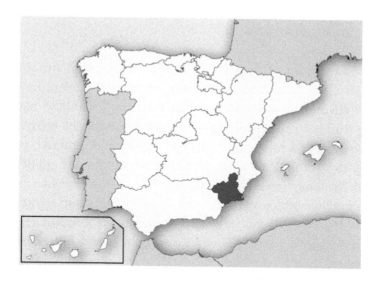

A Dusty Little Corner

Murcia - Lorca

It was the silver-haired route to the region of Murcia. I don't know what it is about Spanish octogenarians but apparently there is something they find profoundly difficult about putting a bag on a rack and then finding a clearly labelled seat. The train to Murcia trundled through strange and new scenery, one I had yet to see in Spain. Hills and ravines with white, chalky land and bright green trees. In the troughs, sky blue lakes and lagoons sat still. Many people – maybe it was their first time too – arched their necks to look, some placing their palms on the windows and pressing their noses up on the glass. This was, however, only the northwest part of Murcia and soon the real region arrived. Hazy, low hills, near barren, slinked in the heat off to the left and off to the right. We were passing through a very wide, very flat and very parched-looking valley floor. Pale, sandy land was coated in planted shrubs, olive trees and covered grapes. It was bleak and nondescript but transfixing because of this.

I opened the door of the carriage in Murcia (the city) and was given a hot, dry, kiss by the 38-degree temperatures that were lurking for me in the southeastern corner of the country. I wouldn't have been able to trudge around for long with the laden rucksack wettening my back so I walked to the first *pensión* I could find, entered, paid and located my room, chuckling at the reliability of the guidebook – 'musty'. Walking around outside, freed from my shoulder bonds, I instantly felt both sorry for, and inescapably disappointed with, Murcia. It is a maligned and almost neglected community that is often the butt of jokes. Many of my friends, and indeed even my housemate, tried to dissuade me from going there despite knowing my aim of visiting *every* community on the peninsula. This may have been a little overly harsh on their part but after walking around Murcia I could more or less see the basis of their argument.

Time and history have not been kind to Murcia. In 1810 the city was looted by those pesky Napoleonic troops and a mere twenty years after that, in 1829, the city was smashed senseless by a massive earthquake leaving six thousand dead, huge numbers of buildings as rubble, and the doors open for cholera and plague to stream in. This wasn't the only way Mother Nature mistreated Murcia: in 1651, 1879 and 1907 severe floods drowned the city and surrounding areas.

Another reason for its current character is its relationship with tourism and development. Until fairly recently it had been one of the least developed regions of coastal Spain. The cause is not that flattering. Speaking bluntly, the region is nowhere near as lush, green or attractive as its neighbours Andalucía and Comunidad Valenciana. It is rather dry and arid. However as the region got richer and more and more people moved in, the property developers quickly had to build new flats and offices, which have swamped the area that would usually have housed the old quarter.

As a result, all the potentially atmospheric narrow streets or grand buildings have vanished on the winds of modernisation and historic catastrophe. The end result is mostly ugly and boring and unattractive. Characterless and uncharming streets fill the centre of the 400,000-strong provincial capital. But despite the overall taste of disappointment there were a few sights that stopped it becoming bitter. Approaching the centre from the south I crossed a fine, arched, stone bridge over the river. It wasn't as beautiful as those at Salamanca or Córdoba but it was interesting enough to at least be noticeable. In the yellow water below, sculptures of fish and other creatures writhed motionless for my attention. Fronting the river on one side was a building doing its best to look like an old theatre and on the other was the grand town hall building, completely smothered with palm trees as if trying to remind me that this was the Mediterranean. With no bearings in mind I followed a shady alleyway towards some distant spire.

At the end of the alley, exposed to the sun, was a wonderful square, the plaza Cardinal Belluga, which houses the Cathedral of Murcia. Put it among the gothic beasts of Castilla y León and you could easily lose it. Here though, as if knowing I was going to feel deflated, it soared, outrageously ornate. One spire, off centre; a small, blue onion dome and a broad, decorated façade commanded the entire *plaza*. Some scattered terraced cafés and a pastel red building, El Palacio Episcopal, finished off the scene. One notch in Murcia's scoreboard. A long and healthy walk around yielded a few more pleasing sights. There was a bizarre statue of a naked man with fairytale horns that stood in front of a regal, crimson, baroque building. A few snippets of some typically Spanish streets and some nice little squares and churches flittered in and out of view as I searched for diamond needles in a haystack. For a provincial capital, however, I was still a little surprised at the lack of anything on offer.

After a fitful and sweaty siesta in my little box room with its pathetic fan and close walls, I decided to head back out and taste the air. Following my heart I strolled back to the cathedral and sat down at a café ordering a beer. The thing I do like about some of Spain's outdoor cafés is that in the summer – unlike in England – little jets spray intermittent clouds of water over the customers. Cooling drops of vapour misted the view of the lit up cathedral while a musical trio (keyboard, accordion and violin) were playing romantic ballads from some bygone era. It was incredibly relaxing and for a split second I thought 'actually, Murcia is quite the finest place'. Then at 11:55 my café closed, the band packed up, and I was jettisoned back into the hot reality of nothing-to-do-ness. I took a photo of the cathedral and, as if my camera had consumed the lights themselves, a few seconds later the building went dark.

It was surprising how quiet the city was. Even on a Monday evening Madrid was buzzing like some hyperactive hive. But in this southerly hub all was hot and peaceful. I showered in chilly water for the third time that day and then fed myself to my weird dreams. I remember one part very clearly; I had discovered some immensely vast area of Murcia that wasn't in the guidebook – an area with a huge downhill promenade, lined with turn of the century buildings under a pastel pink sky buffeted with soft, white clouds. I awoke disappointed, knowing that that place didn't exist.

*   *   *   *

The next morning wasn't much cooler as I took the local *cercanias* to the nearby 'historic town' of Lorca. The train passed once again through the savagely continuous terrain of Murcia. Craggy hills and struggling vegetation browned in the violent sun. The views of the region were becoming dreamlike. I found that if I just stared out of the window I would lose myself in everything. The drowsy, heat-gripped landscape seemed to be closing in around my train, around me. The metronomic nature of the railway tracks coalesced with the repetitiveness of the scenery. The effect was a little strange. If Daliesque creatures and clocks melted into view I wouldn't have been surprised. Before a sultry, feverish madness set in, our train stopped.

'Passengers for Lorca, this is Lorca.'

I didn't have long there but according to the guidebook I wouldn't need much time anyway. I walked straight, and up. Up was always good. Up gave me perspective. It was only a short way before I was at the top of everything by a little broken church near a hilltop. From a height the fuzz from the heat created a limited and claustrophobic view of the town and its surroundings. I could only see the imminent: the end of the settlement. It was a far cry from the clean, cool air at Montserrat.

It was then, for whatever reason – the heat, fate, karma, overworking – that my right flip-flop broke. The material that wove between my big toe and my index toe had frayed and snapped. I was at the top of a hill, under the high sun, map-less, in a town where I had never been before, and with only one flip-flop. 'Right, better head back down then', I thought to myself. Murcia's large immigrant population spread to Lorca as well and up in the hills were to be found tiny houses buckling up into each other. Some were no more than huts with a few facilities. I felt like I was back in Guatemala as non-Spanish faces peered out at me from pockmarked, crippled buildings. A man walking down one of the channels that helped form the jumbled mess of streets, held up his arm and called out to me.

'Have you broken it?'

'Yeah!'

'Be careful not to burn your feet!' he smiled.

'I will walk faster then!' I replied.

I half-limped further down, avoiding broken glass and the odd grubby and forgotten plastic toy. A little boy whispered to his friend and laughed at me 'Haha, you've broken it'. Smart-arse. I smiled a kind of 'silly me' smile back at him and shrugged my shoulders dopily. Two-shoed smart-arse. The concrete and tarmac scorched the sole of my foot. From the earlier summit I had noticed a large church building so, using my fairly reliable internal compass, I headed for it in what was, hopefully, the right direction. Luckily for my feet, it was. Also lucky was that I had finally stumbled upon somewhere that was mentioned in the guidebook. With no map in it just having a book telling me street names was about as useful as giving someone a solar powered torch in a very large, very dark cave…and taking away one of their flip-flops.

The building was the Colegiata de San Patricio on the small, but handsome, Plaza de España. On the same burnt-honey square was Lorca's fine 17/18th century town hall, which was initially used as a prison. The streets immediately tapering off from this point were also quite fine. Pretty and Spanish – white with cream balconies, little black railings and the odd brimming flower box here and there. I felt a bit silly hobbling through the area with one shoe on but nevertheless the Colegiata, with its dirty, yellow, fifteenth century ridges and family of whirling swifts didn't seem to mind.

The good, however, was over too quickly as I soon re-entered the more Murcia-styled town area; all ugly flats and soulless blocks. In a Chinese-run bazaar shop I managed to buy some cheap rubber flip-flops. I didn't know whether it was primarily because of the financial crisis but the Murcia I saw seemed to all be 'on sale'. Almost every shop was offering *rebajas*. As well as the normal places to buy things there seemed to be an abundance of budget shops, bazaars and tat-sellers – more than I had seen elsewhere. It cheapened the atmosphere. Took away the romance.

Murcia, or the Murcia I had witnessed in any case, seemed to have been left behind by the rest of Spain, financially, geographically, progressively, culturally and infrastructurally. I couldn't figure out how it could reverse the damage already done to it. How it could pull itself out of its own self-induced quagmire and promote itself. In the El Corte Inglés bookshop – I had to escape the heat briefly – in the travel section, the book on Murcia is the thinnest of all regions. A testament to its plight perhaps? Murcia was a candidate city for the 2016: European City of Culture. Many of its competitors were from its own family but it didn't get past the first hurdle.

The candidate cities for Spain's initial selection included: Oviedo, Santander, San Sebastián, Pamplona, Zaragoza, Burgos, Tarragona, Segovia, Cáceres, Córdoba, Malaga, Alcalá de Henares, Cuenca, Murcia, Palma de Mallorca and Las Palmas de Gran Canaria. In early 2011, the group of Spanish cities selected to continue further in their campaign were: Córdoba, Segovia, Burgos, San Sebastián, Las Palmas and Zaragoza, with Córdoba leading the bunch. I personally was disappointed to see that Pamplona had not gone on to the next stage as I felt it had a lot to offer. To be honest I really didn't think Murcia stood a hope in hell of winning in the first place but it was positive that it had tried. I would like it to have had more of a chance though. Not because it deserved it, but because I think it needed it. The win could have provided a much needed financial and cultural boost that some of the other cities didn't really need. Unfortunately poor little Murcia city in poor little Murcia community will have to wait longer for its renewal.

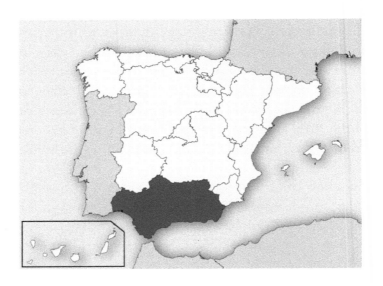

Quintessentially Iberian

Almería – Algeciras – Gibraltar – Ronda - Cádiz

Coming in from Murcia in the east our little bus entered the strange province of Almería in western Andalucía. If I had thought Murcia was dry and desert-like, the lands in Almería were a bit of a shock. All green nearly vanished. It was a land where chlorophyll was fighting a losing battle and the fiery yellow ball in the sky looked devastating. This was desert.

Almería is a famous name in certain Hollywood circles. Many films were shot there in order to take advantage of the countryside while still being able to stay in Europe. The list is impressive and long. Some of the more notable entries include: The Magnificent Seven, Lawrence of Arabia, A Fistful of Dollars, For A Few Dollars More,

The Good, The Bad, And The Ugly, Once Upon A Time In The West and Mad Max III. It was obvious why the area was chosen. Low, tumbling hills rumbled off into heat-veiled distances. Old straw, and dirty soil, were the only colours in the land. Scalped earth and barren waves provided an instant twin with the American Wild West. It was easy to imagine some man with no name trotting lazily down a ridge; some far off smoke trailing from the mouth of a recently fired six-shooter; a flurry of bandits fleeing, sending up clouds of dust; crickets creaking; earth shimmering; and a cigar suffering in a stubbled jaw.

'Ladies and Gentlemen, Almería!'
Leaving the bus the difference in climate was instant. Almería is a fairly large port. Port meant sea, sea meant breeze and breeze is what there was. No more did I have to deal with the lifeless, clingy air of Murcia. A decrease of a few degrees and a little bit of wind can make a lot of difference. It was more humid there but I happily accepted that in order to have the wind kiss my face and have my lungs like me again.

My first stop was the tourist office, as per usual, where the gorgeous blonde girl working there reeled off a list of some cheap places to stay. Oh, for an ounce of that *chulo* courage to enquire whether her flat was on that list! I strolled along the port a little from the very showy old station entrance – a melée of red bricks and painted tiles laid out around a clock – where a piece of rail track, El Cable Inglés – an old, and now protected, loading bay for mineral ore – ran off. It started its journey on a stone arched bridge and then ran on an aerial, iron walkway similar to the ones in New York that used to carry the trains. The track carried on like some great metal caterpillar toward the sea front, where it stopped dead. Heaving metal buckled and halted by both sea and logic. A fairly fine palm-treed promenade walked down the side of the sea, past statues of frolicking dolphins and twisted abstract sculptures, and past some oddly designed building-fronts. I took a right and headed up a road that, according to pretty-gorgeous-blonde's map, burrowed right into the heart of the city.

The streets were small and low level, old looking but probably quite modern. I bore left down Calle Infanta into the subdued, but classy, square that housed Almería's strange sixteenth century cathedral. It looked like the potential offspring if, one night, a usually chaste and conservative building of the cloth decided to get a bit frisky with a dashing castle that was passing through town. The city's fortified cathedral is the result of a beleaguered history and the melding together of both gothic and renaissance styles. It needed to protect itself from north African pirates who would often raid the port and so, over time, became the hefty, bulky beast it is today. It was hollow and gaunt and a little underwhelming inside and, despite having the typical imposing golden reredos above the altar, was neither grand, tall nor gilded enough to set it apart from its cousins.

Yearning grander things I sought out the city's *Alcazaba*, the Arabic fortress. I flip-flopped up through an unkempt but appealing zone of two-storey alleyways called the 'cave quarter' and found it. It was too late to enter but nonetheless the views from the entrance were sweeping enough. I walked around the back of the *Alcazaba* along a dusty track where a few cars were parked. An old man was slapping fruits off a cactus with a piece of wood; a far younger man was taking a photo of his girlfriend; and flies were trying as hard they could to land somewhere fleshy. The hill atop which the *Alcazaba* stood slinked down into a tiny basin and then almost instantly rose back up again to another small peak. From one peak to the other a fortified wall was stretched. On the second peak, next to the connecting turret, a rock plinth held a large white statue of San Cristóbal. He stood in the ruins of the San Cristóbal Castle. At the time I thought it was Jesus. Size wise it might not have been as epic as the geography made it seem, but the evening sun threw dramatic shadows and lit up the whole scene a weary, beery sandstone colour.

The further away the hills the more they were consumed with the gradual lazy darkness of the Andalucian evening.

Before the sun fell I dipped into a quiet, local-looking place and asked if they had any soup. They didn't, but I had already taken my place. Not being very good at turning things down – damn the middle class! – I was soon happily smothered by a *menú del día*. An *ensalada de verano* – a tasty, cold, potato, egg, tuna, onion and pepper salad – was followed by spineless piece of fried cod and then a juicy wedge of very fresh melon. Such was my 'soup'. The walls of the bar were covered completely with photos and posters of a taurine nature and, although the waiter/owner appeared a little grumpy and emotionless, he seemed very generous. Even though I speak Spanish, I could still easily be toppled by a rapid-fire Andalucian tongue. I smiled and nodded when he machine-gunned me with the different types of fish he had on offer.
'Ahem, *sí*, that last one sounds good...'
'The cod?'
'Ah, good, the cod, yes, thank you, the cod...'
I watched the news on the bar's TV for a while: celebrations in Seville for their star World Cup team player Navas; celebrations in Amsterdam for the Dutch who valiantly came second; and then two days of violence in Northern Ireland. In a macabre way it was nice that sport bumped bad, but clearly more pressing news, into second place.

I meandered leisurely back to the port past the cathedral and some smart shopping streets that reminded me of Madrid and phoned my parents to let them know I still had a pulse. Travelling alone it was easy to miss taking part in conversations. I missed familiarity. As much as I loved my trip I often caught myself thinking 'I wish I were at home in England with my family and friends'. In reality it was just the absence of a life where there were, and are, no worries and no stress. That irritating expression 'home is where the heart is' is often annoyingly true.

*   *   *   *

At the despicable, but thankfully balmy, time of 7:45 I caught a bus, the only bus, to Algeciras. It wasn't ideal but it would have to do. Some days on the trip were too short. Some regions on the trip didn't get enough attention. Murcia was an example of this. But in order to further the journey, sometimes tricky choices had to be made. Leaving promptly at the allotted time the bus was expected in to Algeciras at 14:50. More than seven hours for only 214 miles (344km).

For the first couple I toyed with the idea of sleeping. As my head bobbed and bounced off the window some guttural tongue woke me up. It was just people talking on the bus. Since first arriving in Almería I had been hearing more and more Arabic – due in part to the southern regions Moorish history and also its proximity to the northern coast of Africa. I don't find it particularly attractive aurally as a language but it did succeed in making the trip feel more exotic.

The landscape for the first leg could be taken into consideration for some Palm d'Or of unappealingness. Miles of impressive coastline were ruined by dirty grey beaches; sad colourless mountains with plastic sheet-covered fruit and vegetable agriculture; and scruffy, drab-looking towns. Things changed for the better when we stopped for half an hour in a place called Motril and pushed on west towards Malaga where eye-catching clean white towns – Salobreña, Almuñécar, Nerja – hugged the now greener slopes all the way down to the sea. They reflected the sun and genuinely seemed to shine. The glimmering silverfish soon gave way to an oversized grouper with the arrival, five and a half hours in, of Málaga. It was a place I had still never visited but whose bus station I had now twice graced. A new batch of people clambered on and we swam away further west.

It was between Malaga and Marbella where I was slightly impressed, disgusted by, and in awe of, the rampant resort development that sprawled all over the coastline and up the creaking arms of land. A corrosive but inescapable burden. From the *autovía* high up in the hills the land-grabbing urban growth was quite a sight. It was beautiful in an awful way. Towers and hotels and flats and houses. A blockish smudge of white, fleshy pink and cream. Thousands of souls. Thousands of crisping blobs enjoying a segment of the south. Though this was no lemon-tree paradise offering morsels of history and culture. It was a hot, dry place next to a blue, wet place with a golden, sandy place in between.

The few glimpses of Marbella that I got confirmed and reinforced its fame as an unabashed and unchecked area of fortune and lavishness. After leaving the plush and full 'Ariel Bold' whiteness of the centre, the real wealth showed its face. Houses, chalets, mansions and palaces were sculpted into the landscape of whatever altitude, on whatever peak or in whatever trough. Picture-perfect golf courses and dazzling pools littered the land around the private homes. This was the area where the super-rich lived; people who viewed the rich of the centre of Marbella as poor. I just hoped some of them actually deserved their filthy gorgeous paradises. I concurred with the little girl when she caught her breath and said to her mother 'I wish we had a house like that...'

Some minutes later than scheduled we finally arrived at Algeciras. The jolly tourist office worker directed me, in an endearing, but off-putting mix of Spanish and English, to a nearby *pensión* where I could lay my head. I found the 'pensión Lisboa' in the old centre of town. It was on a pretty little street called Calle Juan Morrison above a bar of the same name. The lady at the desk was absurdly friendly,
'Hello, my name is Rosa,' she beamed.
She produced information and scribbled on my map

'Here is us, this is the main area and on this street you have a McDonalds.'

'I'm alright for that thanks.'

'You don't like McDonalds?' she smiled broadly, 'She does' nodding to the giggling daughter standing next to her, 'Are you going to Africa?'

'No, but I'm planning on going to Gibraltar.'

'Oh, fantastic! Be careful of the monkeys.'

'It's ok, I know kung fu.' The girl covered her face with giggles and hid behind her mother.

In his spectacular book "As I walked out one midsummer morning..." Laurie Lee said of Algeciras, 'it was a scruffy little town built around an open drain and smelling of fruit skins and rotten fish'. The *zona central*, which although will never receive high praise for being an area of architectural artwork, has come some way since Lee's 1935 visit and was just about twee enough to go some way towards building a case for Algeciras against the tide of unfair comments ranting about its ugliness. I would, however, not have expected it to be a looker as I would have expected Murcia, what with Algeciras being the seventh largest port in Europe and ports not tending to be the most visually pleasing of places.

At the Plaza Alta, with its borders and central column built from kindly looked after Andalucian tile work, I sat and had a couple of beers. For *tapas* I received two hard-boiled egg halves filled with tuna and then a small dish of *salpicón* – a salad of crab, tuna, onion, pepper and other bits. People came and went; some English-speaking Indian lads looking for cigarettes; a couple of elderly ladies having coffees and luminous jams on toast; a lanky German couple lounging on their chairs in a very lanky and very German way. I left my table and went for a wander. The main road wound up and up away from the water out of town passing a gleaming, but quiet, five-star hotel on the right and a grey, soulless block of flats on the left. Looping back in the direction of the centre I found some attractive houses but they were not numerous. I think it would be true to say that based solely on the aesthetic Algeciras *was* the ugliest place I had visited in Spain, but not the most characterless.

In the evening I strolled again through the centre. Ladies in basic kaftans and hijabs walked around languorously with excitable children, while groups of Arab men gathered in doorways and on benches hacking up words and laughter. Finding a tiny supermarket I bought some cheese, a wheel of Arab bread and some intriguing halal *chorizo* and made myself a North African sandwich. In the comfort of my room I clicked the fan to factor 3 and fell asleep to the feeble wind.

*   *   *   *

Something was barging itself into my dreams.
Stop it!
Some romantic entwining with a vision of beauty was being infringed upon. A flight across the lands of some unknown world was being interrupted.
Get away!
My descent into the profundities of the mind, easing my way to the bottom, to the meaning of everything, being badgered by this thing.
Cloud of thought, pfff!
Blurry vision.
Heavy eyelids.
Bloody alarm clock. It was only remembering what that day meant that got me out of my voluptuous double bed and into my shower.

At the bus station I caught the M-120 local bus to an oversized fishing town called La Linea (de la Concepción). It passed through a couple of grimy areas as well as the 'La Fontana' five-star hotel-club offering a 'streptease', yes that was the spelling, before arriving at its destination. The bus was slow as long queues of cars and freight waited for entry into the little scrap of the British Isles. I disembarked and stood and beheld the green and white fin of Gibraltar, 'The Rock', standing alone. Britain.

I couldn't help but smile when I saw the Union Jack fluttering about as I walked with some other pedestrians to the little passport control, where a bored looking man just waved us through without really checking our documents. It felt more like a silly formality than a strict passing into another country. We were halted by some traffic lights as a Monarch flight, probably Madrid bound, took off in front of us and shot across the runway that had to be walked over in order to enter town. Another Monarch plane then roared into view as it landed. Green light, barrier up, walk past a Gibraltarian policeman looking like any British copper, scurry across the concrete runway towards the settlement, giggle at a red phone box, chuckle at a red post box, smile knowingly at the British traffic light buttons, find the entrance portal to Gibraltar and enter.

'Main Street' was the first place inside the city. It was funny and odd. It looked like a collection of Spanish buildings had got into a fight with an English shopping street, realised neither would win, and formed a truce. Some English brands, lots of duty free shops and many unknown companies and tourist trap affairs littered its length. Firing off Main Street were a variety of other unbelievably theme park named streets; Parliament Lane, Winston Churchill Avenue, Secretary's Lane, Flat Bastion Road – to name but a few. I changed my money into Gibraltarian pounds – legal tender that looked like monopoly money – and made my way past a selection of twee looking pubs to the cable car, which led up to the top of the rock to a place logically named 'Top Of The Rock'. From there I was able to investigate the myriad sights that the lonesome British mountain maintained.

On the summit three things were striking. Firstly the immediate sight, and proximity of, a Barbary ape (actually a monkey). Secondly the intense stupidity of a tourist trying to touch the animal – how I hoped one of the furry critters would use them as a scratching post. The third thing was a view, the kind of which I hadn't seen since Montserrat. It was a view in three parts.

Looking west: the ugly scar of Algeciras and its hills, and further to the right the smoky blemish of San Roque every so often belching out black fumes to ruin the pristine blue above it.

Looking north: the fine crest of The Rock speared out and filled the world in front. A fine layer of green atop a grand cathedral of white; the dividing line between the views of hell and heaven.

Looking east: to mystic visual poetry. Shifting my gaze right I saw faint hills that seemed too coy to show me their full detail. Further right again and I had a view to liquefy my heart in a blender of wonder and slosh it around my throat. The Mediterranean was vast and endless before me. Blue. The perfect blue. A blue I wished everything was. And boats, tiny giant oil tankers arranged in an epic echelon, imperceptibly moving towards the port. I don't know why it affected me so. Maybe because I feel I have an affinity with water. It calms me. Also, most people were interested in the crest or Algeciras or that first ape, to bother with a view of almost nothing. Had I heard a far-off mournful foghorn I might have cried. Aware of the potential emasculation I would later face on paper I set off on a walk.

A little band of apes was near an open pen where they chewed at some stinking, hot fruit. They sat, not really bothered, next to dumb tourists wanting a photo with them. I wanted a photo. Then a battered old outpost and a young Russian couple amused me for a few minutes before I pushed on south down the mountain. I found a plaque on a boulder next to a very steep, very high set of stairs relaying an interesting story of one of many failed attempts to take control of the area:

'Led by a shepherd 500 Spanish soldiers climbed the east face of The Rock in 1704 from Catalan Bay to surprise the garrison, but they were discovered and made prisoner. The shepherd's path from near this spot was scraped away soon afterwards'

I peered over and then up. Only goats would have been at home traversing the slope so I wasn't surprised that this point of entry wasn't the most successful, despite its secrecy. I then thought sod it and climbed the very steep, very high set of stairs, which turned out to very steep and very high indeed. I was rewarded with a whopping view and, slightly lower down, an eerie ex-military gun post.

The heat was starting to intensify so I was quite glad when St. Michael's cave finally arrived. Squeezing past a group of blonde, tanned Germans photographing the monkeys I went inside. St. Michael's is a network of limestone caves that have long commanded the respect and attentions of both inhabitants and visitors. They were first mentioned when Pomponius Melia, a Roman travel writer, came across them in 45A.D. Despite the throngs of tourists that I hated for no other reason than that they were there, the cave was still oppressively beautiful and was larger and vaster than I thought it would be. A spotlit mess of layered stalactites and more simple stalagmites covered the walls and ceiling. During the Second World War the cave was used as an emergency hospital although now the main cave is used as an auditorium for plays, ballets and concerts. The area was still intact, albeit with red, plastic chairs. Vivaldi's 'Spring – 1st movement' was stuck on repeat in the background. I sat on one of the chairs and let the strains of the violins echo round my skull.
'*Yah, das is ein spectaculär!*'
A bolshy German tourist brought me back to the real world. Only one day. Press on. Mission Gibraltar.

It was over two km to the other end of The Rock. It wasn't far but it felt it in the 30+ heat. Pearls of perspiration were crowding my forehead and had started using my back as a slide. I had never experienced so much heat in a British town! I huffed and puffed my way along a fairly sleepy road down the west flank, occasionally having to hug the wall as a tour-taxi-mini-bus thing whizzed past ferrying lazy visitors to the sights. More monkeys, more sun. The road seldom offered shade. My water was running low and tasted warm and metallic. Hotel tap water from the morning. It was viewpoint after viewpoint, Algeciras after Algeciras until finally arriving at the northern tip and 'The Great Siege Tunnels'.

Now is time for a potted history of Gibraltar. The Rock, as far as modern civilization is concerned, has always held the interest of whatever nation was hanging about. The Phoenicians, Carthaginians and Romans all took an early shine to it, but mostly for religious reasons. Archaeology has shown that the area was used for religious offerings, but little else. The lack of fertile soil, natural resources or fresh water also contributed to dissuading early settlers from creating something more permanent. In 711 a Berber army, under the command of Tariq ibn Ziyad, swept over the region and pummelled the borders controlled by rival Christian factions. The city of Gibraltar was founded in 1160, its name originally being *Gibel Tariq* – the 'Mountain of Tariq'. What followed was three hundred years of conflict that ended in 1462 when a small Castilian force launched a surprise attack while the town's senior leaders and townsfolk were paying homage to the new Sultan of Granada. The garrison surrendered and the era of Spanish rule followed.

In 1501 Queen Isabella I of Castile charged all future monarchs of the country to 'hold and retain the said City for themselves and in their own possession; and that no alienation of it, nor any part of it, nor its jurisdiction shall ever be made from the Crown of Castille'. Despite this grand statement the Spanish didn't really look after it at all and it fell into decline. Marbella became the big, southern port, as Gibraltar's economic value was very limited and its terrain remained fairly inhospitable. It was instead used as a prison camp for Christian renegades and Moorish POWs. Its weaknesses were taken advantage of in 1540 by a raid of Barbary pirates who slaughtered many and seized hundreds of hostages. Finally the Crown responded and, in 1552, fortified the town somewhat. Despite the Dutch who attacked the shipping lanes and Spanish fleet in the early

1600s and a couple of early English pops in 1620 and 1625, the island, with its overcrowding, unsanitary conditions and disease, *did* remain Spanish. This changed, as did a lot of things, with the War of Spanish Succession.

The much-maligned dictator/leader/lord protector Oliver Cromwell once said, fairly humorously but also correctly, of Gibraltar: 'if possessed and made tenable by us, would it not be both an advantage to our trade, and an annoyance to the Spaniards, and enable us to ease our own charge?' In 1702 Queen Anne formally declared war on France, a favourite pastime of the British. After Charles II died childless, the question of who was going to inherit the Spanish throne was left wide open. The dispute, and then war, was between Prince Phillip of Anjou, of France, and Archduke Charles of Austria. The two sides ended up consisting of the French, Bavarians and Spanish loyal to Phillip against the combined forces of the Dutch, British, Prussians, Portuguese, Hapsburg Monarchists and Spanish loyal to Charles. In 1704 Gibraltar surrendered to the British and in 1713 the War ended, with Phillip on the throne but with Queen Anne still holding onto her new territory.

Throughout the rest of the eighteenth century the Spanish continued to lay siege to the island and bombard it. Early on the British offered to sell it back to Spain but the proposals were vetoed by the British Parliament following protest from the locals. They didn't want to be handed to the Spanish. Spain's aggression culminated in the Great Siege in 1779. The fourteenth, largest and last attempt to take the island left the town in rubble, with diseases spreading like wildfire and starvation creeping around every corner. However, the British held fast. When the three and a half year siege ended Britain ceded West Florida, East Florida and Menorca to Spain, but not Gibraltar. This is still a bone of contention today leading to cries, either serious or in jest, of '*Gibraltar Español*' during the odd protest – always from mainland Spaniards who feel they deserve the land back, and never from the happy people who actually live there. The upside of the Great Siege is that it left its mark in a way that one could revisit it, and feel and see the history.

Not as airy as the cave, but cool enough, the tunnels went down and down - occasionally punctured by a windowed gun chamber - culminating in the St. George's chamber, a seven-gun battery. The rock had seen so many wars and swatted away so many sieges it was plain to see why people said it was invincible.

Descending Ellis Road there was the 'City Under Siege' exhibit, which was small but rather emotive. At first I didn't know what I was seeing. I thought it was simply a museum, but soon realised it was the artillery blasted remains of old Gibraltarian buildings. Nothing of them remained except for scattered husks. I imagined the hellish heat as soldiers, parched and starving, struggled to fend off the forces of two powerful nations and villagers screaming as their homes and livelihoods were smashed from existence. And there I was 'suffering' in a t-shirt and shorts allowing a breeze, sun cream protecting my skin and water to keep me from harm. The fact was driven home at the tiny, hidden, underground Heritage Museum in which there was a tasteful and solemn memorial to those who had, over the years, died in service at Gibraltar.

The Bunsen burner Andalucian afternoon soon drove me back down into the centre, past a weathered tapestry of different style houses. Typical Spanish flats, all youthfully painted, sat next to more British styled brickwork and a shrunken church, looking as if it had been airlifted from Bath and decided to stay on account of the good weather. My stomach groaned. It was gone five and it hadn't really been fed yet and my head was beginning to throb with the lack of sustenance. I came to Gibraltar with one culinary thing in mind; the oh-so-English Fish 'n' Chips. I found a tiny pub cradled in the shade of a high-walled street called Bell Lane. The Aragon. After a longer wait than I would have expected at my outside, four-bench, area a well-fed, middle-aged woman jollied out.

'Are you waiting for someone?'

'Yeah.'

'Mary! There's a young man out here wants serving.'

Another well-wintered, middle-aged woman tumbled out of The Aragon.

'Sorry love, what can I get you?'

'I'd love some fish and chips, with peas.'

'You don't want salad?'

'Salad? No.'

'To drink?'

'Have you got any ciders?'

'Strongbow?'

'Perfect. I've been waiting a year for this so I'm looking forward to it!'

As I waited for my English staple I was slightly confused as to what was really the main language in Gibraltar as I had been hearing a lot of Spanish. Indeed, sat there I heard passers-by switch from Spanish sounding Spanish to English sounding English in an instant. Also a lot of the more olive skinned Gibraltarians spoke English with a near imperceptible, energetic, tangy lilt. I suppose you could call it an accent. The fish and chips arrived.

You can say what you like about English food – and the Spanish, they do – but we have the market covered with regards to hearty or feel-good grub. And I did feel good. Buttery batter sat firm around a vigorously fried, but moist and fishy, piece of cod. It was classically complimented with salt and vinegared chips with tomato sauce and my peas. My amber cider clinked with ice and fractured the light that entered my banquet of one. As I ate I overhead two women chatting:

'Hello Susan!'

'Oh, hello!'

How could I not overhear, and how I wanted to. One of the ladies, the more boisterous of the pair, was the owner of the Midtown Bookshop, which sat next door to The Aragon.

'We've got new signs now!'

'I can see. Very nice.'

'We got them done here.'

'Isn't it cheaper over the border?'

'Yes, but you never know what you are going to get. Just the other day I was walking over (something) road. Them new people are there with the (something) shop. They got their signs done in Spain and its got typos. Shepherds Pie instead of Shepherd's Pie. Can you imagine that!' she laughed.

'Goodbye Mary.'

'Goodbye Susan.'

Was I really on one of the most southern tips of Spain? The seemingly bilingual, as I think almost everyone in Gibraltar is, waitress removed my spotless plate. I couldn't resist treating myself to some tea and scones with jam and cream before I left.

'Would you like it in a mug?'

'I most certainly would.'

I finished my food with an internal, exuberant flourish that outwardly surfaced as a smile and a contented sigh. I nipped into the bookshop a few minutes before closing time. As well as needing another book to accompany me on my bus trips I secretly wanted to talk to the owner. I calmly looked at the classics section, perusing the titles. Should I go for short and sweet, maybe Dead Poet's Society, or maybe something heftier like Welles. I opted for a compromise, Vladimir Nabokov's "Lolita".

'Do you have many Spanish books here?' I enquired, yearning conversation.

'We currently have two Spanish books in the shop. If people want Spanish it's cheaper to get them on the other side of the border due to tax. Our English books are cheaper though.'

True. Books in Spain are in general very expensive, whether they are English or not. In the UK books are considered educational and are therefore not taxed in a certain way thus they are quite cheap. Average paperbacks range from £5.99-£8.99. In Spain those same paperbacks are priced between 15 and 20 euros.

I changed the topic:

'If one Gibraltarian passes another in the street how would they greet each other?' I realised it sounded like a joke, but thankfully she didn't.

'Well, it depends. I mean you must realise that in Gibraltar we also have our own dialect. So maybe we could say *'paga el switch'* for flick the switch,' she started giggling heartily.

'I never knew.'

'And over the centuries many have married in and out, so some people are from the English Gibraltarian heritage and some have Spanish roots.'

'So it's like a big mish mash.'

'It's a mish mash exactly.'

She then told me how the fish and chips lark is really just for the tourists. I confessed to having enjoyed it nonetheless. Gibraltarian cooking is again a warped mixture of things 100% recognisable as English and dishes that are unmistakably Spanish. On the same page of a little cookery book she showed me there was a recipe for tea cakes printed intentionally and comfortably above *torrijas*, a Spanish bread and butter pudding type thing.

'Of course, *paella* is in here, but on the whole this book is pretty precise when it comes to what we actually eat.'

I had the image of the original British inhabitants eating their hot pots and pies and gravy. One day Mrs. Tubbs, the captain's wife, thought she'd give *chorizo* a whirl in the lamb stew and via word of mouth, and taste of spoon, a Spanish element was introduced into the local cuisine. I am sure it started off apprehensively, with a sprinkle of paprika dust on the morning eggs, or adding rice to the fish instead of potatoes, before one day a dam broke and the buxom

Gibraltarian lady announced it was kidneys in sherry, *morcilla* and spinach, and red peppers stuffed with cod. And how the men must have cheered as their bellies shrank and their hair took on more of a gloss.

On my street back in Maidenhead, one of my neighbours is a Gibraltarian family. They have lived in the UK for around thirty years but still occasionally go back on holiday to visit their old home. Carmen and Manolo and their son Eric live in a very British house on a very British street in a very English part of the country. Berkshire, Home County, River Thames, afternoon tea and all that. One afternoon I went round their house, to their warm living room, and quizzed them about their ex-home as we sipped Earl Grey.

'Do you guys feel Spanish at all?'

'Hah!' spat Carmen with a throaty laugh, 'No! We are British and we are proud to be so!'

'Absolutely not!' added Eric.

'Why do you think Spain keeps protesting about Gibraltar when the people want to be British then?' I asked.

'They still believe it is part of their territory and have no respect for our sovereignty,' he finished.

I thought it interesting that he said 'our'. He was British, no doubt, despite being the product of a Maltese family on his mother's side and Spanish on his father's. Their opinions are mirrored, or backed up, by hard facts. In a 2002 referendum a proposal for shared sovereignty between Spain and Britain was rejected by 99% of Gibraltarians, an overwhelming majority. We then continued talking in Spanish as more tea was served and some biscuits were brought out on little china plates.

According to the bookshop owner the assistant, or daughter, had apparently studied in Valladolid so I mentioned that I had recently visited it.

'They say we here speak like the Andalucians, cutting off our words and the like – haha – there they speak very posh.'

'My kind of town,' I winked as I made my way to the door. 'It was lovely to talk you both.'
'You too love. Tell Manolo and Carmen to come and visit us here again!'

It was evening and some shops were beginning to go to sleep. I passed a pub called the Clipper, which had a smashing russet-red haired bar girl hanging out of the window. It had a sign sporting the late, and personally much loved, Cutty Sark. I toyed with my conscience. I wanted both to try and flirt, maybe start a passionate long-distance relationship, and to have another cider. Even though it was evening, the sun was still fully in the sky and making me thirsty. Instead I decided I should grow up and stop being so mildly creepy so, after standing like a lemon at a crossroads for more than a minute, I crumbled and slunk away into the evening heat towards the airport and the heavily trafficked exit road.

A quarter of the way across the runway an alert went off 'beep, beep, beep – PEDESTRIANS, DO NOT STOP ON THE RUNWAY!' Jesus Christ, I smiled to myself, this is a bit exciting. It was the last crossing before the barriers went down to let a plane land. I secretly hoped a budget airline would hurtle into view as the alarm system blared – 'PEDESTRIANS, RUN FOR YOUR LIVES'. I would pick up a dame with a broken heel and in the last seconds before being wiped into splattered atoms we would dive to safety. I would get a kiss and a crowd would be applauding. The police and, why not, the plane crew would salute me. From Gibraltar with love. On the contrary I had to hurry a little and just ended up panting, as I scrambled for my passport and found myself back in Spain.

The last Saxon dribbles were heard dissolving into a variety of buses headed off round the South. Not me. Although I had my Spanish to keep me company in my bubble of linguistic isolation, I was still a little lonely as I sat in my room with my book and with no one to talk to. Falling asleep that night my head wrapped around the lyrical wonderland of Zabokov's words and was tenderly buffeted by the cooling push of the electric fan.

*   *   *   *

The train to Ronda left at midday. I was still waiting in line ten minutes before it was supposed to pull away because two groups of idiots were holding up both ticket offices. Pouting and exhaling noisily I crossed my arms: *the* display of English irritation. I was so angry I could have written a letter. But fortunately, with only a few minutes left, the mentally deficients finished fiddling with timetables and purses and I was free to buy my ticket and find my seat in the excessively spacious carriages.

The scenery north of Gibraltar, after the first hour or so on the way to the '*pueblo blanco*' was, at times, monstrously beautiful. Shooting in and out of mountain tunnels I grabbed snatches of the extraordinary tight valley we were travelling through. It was like a pair of flamenco dancer's legs and she was flirting with my vision. I was glued to the window. The high sun dappled the green and orange slopes with little, bobbly, dark shadows. A river wound along the valley floor from where the hills fired up. The water was clear and wavy with the greenest, swirling algae. Blotchy, heliotrope-flowered bushes and the blurring from the speed made the world look like some lost Turner. The sky was impossibly blue. The sea in air. The train looped around the back of yet another pearly white town and then hauled itself up an incline towards Ronda, the big daddy of the 'white towns' – a string of whitewashed settlements that are peppered over the whole region.

It sat, stuck to the top of a hill, creeping over a gorge. It was almost fully white and it glinted. Following the signs, again map-less, I strolled, inexplicably confident in the direction of the centre with my constant friend, the sun, who struck upwards and caused the world to shine. My first taste of Ronda's blinding glamour was the small, pure white – everything was pure white – bullring. Outside, statues of *toreros* unmovingly swept their capes past invisible bulls while a decorated horse stood in the heat, swatting itself with a thick tail, waiting for the next tourist wanting a twee photo. Leaving the smooth square I followed the 'main', but quiet, road to a bridge. This was *the* bridge. The bridge of Ronda. The Puente Nuevo. It is a giant bridge that was built over a period of forty years (1751-1793) and claimed the lives of fifty builders. It stands holding apart the Tajo gorge; 98m wide and 120m deep.

The view, in an effort to continue the theme of being utterly unoriginal, was undeniably epic. The sight was of the thick stone arms of the Puente Nuevo in between the two land masses, like some stoic peacemaker keeping two giants from fighting; white houses were built to the edges of the cliffs where birds whirled; and the far off reaching fields and ghostly heights of the Sierra Nevada. The heat was awesome and the glowing nature of the walls made it more potent. I wanted to see the bridge in its entirety. Where is the fun in only looking down from a bridge; I wanted to look up. Crossing a shadowless path through some pretty, cobbled lanes I came to a small square with a quiet gurgling fountain. There were some steps. I weighed up the options:

1. Do the non-touristy thing and descend the mountainside in the heat and sun and inevitably sweat-ruin a t-shirt for the sake of a view.
2. Follow the other packaged tourists and 'baa, baa!' my way around the sights on the map.
3. Get drunk in a bar with a bottle of Spanish wine because, in life, that is always an option.

I chose the first and readied my Murcian flip-flops for a pounding.

There was near to no shade and the sun seemed to be beating in time to the painfully loud cicadas that were screaming in their steaming, twiggy kingdoms. I passed a red-faced, wheezing couple, sporting slanting eyebrows that communicated both their desperate condition and the imperative nature of my turning back. I never quit on a view. The steps ended in a crumbly broken heap after which a dusty, bumpy path took over. At the 'bottom' – the end of the path where a smashed Arabic archway stood – I was suffering with the volume of liquid leaving my pores. I ran my hand down my chest and it came out glistening. My blue shirt was blotchy with dark smudges where my sweat had absorbed into the fabric. There was one more wilting couple, drinking water before the big uphill, and then there, turning, was the bridge. It was staggering. I had seen photos of it and had seen it from above but to have it looming over like some ancient skyscraper, and with water jetting out its base collecting in an opalescent, lime green pool was so worth the state I was in. I wanted to get up close to the walls to touch and inspect the beast.

The path went a little more 'off road' after a blasted away building and gate. Should I be going this way? Before I managed to find an answer to the question, hot soil and warm rocks were getting in my footwear and I was trying to keep my balance in that wilder terrain. There were two routes. The first of which led down through soft earth and vegetation to a shrouded wall continually sprayed by an exit stream of water. I wanted to get to the very bottom, to the pool, but everything was either too wet or too overgrown for me to get through in my fairly inadequate clothing. It had gone jungle.

The second path was more productive. As I neared the foot of one of the bridge's gargantuan legs, a path and a little rusty railing appeared. A small filter channel of water ran alongside it and disappeared into the wall – through the leg. A vein. It wasn't deep so I took my shoes off and sunk them in. The cool water smothered my feet and it was good. Igniting my phone light I wandered into the cave that bled into the leg. Pond skaters darted around my shins and the darkness became more absolute. I was inside the Puente Nuevo. I felt fairly honoured. I couldn't say how many people had done it. After a while a combination of deepening water and, to be honest, becoming a little unnerved by my location, I backtracked and sheathed my two soggy swords back in their sandaly scabbards.

Continuing under the enormous arch I soon realised that I was not traversing some tourist-ready path. Health and Safety would have had a field day. It was a service path and it took me through to an area on the gorge floor where some battered old buildings and water gates, whether used or not, seemed to control the flow of water. It felt like an open-air museum piece. The little rivulet where I had bathed my feet followed the path in a lower, deeper channel until coming to a stop at one of the gates. It was probably used to balance out the flow rate like a dam. Unlike a museum, however, there were no information panels to confirm my thoughts.

I savoured my last few moments of innocuousness before plodding back up the hill and steps, stopping at any and every polyp of shade that hung grossly off tiny trees and branches. The worst time for heat in Spain is between 3 o'clock and 5. The worst time for a strenuous walk up a steep hill I found out was also between about 3 o'clock until 5. Back at the little square, I splashed my arms with water from the fountain and sat down. A relaxed, virtuoso, Spanish guitarist was sitting under an orange parasol producing lemony tunes while arpeggios glided up and down the neck of his guitar with a dreamy brilliance. The heat, the cooling water in my eyes, the warm strums from the guitar, and the little plaza all came together to form an image that was stereotypically Andalucian. My moist eyes and the over-saturated colour of the scene made it a little imaginary. I phoned my parents briefly so that they could hear what I was hearing. Holding the phone aloft towards the guitarist I heard my mother audibly groan through the tinny speakers.

Another hour was spent wandering around the *casco histórico*. It was so idyllic I wanted to buy a summerhouse and grow vibrant citrus fruits in the garden and have flamboyant flowers streaming over its white walls. The area was full of slim, cobbled lanes the colour of snow, under a very blue sky. Exiting the tiny streets I sat and had some lunch: a fine *gazpacho* and the classic plate of eggs, chorizo and potatoes. My drinks, however, weren't included in the set menu. It was my fault. I should have read the menu more carefully before ordering two glasses of wine. Something that bugs me in life, especially as a student of languages, is simple translation mistakes. For example where I was sat the menu offered an *ensalada mixta* – a mixed salad. *Mixta* is an adjective but still they so often translate it as 'mix salad', which is just wrong. So, still a bit miffed about the drinks, on the back of my larger than expected bill I helpfully wrote 'mixta = mixed!' and placed it on the table and left with a cocky grin on my face.

The evening sun threw the sultriest of shadows on the world as the train returned to Algeciras. The last memory of the north-African flavoured port was the thick smell of cooking halal meat and sweating vegetables washing out into the cool sea air.

*   *   *   *

My last stop in Andalucía was the ancient port of Cádiz. I left the bus station and, slightly disorientated, bumped into a German guy. Well, he bumped into me.
'Halo, you speak English?'
'I am English.' I always got a kick out of saying that.
He was worriedly asking me if I knew any streets with cheap hostels. Of course I didn't, so he – Roman – and I teamed up and went in search of some.
First to the tourist office:
'Is there a list of cheap hostels?' I asked.
'Cheap? In summer? Doubt it,' said the lady.

Roman and I followed my rough guide and managed to find a funky, hippy-ish and 'backpacker friendly' hostel called *'Casa*

Caracol', 'snail house'. I shouldered open the blue door and we shuffled in. It was a buzzing room full of tie-dye t-shirts, piercings, body hair and grubby clothes sweating into rucksacks. Some pans were clattering around a communal kitchen and a few attractive German girls were eating sandwiches at a table whilst looking utterly out of place. My kind of hostel - rough and ready and cheap.
'Hi guys, you got a reservation?' said the girl working at the counter.
'No. Do you have any rooms free?'
'I'm afraid tonight we are completely full.'
'Shit,' wheezed Roman.
'But if you hang around a bit the owner is on the phone to a friend with a flat who rents out rooms. He might have space.'

The girl, Jo, with her pretty eyes, downy face and heaving, slightly sunburnt, British cleavage, tapped the shoulder of a wiry Spanish man who had just come off the phone. She explained our situation to him. He told us that in that precise moment it wasn't looking hopeful so, as a compromise, he let us leave our bags there and took us to a cheap, but good quality, tapas bar, where we could wait for the outcome.

Roman wore a blue shirt with a red Arab style scarf and had a kind, slightly bug-eyed, face, touched pink by the sun.
'For sure I will stay on the beach this night. I did it in Marseilles and it was great. Here will be fine.'
Vegetarian Roman had two helpings of toast with a blue cheese and walnut spread. I had potatoes in a peanut sauce and chicken escalope wrapped around ham and cheese. I always strived to choose the healthier option if it was there. I had a beer too. We enjoyed the warm shade as we waited. He was doing some travelling in his holidays before going back to study, while I was doing some travelling in my holidays before going back to work. We were very similar. Almost the second we had finished, the spindly owner, with his mysterious limp, scuttled up to the table.
'You guys are in luck. My friend has space. I take you there now.'

We walked up through some alleyways past a pub where a man was enthusiastically bleating to a Spanish guitar he was playing. The conversation was held in a mixture of Spanish and English – about Spain's World Cup win – until we arrived at an inconspicuous little wooden door. Limpy took some keys out of a tattered, white envelope. He fumbled choosing the right one and with a little shoulder barge opened the door. Inside another door, then up two floors via a tiny, tiled, white square staircase, through another door and we were in our house. He plopped the little metal key into my hand, waved, nodded his head and hobbled off down the stairs.

Our flatmates were a scruffy, weed-smoking skater couple who originally hailed from Madrid and, tired of the hectic lifestyle there, decided to try and start a new, more laid-back, life for themselves down in the south. They were warm and welcoming. Roman had an instant connection with the guy whose second name was Zimmerman. My connection was that I had lived in Madrid but I had to hold back from pouring forth my love for the city, as they clearly hated it. Zimmerman sat there, in his shabby red t-shirt, with a spliff hanging in his mouth while his girlfriend, slightly more presentable, prepared them a salad. Their faces were placid but tired looking, with heavy bags, but they were animated and enthusiastic to have new visitors.

Apparently the guy who owned the flat, and also lived there, was in bed asleep, ill, possibly due to a hangover and had been robbed the night before. We therefore didn't bother waking him up and when we had finally sorted ourselves out with sheets and pillowcases Roman decided, as he was going to be there for two days, that he definitely needed a siesta. We were sharing a key to our two-bed room so I told him to sit-tight, well, lie-tight, and that I would be back in a couple of hours. Nodding sleepily he reclined on his creaky little bed.

Cádiz was mine for a while. The Cathedral was unlike any I had seen up until then. A large whitewashed, blockish towered building, topped with a striking golden dome. It sat like some vast ivory sphinx overlooking the sparkling mass of the Atlantic. Walking along the promenade I felt my back wettening in the very moist sea air. It felt, and looked like, the *malecón* in Havana, Cuba. There was a large sea wall with corroded boulders splashed at the base by waves and whose arms wrapped wide around the bay. I came across a beach loaded to the point of disintegration by a fleshy army of holidaymakers and local beach bums. Privacy and seclusion were not to be found there. On the other side of the city I found the water again. Cádiz is on a spit, surrounded by sea on three sides. In the centre of the old part of the city is a wonderful jumble of interlocking streets that shoot off in all sorts of directions. Almost all were crumbling and peeling under the combined attack of both age and the sea-air that curled around corners and bit by bit launched itself at the paintwork. It was the attractive result of some millennia slow war of attrition that the buildings were losing.

'*En el nombre de Dios!*' a wedding in a church was being held with the doors wide open. Some fishing rods flicked and twitched as the floats bobbed expectantly in a sapphire sea pregnant with fish. My watch showed 17:45. Time to return to my snoring German, I thought. I knocked the pre-decided two knocks and entered, hearing a salutatory groan.
'Can I open the windows,' I asked.
'Yah, but slowly, bit by bit.'
I did as he said.
'Arrg, holy shit,' he squealed as he rubbed his eyes. A quick face-slap and shower later and a freshened Roman and I were conversing with our flatmates as they ate dinner.

No sooner had we begun to relax in our new surroundings when another lodger arrived. A lanky, grubby German, who Roman had briefly talked to in Casa Caracol, shuffled in. He spoke, as so many

Germans do, with near flawless English, but he was a little oddball and behind his eyes seemed to flicker a cognisance that didn't promote itself beyond the grey meatloaf of his mind. As a result I never really felt comfortable around Theo. He had been in Cádiz for five weeks and was there only a few days more. The problem was that he had been kicked out of his flat.

'Yah, so we already had a warning for making too much noise. The neighbours, they said one more complaint and we will have to kick you out. Then we [his Swedish housemate and him] let a couple of German guys stay on our terrace. They made some noise man, so we asked them to leave. One guy was on his way out but then the other guy kicked off. Went kinda crazy. After an argument, a loud argument, my Swedish housemate and he had a fight. My housemate broke the guy's jaw. With one punch. Well, he does martial arts. Next thing there's like loads of police cars downstairs and policemen, so more noise.'
There was a pause as the animated teenager stopped
'So you were kicked out?' I offered.
'Yeah, we were kicked out.'

We went shopping for alcohol in an effort to save money. We also bought bread, cheese and a pasta sauce that was never used. Back at the flat, after some of the aforementioned bread and cheese – which Roman had bought and actively offered me and begrudgingly offered the provision-less Theo – we were encouraged by our housemates to go and enjoy the evening sun up on the roof terrace.

A higgledy-piggledy of ups and downs and antennae and washing lines stuck up into the dimming cerulean of the sky. Streets wandered off to unknown corners, seemingly distant voices swam around below and a flash of cathedral finished off the view sending the last whispers of the faithful up to whatever deity they were so much in love with. We had an iPod, speakers, a creaky wicker bench, two bottles of white wine – not for Theo – and a bottle of

Sherry. The Cádiz province is the home of sherry and about 35km away is Jerez de la Frontera, which is the centre of the production zone. We drank steadily but never fast. At one point Zimmerman joined us with a beer and we chuckled at a man on a distant terrace plumping the leaves of his marijuana plant before carefully taking his fronds inside.

'Weed doesn't like the cold,' Zimmerman said with a knowing smile. Roman was getting antsy about the time, as it was almost 10 o'clock. 'Don't worry it's only 10. It's early,' I warbled silkily, beginning to smoothen under the cushion of alcohol.

'You have been in Spain too long. If there are German girls there they have already gone!'

He had a fair point. A couple more drams of the hollow tasting – nothing on your tongue but flavour in your throat – *'oloroso'* sherry and, after asking some directions in a rather frazzled manner from a family dining outside, *and* picking up a bottle of *tinto de verano* on the way, we arrived once again at our helpful snail house.

Inside was not the party we had been told it might be but we joined the group and it grew as the evening went on. A few of the young workers at the hostel, some Germans and a couple of Italian girls, one of whom, Ilaria, I fell madly in love with as soon as I set eyes on her. Wildly attractive, she glowed with a tanned innocence and had an intelligent and cheeky gaze. She had sparkling brown eyes and shiny chestnut hair that tumbled about her where it liked. She loved classic rock and wore a short dress. Fantastic English, set-off with a slight bouncy Italian accent, fired off a playful and often sarcastic stream of the Queen's. We all continued drinking. I was handed some acrid, cheap red wine in a plastic mug. Through the evening I tolerated foreign conversation and stuffy temperatures as I repeatedly worked my way back to Ilaria to swap music tastes or share schoolyard banter. If I was speaking to someone at one end of the table and she at the other I would be thrown corny winks. They were plain to see, but I felt that they privately drifted between us. The touch of an arm or a playful slap crumbled me. She was utterly romantic and she added me there and then on Facebook using the hostel's computer.

'If you ever come to Milan, you are welcome to stay.'

'OK guys, it's 1:20 in the morning, and time for non-residents to leave,' said the severe looking hostel worker, with his drunk gaze and heavy lids.

And with that the bubble burst. 1:20? Strange time, we thought. Either the chap was just doing his job or, as I prefer to fancy, he was jealous of my well-meaning lechery. Roman and I walked to the top of the street where Theo was standing with another guy. After talking rubbish for a while I heard a door close. Ilaria was outside on the phone. Oh, for one last word! I tentatively slinked back down to the hostel and when she finished her call we chatted for a few moments. She irresistibly told me how she didn't have a boyfriend as such and was looking for some fun in her life. I am fun, I thought. She had to go back inside. And 'poof' the night ended. I fell asleep in an intoxicated reverie with one stabilising foot on the floor. Sometimes being a romantic is very much drawing the short straw.

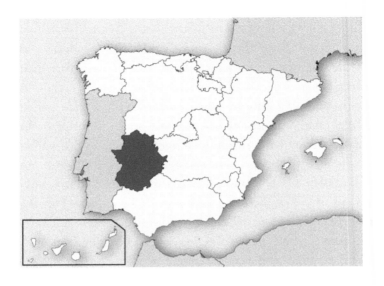

Pimentón Picante

Mérida – Trujillo – Cáceres – Guadalupe – Miajadas – Villanueva de la Serena – La Vera

It was hideously early. Roman was completely knocked out and snoring but he was awake when I returned from my shower and bid me a croaky farewell. I had a stomping headache. I hadn't really had much to drink during the trip so the quantity of alcohol consumed the night before, combined with the heat, left me with a jackhammer pulse in my temple as if something were trying its hardest to bust out of my skull. The dawn had not even thought about breaking as I left with my trusty baby-blue backpack. It was five something in the morning and the heat was gentle.

It was a chore getting to Extremadura, the next region. First was a train from Cádiz to Sevilla. I curled up in a ball on my seat and tried to get back to my land of dreams, through the thump in my head. At some point in the early stages of the journey a lady wanted to sit next to me. Perhaps she had a booked seat, even though the majority were empty and she had been sitting in another place further down the carriage. She was there with her family: two little kids and what was presumably the grandmother. I guessed they wanted to sleep too and didn't want to have to deal with someone waking them up and telling them they were in their seats. I grunted a good morning and closed my eyes again.

'Where are you going?' murmured a sleepy voice. The lady was talking to me.

'Mérida via Sevilla,' I answered lethargically back.

She asked me a few more questions about who I was and I struggled to answer under the combined weight of my disgusting hangover and my strong desire to catch some shuteye. I really didn't want to talk to her. Soon enough she gave up and, along with her kids, fell asleep too. The surrealism ended when the sun creaked up over the horizon, setting Andalucía aflame with light.

An expensive taxi ride through the sleepy outskirts of Sevilla took me to the bus station. The land between Cádiz and Sevilla was almost as dull as the scrubby countryside between Cádiz and Algeciras. Endless brown, dead-looking fields were punctured by the odd limp-looking hillock, lonely wind turbines, or the occasional intriguing village in the middle of the utterness of nowhere.

At the Mérida station I waited outside for my ride. It was mid-morning and I was slightly shocked by the heat. Strong, dry and tangible. Elena and Carlos pitched up a couple of minutes later in a rattly old car. We all ran to each other and embraced. I hadn't seen them for a week, which in itself wasn't very long, but after the tiring, sweaty days of the South it felt like an age. I gratefully dunked my rucksack in the back of the car and we motored away from the station into the town. It felt so good to be with them. I felt safe and looked-after. I didn't have to do anything for a while. I could name a place and we'd go there. If I needed something we could sort it out together. I had two *Extremeños* showing me their region. And show me they did!

Mérida is a real Roman city, founded in 25 BC. But it still retained its splendour under the Visigoths (fourth to eighth centuries), staying strong under the Christians until it took a beating during the period of the Napoleonic Invasion in which it lost a lot of the buildings that made it so fine. Today it is no longer as important as it once was, but still remains the capital of the Extremadura region.

We parked the car and snacked in a local bar before heading to buy our tickets for the Roman sights. Elena told the man that she had a student card but that we didn't. The man at the till looked at us through thin glass, waved his hand and said it didn't matter and went ahead giving us all student prices, two-thirds off the original cost.

'People from Extremadura are very *humilde*. That is one of our characteristics,' said Elena wagging her finger, making sure I got the correct representation of her people for my book.

First we visited the Mérida museum, a grand showcase of all the excavated statues, bits of wall, mosaic, metal-ware and coins that had been found. The temperature was rising sharply as the sun crept up. When Elena mentioned the '*humilde*' trait, I thought she was just saying it to boast about her people. On entering the museum however, the lady working there decided to let us three through for free. Elena didn't know why, I didn't know why, and Carlos shrugged his shoulders. Maybe Elena had a point.

After the museum it was time to go and see some of the town's celebrated sights. The heat had now reached its peak, few people were walking round and everything felt heavy and hot. It was averaging 43 degrees and the sun all but hurt the skin. It felt similar to when one holds one's hand next to a flame or hot lamp, not in it, but near. It didn't feel like it was burning, just that it was heating me perceptibly. The streets, where previously waiters and owners of restaurants had tirelessly been badgering us to come in and eat, giving us leaflets, telling us it was the best and freshest and well-priced menu we'd find, were now empty and silent.

The amphitheatre at Mérida was inaugurated in 8 BC and was a place for the 15,000 strong audience to watch fights between gladiators, between animals or between animals and men. Images of Russell Crowe's film came to mind. Its size was telling. Mérida was once an important Roman capital. During the Empire's height all of Spain and Portugal were under its rule. The peninsula was separated into various provinces: Baetica, which shares an area similar to modern day Andalucía; Lusitania, which spread over what is now Extremadura and most of Portugal; and Tarraconensis, which comprised everything else. *Tarraco* (Tarragona) was the capital of Tarraconensis, *Corduba* (Córdoba) the capital of Baetica and *Emerita Augusta* (Mérida) the capital of Lusitania. Even though the Mérida of today is scruffier and less important that it was once, it still retained the shadows of its greatness.

The path headed round, through, and up and down the amphitheatre before carrying the visitor to the theatre. A certain Marco Vipsanio Agrippa, who had the ear of the Emperor, promoted and eventually saw built the 6,000-capacity building in the years 16 and 15 BC. I had never seen a ruin like it, as much as it was ruined, which it wasn't really. A wide arc of chairs rose up and faced a stage that was backed by a two-tiered façade of columns and statues made of slightly duck-egg, blue-grey and orange sandstone. Here was a ruin where one didn't have to use the power of imagination to dream up some early performance of 'Carry on Caesar'. The only downside was that there was modern staging and lights rigged up for an evening performance and it detracted somewhat from the genuine feel of the place. But only somewhat; not a lot. It was veritable marvel.

The heat was actually beginning to hurt in earnest. It wasn't sweaty heat but it was still uncomfortable. The thermometers tiptoed above 44° and I could actually feel the sun doing its best to flash fry my arms and neck. We searched for somewhere in the dead streets to eat. Elena and Carlos argued as we got lost around alleys where there were no eateries.
'I told you we should have gone to the place back there!'
'You were the one that wanted to find somewhere else!'
And so forth.
Eventually we stumbled upon a miniscule bar that was not only dirt-cheap but was utterly local. No 'Come, come, tourist, special menu for you' salesmen here. The food wasn't interesting but was, on the whole, delicious. First up was a strange, watery *gazpacho* that tasted nothing like tomatoes. Carlos and I shared knowing looks accompanied with sceptical raised eyebrows. Elena looked pleased she hadn't ordered it. Then, plate after plate of new delights arrived from the fat, dopey but charming waiter: *pastel de atún* (tuna cake; a tasty but unsettling slab of brown fishy 'cake'), *lomo con ajo* (chunks of pork loin fried in lots of oil and garlic), *prueba de cerdo* (literally 'test' or 'proof' of pork: small boulders of fried meat in a sharp sauce) and finally a molten pot of my favourite gum-slapping mature Spanish cheese: *torta de la Serena*; typical of Extremadura and served simply with bread. We rounded the meal off with two, hulking jugs of cold, fruity and quite alcoholic sangria. A little happier and light-headed we went out again and braved the screaming Meridan heat.

We only managed to get halfway across the Roman bridge that crept out over the Guadiana River before turning back and fleeing to shady pools of ever-thinning shadow. In fairness to us, it *is* the longest of all existing Roman bridges, clocking in at an impressive 721m. And it was *very* hot. Before carrying on into the silent streets we bathed our arms and faces and feet in a fountain. Just us three, splashing about and attempting to lower our body heat. We contemplated taking a tourist toy train around the remaining sights. The lady organising it was having trouble, at this hour of the day, drumming up business and urged us to wait a while and see if more people showed up.

As we sat on the baking stone benches, one of which comically burned Elena's hindquarters, a homeless man came up to us. Initially I felt, guiltily in retrospect, a little uncomfortable. The 'Oh balls, I'm going to either give him some coins or look like an evil bastard by unconvincingly lying that I have no money on me' feeling. He produced a little wooden flute and started to play a tune, badly. When he finished that he, out of nowhere, recommended to us a restaurant in Trujillo, a nearby town, called La Troya. He pocketed his flute and talked with enthusiasm about the quality of the food, the size of the portions, and the low prices. Whether he had visited this place once, was making it up, or was a regular patron, we didn't know. He then very politely asked for some money. Elena extricated her leather purse and gave him a few euros. He bowed with his hand on his heart, 'Thank you very much', and wandered off to who knows where.
'This is why we are so poor in this region,' Elena started, 'We feel we need to give all our money away. This is *humilde.*'

We walked, and occasionally drove, round the remaining sights, notably a Roman circus and some stunning aqueducts, and decided we couldn't take anymore of the claustrophobic air. So, we did what the fine people of Mérida had done a couple of hours before, and ran away.

In the car I nearly passed out. The little digital temperature gauge read 52°. For a moment we just sat in silence as the old banger's air conditioning did its best to churn out cooler air. I felt a little sorry for it as it crackled and creaked at its maximum setting. With the climate more acceptable Elena swung round stating:

'Let's go to Trujillo and have a drink.'

Trujillo sticks out, a brown medieval bulge of turrets and towers, in the midst of a vast straw-coloured ocean of scrubland, unattractive but hypnotic. The little car snaked up some weenie streets and came to a stop just short of the main square. Its majestic palaces and mansions are courtesy of the fifteenth and sixteenth century *Trujillano* conquistadors, who had returned enriched from their expeditions and decided they should have something sprucy to live in.

We sat drinking in the golden main square. It was broad and lined with stone buildings with a church and a fine statue of the conquistador Francisco Pizarro, who was born in the city and is credited with conquering Peru for Spain. It was serene as the locals were still evading the heat of the day. There, among the row of establishments that would later burst into life, was something I didn't expect to see. 'La Troya', standing as conspicuously as it could. Centre stage. The beggar from Mérida didn't lie. We walked along cobbled streets and past perfectly preserved throwaway churches up to the high walls of the reconstructed castle atop the hilly outcrop that the town was sprawled out on. It commanded vast and poetic views out across impossible plains of that scruffy desert-like Extremeñan landscape. From there it was awesome. I walked a little ahead and alone in order to give the couple some time to wander and gaze longingly at each other and their surroundings. It was a romantic place and I felt a quick pang of loneliness before shrugging it off with a manly sniff and a booming cough.

It wouldn't have felt strange if the clip clop sound of hooved-feet echoed down a lane, shortly to be joined by a whooshing sound and then a man, with a long sword, black coat and large tricorn hat, galloped past me to some unknown affair behind the grand walls of the city. It was truly preserved. Not in a touristy 'Look how well we've looked after the place' way but more 'Look, we've not bothered to really touch the place'. Trujillo still remains a fairly unvisited jewel in Extremadura's newly emerging crown and this, coupled with its location, out in the sticks, has only aided its preservation. From the summit we trickled down some ancient lanes back to the main square. It was early evening, well, about quarter to ten, and it was finally starting to dim a little in the sky. During our brief foray, the locals had been released from their cool cages and had filled up the cafés and outdoor bars and restaurants.

We drove to where Elena's parents lived in a large, farming town called Villanueva de la Serena. Elena continued her game of annoying me by only playing the most dire and unequivocally torrid Spanish pop on the radio. Every time a song I liked came on and I all but begged her to let it play out, she would change it so some other garbage that sludged out of the speakers. Carlos didn't mind either way, and he, with his stubbled chin, dark sunglasses and relaxed attitude, was busy focussing on the road. He drove better than most Spaniards I knew. I moaned and squirmed all the way home as she giggled an evil giggle.

Elena's parents are saints, nothing more, nothing less. They were an undeniable plus point to my trip and my personal experience of the region. I had met them briefly before, in Madrid, but often only in passing. Her mum, the blonde-haired and slim Petri, would always bring boxes and tubs, full of homemade food, for her darling child when she visited. The bright side was that I was always given some; meaty soups, fried *croquetas*, cold meats and sometimes cakes and sweets. She was even more giving in real life, as was dad, Angel, a broad shouldered, boxish gent with a serious face. Over dinner Petri constantly, in that motherly fashion, plied me with more food than I really needed and kept fussing that maybe I hadn't had enough with my four pork chops, quarter of a tortilla, forest of salad and mountain of bread. Angel was more concerned that I really wasn't getting enough different alcohols down me.

'Angel, the boy's had enough!' Petri niggled at him as he filled one glass up with some sherry, whilst topping up my Extremeñan red wine. *I* wasn't complaining, neither at the liquoring nor at the force-feeding. It felt like I was being abused by an overly friendly restaurant harbouring clandestine thoughts concerning a fattened me in a bubbling pot, as onions and sliced carrots bobbed in the broth around me.

We talked a while outside in the hot evening air; Angel, with his quick and tricky accent and Petri, the teacher, with her crystal clear enunciation. We talked about the coming days, my impressions of their country and how I was going to proceed to the next region. It eventually turned into a logistics committee. Petri's eyebrows arched as she saw me blink sleepily.
'The poor thing. He's tired. Go to bed, we can talk about this tomorrow.'
I was whisked away to a little bedroom where, on accepting it wasn't going to cool down further, I fell into some hazy heat dreams.

*   *   *   *

We woke a little later than planned and then ate breakfast a little later than planned and so ended up leaving the house a little later than planned. Elena wasn't best pleased at the unplanned lateness. Her parents dropped the two of us off at her flat in her birth town of Miajadas – a place famed for being the centre of Spain's tomato industry. Elena had to sort out some papers. She then slept on the sofa like a cat until Carlos arrived. This then caused us to get to Cáceres later than planned. Elena was grouchy all morning and snapped passionately at Carlos in that Mediterranean hot-blooded way. All fire, no depth. I thought it best not to protest at the music choices although I occasionally emitted little grumpy huffs and groans that I am sure she heard for she would either turn up the volume or start singing along. Fortunately by the time we reached the provincial capital of Cáceres, Elena's shoulder chip had fallen off and she had returned to her usual wry and bubbly self.

The city, a UNESCO World Heritage City, was founded by the Romans, enlarged by the Visigoths and flourished under the Christians during the *Reconquista* and Discovery of America. Cáceres outwardly was not particularly attractive. A brawling mass of orangey-brown coloured flats and shops. Inwardly it was like Trujillo had been popping muscle gain pills. We parked the car by Sira, one of Elena's childhood friends' flat and walked into the centre. It was still abusively hot but noticeably more skin-friendly and manageable than the furious tirade that attacked us in Mérida.

The *casco histórico* appeared seamlessly. We wandered around its high medieval walls as Sira graciously and effusively played tour guide.
'This is the statue of the lady who started the newspaper I write for. Oh and this is the statue of San Pedro – you have to kiss its feet and make a wish. Over there's the main square that unfortunately is under construction. And this is the Museum of Cáceres'. She was short, like Elena, with blonde hair, light skin and a frequent smile offset by a little shiny ball piercing in her lower lip. She was smart and enthusiastic and had a guttural laugh that often tailed off with a snort, which only served to further her giggles. She understood my mission and took it upon herself to see that I got the full Cáceres welcome. *Humilde.*

Concerning the historic centre; almost as soon as we had entered it we left it and filtered back into the tan-coloured streets. Sira was taking us somewhere 'cool' to eat – the romantically named Vivaldi bar. After a *caña* and some free tapas we ordered some proper food. Sira seemed to know a lot of people in the city and she was constantly out of her seat embracing patrons on the other side of the bar, finally settling when the dishes arrived. The majority were culinary delights that I had never tried. My hosts walked me through them: *chipriones*, fried little squids; *mejillones rellenos*, stuffed mussels;

huevos estrallados, a gloopy mix of fried eggs, potato and meat; and *solomillo* with *torta de la serena* sauce, little cutlets of steak served with a molten pot of that regional cheese. It was quite a feast given the surrounding temperatures. I didn't have much of an appetite but the thing about Spanish food is that it's moreish and it sits there on its little plate looking at you with non-existent eyes screaming 'Eat me'. It would be a disservice to the memory of whatever animal lost its life *not* to eat it.

We waddled, fattened like fed lions and a little 'merry', back to the flat. After sucking in our slightly more distended bellies, we changed into swimming costumes and lolled around the ice-cold pool. After some lengths and a cannonball dive, I was hiding in the shade as the Spaniards soaked up the rays. I didn't want to be burnt. It was a sign of the potency of the summer in that part of the country when even the Spanish had to put on cream. Carlos' cousin joined us; a wiry and jolly fellow who looked as if he had been stretched out on a rack. A little later an outrageously attractive friend of Sira's, Lara, joined us and I attempted a dashing mix of wit and charm as she lay back in her tiny bikini. I called her 'Crofty' and then had to, at some length, explain the joke about her being named after Lara Croft while simultaneously sucking in my stomach. She had heard it before but laughed nonetheless. Forgiven because I was a *guiri*.

In the late afternoon, drying off in the flat, Sira suddenly started: 'Let's drive up to La Virgen.'
Elena, Sira, Carlos, his cousin, and I piled into the little car and hurtled round towards a fairly built up hill, away from the centre, on the east side of the city. A small road wound upwards. Carlos swung the car round each corner so that Elena and Sira could act out that childhood game of slamming one's seat-belted neighbour into the car door or window by using the momentum of the turn. I thought I had better not join in for fear of crushing one of the *petites dames*.

At the top there was a darling little white church, el Sanatorio de Nuestro Virgen de la Montaña, and a near 360-degree view of Cáceres and its surrounding province. The heat had left a milky haze over the land above which searing blue skies showed off their bigness. A large statue of Jesus, arms outstretched, stood golden with a half-moon hovering in the heavens behind him. Some sweaty runners and cyclists were drinking up the vista or popping into the church for a quick prayer and *signum crucis*. We gazed from our cool crow's nest and then lazily came to the unconscious agreement to return to *terra demitta*.

As the light finally changed places with darkness we went to a large park with a pond and an outdoor bar, sat and ordered drinks. Over the next hour more and more people joined the group. Extra white, plastic tables and chairs had to constantly be pulled up. Elena whispered that she didn't know half of them. But this was Spain. If you were a friend of a friend you were more than welcome, no questions asked. Crofty arrived in a white summer dress, then some old friends of Sira and Elena's turned up and got straight down to swapping anecdotes. It got to the point with the number of visitors that even the Spanish stopped getting up and kissing every single newcomer. I had long since bothered. Head nods would do fine. The final count was more than twelve.

We ordered beers and various plates of severely salty, deep-fried foodstuffs; oily plates of *chipirones*, pieces of meat, chips, and mushrooms. It was a rare moment of utter unhealthy eating and I was a little surprised. The Spanish are usually so focussed on the good, the healthy and the fresh. The months of banterous tutting from Elena, as she surveyed my home cooking, helped certify this fact. I had been eating good food for a while and this new stuff, despite my hunger, was a shock to the system.
'You OK Lucas?' asked Elena with a furrowed brow.
'I'm full.'
'You, full? No! I don't believe it.'

She had a point, usually my appetite borders on the obscene.

It was an almost overwhelming experience. As well as the food, I had the age-old problem of trying to keep up with the speedy, in-jokey, food-in-mouthy, Spanish that was being shouted over itself by everyone. There was a conversation to my left, to my right, over there at the end of the table, and I couldn't really join in any of them. Occasionally the one I may have been listening to would stop and enquire 'Have you understood?' Elena would then proudly, and sweetly, interject and state 'He understands everything, he always understands everything'. Sometimes, and this time was no exception, she would ask me to prove how far my Spanish had come. Her favourite moment being if someone shouted '*gilipollas*!' – arsehole.

'Luh-ke,' she would say, 'tell them what you know about *gilipollas.*'

I would then speak,

'*De gili nada. De polla, un metro. Bájate las bragas, que te la meto!*'

Gili on its own has no meaning, *bájate las bragas, que te la meto*, translates as 'Drop your pants and I'll give it to you' and I'm sure you will be able to work out the intentions relating to the metre long '*polla*'. Laughter would erupt and I would be a king for a moment. But only a brief moment before the flurry of words churned forth again.

I received a text from one of my best friends (Laurence), at home, stating that he had asked his girlfriend to marry him. My little old chum was engaged. I was ecstatic and homesick all at once but had no credit left to text him. A little voice in the back of my head said 'Why aren't *you* in a relationship? Why don't *you* have a proper job? Why are you wasting your time travelling around the world? You're just filling a hole aren't you? What's it like to have never found love?'

'Lucas,' interrupted one of Elena's friends, 'a last beer?'

'*Sí!*'

Love could wait another month.

Around midnight there was yawning and the scuffing of chairs along the floor as people started to leave. Not wanting to camp in Cáceres, we too left. Instead of driving the slightly further route back to Villanueva de la Serena, where we also ran the risk of awaking Elena's parents, we tacked back to her closer hometown of Miajadas.

*   *   *   *

I woke up a little confused by some strange dreams. As I became aware that I was in my own body and...yes...this was reality I showered as Elena slept. Firing up her father's computer I loaded Skype on the off chance someone was online. The one person I was thinking about talking to was my friend Jon and he, riding prettily on that aforementioned off chance, was online. Jon lives with his girlfriend Lauren in a twee little cottage in a twee little village in Oxfordshire. They have a twee cat, twee clothing, a twee fireplace, two twee axes and are wonderful human beings. We talked about Laurence's wedding and how proud, shocked and pleased we were.
'I had an idea for the stag do' Jon said, smiling a Machiavellian smile.
'What's that then?'
'Well, I say we get him drunk, put him in a box, and send him to North Korea.'
'Kaleigh won't be happy about that.'
'Nah, she'll love it.'
[Talking with Kaleigh upon finishing my trip led us to the revelation that she would in actual fact *not* have been too pleased in finding out that her husband-to-be was trapped in a closed country headed by a totalitarian dictatorship. We disagreed.]

Elena was once again grumpy. Carlos was going to arrive late and Elena was left sleeping on a sofa as she waited. After he got to the house she pouted and huffed for a short while until her Iberian anger blew over. We were headed to Guadalupe but Elena first wanted to do a spin of Miajadas and then pass through Escurial. Miajadas isn't an attractive town, but it boasts a vastly oversized, block-like church with birds circling its tower. It wasn't a tourist attraction, it was just real life.

Escurial was a miniscule village along a dusty road that was, like most Extremadura villages, built up around the medieval church. On the steps in front of the main door several old men in light shirts and blue berets sat talking, hands resting on walking sticks. Elena asked them for directions to the pharmacy. They all laughed as they gave conflicting directions.

'Sorry *señorita*,' they said with meaning.

We turned the car around and pulled up by a young couple, 'Yes, it's just there on the right'.

'Why are we going to the pharmacy?'

'We are going to say hello to my friend Silvia who works there,' Elena replied.

We entered the tiny, unsignposted building and Elena ran over, squealing, to embrace her old friend. Silvia was a good-looking girl with a warm smile. As with everyone, she had heard about me. We talked briefly, but she was very busy working and before we had the chance to toy with the idea of starting a dialogue we left, dust clouds storming out from under our tyres.

On the way to Guadalupe we drove through village after little white village: Alcollarin, Zorita, Logrosan, Cañamero.

'Most of the young people in these towns went to my school,' said Elena, gazing out of the car window.

I pondered village life. Not twee, village green, cricket playing, Ye Olde Pub bearing, cream tea eating, 'Hello June' saluting, the local town is only a ten-minute drive away, village life. But the dusty land, searing heat, water yearning, middle of nowhere, few jobs and nothing-to-do, village life. I had been living in Madrid. This was very much the other end of the spectrum. Extremadura was one of the largest regions and had one of the smallest populations – a fact that kept hitting home as we covered ground.

The never-ending scrubland took a backseat as a murky pocket of green finally appeared. A steep climb led up towards the hilltop monastic town of Guadalupe; a nugget of prestige and loveliness in an otherwise barren landscape. The village spread out from the highly venerated and decorative monastery that sat on the summit. Inside it was dark, but felt classy and was golden. Away from it filtered out small picturesque lanes, all wooden beams and flowerpots. Small wells often stubbed out of the ground surrounded by hot, noisy swarms of wasps. Few cars could traverse far in so it was fairly peaceful and, away from the religious behemoth, vacant-looking. Off in the distance, providing an attractive backdrop, were subtle hills that didn't divert the attention.

The town and its monastery were important for another reason. It was there, in that most sacred and bold of buildings, that Victoria, Elena's excitable, beautiful, witty and intelligent older sister married her long-term partner Angel, a sweet man, quick to laugh and eager to give. *Humilde*. Elena recalled the day with a swelling sigh and faraway smile.

'We had the monastery for the wedding. We all walked, well, processed, up the main street here. Everyone was looking at us. Everyone was taking photos. Vitor looked amazing in her white dress. We all looked beautiful. It was something special you know?'

When I get married, if I get married, it'll be out of love, untainted by God's will or doing. For a location however I still believe churches outdo most places, maybe tying with country houses. For a wedding I had a hard time thinking of somewhere to surpass the poetry and idyllic placing of the Guadalupe monastery.

Another thing Guadalupe is noted for, among Spanish people anyway, and among *extremeños* definitely, is being a purveyor of the finest products the region has to offer. It was littered joyously with artisan shops. Each so aesthetically put together and laid out that they looked as if they could have come from a 'Tastes of Spain' section of Harrods. The prices were, of course, higher than in the supermarkets but the quality was superlative. I bought two giant, deep purple, *morcillas* – a speciality of Extremadura; a gift for Mr and Mrs Gutierrez, and some Guadalupe bread; big, crusty and fluffy inside with a buttery taste.

Laden with goods and smiles we found that trying to get out of Guadalupe wasn't as easy as it was getting in.
'Don't worry, I've got maps on my iPhone,' said Carlos confidently, plugging the details into his beloved device.
'Turn left, turn right, turn right,' it bleated in tinny Spanish. None of the directions worked.
'I think it's confused,' offered Elena helpfully.
'Yeah, it's confused,' confirmed Carlos gripping the wheel after a long stare at the screen.
Fortunately my chauffeur was Spanish and he had years of experience navigating impossibly slim streets never designed for automobiles. We bumped and bounced up and down and around steep little roads until we were once again flung back into the savannah-like countryside.

In Villanueva de la Serena Elena's mother gorged us on courgette soup, steak, Guadalupe bread and quivering, just boiled fingers of that blood sausage. It wouldn't have been the real Spanish experience had a siesta not reared its dozy head and, as soon as we had cleared everything away, everyone did their best impression of a cat and, finding a soft spot, all but passed out for an hour or so. I generally never bothered with a siesta – I didn't usually get tired after a lunch and I found it a bit of a waste of time, literally – but this time, what with the heat and the small ecosystem recently banished to my acidic depths, even I closed my eyes.

I came to about forty-five minutes later, confused. Simultaneously, and through sticky, dry lids and lashes, I saw, through one eye, Elena's aunt greeting me with an understanding smile and, through the other, a crocodile ripping flesh from some once graceful animal on a muted wildlife documentary. Elena had many aunts, one of whom was bed bound and ill. We were to go and visit her, with some biscuits. I splashed my face with water and grabbed my flip-flops.

A couple of roads away from Elena's smart, modern flat, was where her grandmother, the venerable matriarch, lived. She was currently housing the unwell aunt. I walked in, a little nervous. This wasn't really somewhere I should be, I thought to myself. The flat was small, old, dim, blue and peppered with religious iconography. Lots of Virgins. Elena went in to see her poorly relative and I was left, a little obscure – red-faced and in shorts – with the grandma and two other matron-like aunts; one with a severe face, the other all giggles and joshing. There was some awkward conversation, but the matriarch was in high spirits and was still sprightly and playful in her mind so it wasn't too much of an ordeal until Elena filtered back in. She then presented a loaf of bread and some biscuits to her grandmother.
'Shall I put them in the kitchen for you nana?'
'Don't be silly. The bread, yes. But we've a growing boy here. Open the biscuits.'

I saw where the family trait of force-feeding came from. She kept imploring me to eat more of the dusty, almond and walnut flavoured cookies. Relatives kept streaming in and out of the flat, a cousin here, an aunty there. I just sat and let the family get on with it. When Elena's immediate supplies of pity and concern had subsided we decided to leave. As I got up, Elena's grandmother fished out a little information photo card bearing the Black Virgin of Guadalupe. She pressed it into my hand, 'This is for you' she said with a smile. I kept it in my journal for the rest of the trip.

We left with one of Elena's cousins, yet another Angel. Everyone was called Angel. With Elena's father we all drove through the uninspiring town to a house just outside of the centre in the '*campo*', country. It was a bungalow, with a big gate, sat in the zone where the corn and tomato fields started. What I was confronted with on entering was some strange, Spanish hillbilly scene. Sprinklers were spurting away, throwing glints and rainbows over the grass. Two men sat on a porch, on deck chairs; one was shirtless (another relative) and the other was missing a tooth. A tied-up dog was jumping about and stretching the leash. I sat down, a little sheepishly, on a chair and entertained the boxer, Fito, as another little dog, Sara, scurried out to meet us in her *I'm-your-owner-and-you-are-going-to-wear-this-so-I-can-pick-you-up* harness.

Angel, the cousin, not the father, was currently doing some university degree in agricultural industry. He was gaining experience by working with the man who was missing a tooth. I more or less followed the conversation. It varied wildly. First they were talking huffily about *chiringuitos*, which are little illegal, messy stalls that people set up in the countryside to sell whatever; food, nick-nacks, beverages. They were protesting in continual agreement about how they were a blight on the environment and lamented how nobody seemed to be able to stop them. The conversation then turned to watermelons. The dentally challenged man cultivated, among other things, these fruits, and joked about the ones they sent abroad.
'They want them small. Small, little melons. Small ones fit for the UK and the US,' he scoffed, then laughed, 'and the pigs'.
His buyers wanted small, attractive melons, not big, juicy ones. So he provided.
He turned to me with a mischievous glint in his eye.
'Do you want to swim perhaps?' There was a pool round the back.
'Maybe, yeah.'
'Do you prefer wet or humid water?'
'Um...wet.'

'Then the pool will be perfect!'

Everyone started giggling.

When a nosy neighbour – an upper-middle aged lady in a dressing gown – started sounding off through the fence about hoses and water levels we decided to make a move.

After the surreal feminine/masculine family nature of the afternoon, Elena and I spent the evening walking around Villanueva. It had a fine church where her parents married and a promenade covered with droves of people.

'It's busy!' I commented insightfully.

'Well, after mass, the people come out and have something to drink, or talk.'

Families spread over the pavements and side streets like bees on honey and the night was buzzing. At a little park, with a fountain flipping about in the evening wind, a purple sunset was dropping hints of the night as bats swung madly through the warm air. Walking back to her house we passed an ancient nightclub called 'Dinosaurio'.

'Any good?'

'Well, it's well maintained. It's been there forever,' I smiled at the irony 'But it's difficult to look after a club so long in a small town.' she added, hinting at the possibility of its eventual extinction.

*   *   *   *

This was my last day with Elena and her family and it turned out to be one of the highlights of the whole trip. It can mostly be put down to the enthusiasm that I was shown by Elena's parents. They seemed to feed on my childlike wonder and burn with an urge to show me as much as they could. We had one day and the whole of the area of La Vera in front of us.

We were, characteristically, late leaving and Elena was, characteristically, unhappy about it. Her short flame of irritation was put out as we practised English in the car driving north through the region. Her parents had packed an enormous picnic for the day. It sat, nestled aromatically, in a variety of boxes and tins in the boot. There was no hiding the sweet scent of the homemade *tortilla española*. Up ahead were some mountains that we were heading towards; little bumps of green on the horizon forming a dark scar between land and sky. We drove through the town of Almaraz, 'famous' for its nuclear power station. Elena had visited the place as part of her degree and I had a key-ring that she had bought me as a souvenir. There was a man fishing near the edge of town. Angel honked the horn and the man waved.

'I bet the fish he catches are pretty big,' I quipped.

'And they probably have legs,' responded Angel with a snort.

A couple of hours later an explosion of green shot up around the car. It was the utter antithesis of the rest of the region. Where the majority had been dusty, dry and near dead looking, La Vera was a paradise, lush and verdant.

'Rich people buy land here, make estates, set up farms and stuff like that,' said Angel, waving his hand around.

The area is rich in agricultural industry. And it was industry that swiped past the window as the car meandered through the countryside. Forests of *bellota* trees (of the oak genus) whose acorns the locals eat either raw or roasted, are fed to the pigs that go on to become *jamón ibérico*, or are elaborated into a regional liquor. *Cereza* – cherry – groves destined to be pies and jams, swayed coolly in the light wind. And then fields after swishing fields of tobacco plants. Spain, according to Angel, is the centre of Europe's tobacco industry and Extremadura is the centre of the country's industry. The European Commission's Agriculture and Rural Development website, as of 2009, states that:

'Italy is the biggest EU producer (36% of the 27 EU member countries' total production), followed by Poland (16%), Bulgaria (12%) and Spain (12%)'

So, even though Spain isn't the centre, it still has a lot of tobacco growing in it. And I could believe this as the fields, and their leaf drying huts, kept coming.

La Vera was essentially a mass of hills, mountains and characteristic streams and natural swimming pools, interspersed with twee, and real, little villages. Some were nestled in the valleys and some were stuck to the slopes. It felt genuine, utterly distant from foreign tourism and forgotten by the guidebooks. Everyone knows Benidorm, flamenco, Seville, paella, Barcelona and sangria. Nobody knows La Vera, and for that reason I felt privileged.

The day unravelled in a pattern. First we would stop at a *garganta* and then visit a village. Having absorbed the atmosphere of said settlement we would drive along the road until we bumped into another *garganta*. And then another village. Each *garganta* was visually unique but followed the same template of a down-flowing river that had crowds of people eating beside, jumping into or swimming around in, its natural pools. In the same way the villages also had an inherent rhythm. They were all low buildings, houses and small shops, with red, tiled roofs, light-coloured walls and wooden beams and balconies.

The first of these villages, and one of the most attractive in the area, was Garganta la Olla. The air was clean and cooler there than in the south of the region. Lack of pollution and increased altitude will do that. A sweet little plaza mayor looked after a small well, while the *prostíbulo* (now a doll museum) stood, all blue, with its head bowed sheepishly in a side street. A *prostíbulo* is a brothel. This one, as many were in the region, was painted so that everyone in the town knew what it was, why whoever it was was going in, and, probably, which building it was that they should spit at. It was a building that provided pleasure to a few of the one thousand or so inhabitants in an area, so vast and distended, where finding love, or contact, or a touch, could have proven problematic. They were historic remnants.

Just on from the naughty house was a bar where we had a quick drink and shared secret chortles with each other in relation to the incredibly loud, merry, but shouty bargirl.

Past more downhill streams and broad viewpoints we arrived, ever climbing, to the Monasterio de Yuste, a small palace on a hill where Carlos I often stayed, and finally died. All the *gargantas* in the area are fed by permanent springs and from the high up road, that passes the monastery, one can see the effects of the life-giving water. A *lot* of green.

My stomach growled and I rubbed my belly unconsciously.
'Let's go to the *garganta* now and eat,' said Petri, noticing me and smiling, 'the poor boy must be starving.'
My stomach had still, even after a year, not got utterly used to the idea of eating at 3 or 4 in the afternoon. We wheeled the car into a dusty little bay and unloaded all the food containers along with deck chairs and a table. We scurried across the road and walked down a sandy path toward the water. There were a few children splashing about and jumping into the stream; some beautiful girls were tanning themselves over on the far side; a group of teenagers sat in swimming trunks, smoking and laughing; and we set our table up a few metres away on a raised flat and took out the food. That juicy Spanish omelette, some garlic-fried pork loins, Guadalupe bread, fresh tomato salad, beers, crisps and sangria. It was a light but filling picnic. After eating, Elena's dad removed his shirt and basked and digested in his reclining deckchair. The girls packed up and joined him in gastric contemplation. But I didn't want to. That was boring.

I decided to burn off my lunch and walked/boulder-hopped upstream. Big, light grey, smoothed lumps of stone endlessly cluttered the *garganta*. The sky was ever so slightly accompanied by clouds and the water was clear and cool. Slender black and yellow dragonflies sat on the warm rocks and zipped away when I leaped over them. After half an hour I came to a pool and toyed with the idea – as I was already in my swimming trunks – of bathing in it privately. I began to put my camera, phone and valuables to one side in the undergrowth, but quickly returned them to my pockets when I heard approaching voices. I didn't much want to share my treasure and nor did I want to look like some pasty weirdo all by himself in a bowl of water half way up a stream. 'It must take effort to be that much of a loner,' they would have thought. It was a group of athletic and irritatingly slim teenage guys. I passed them without saying hello and making sure I jumped better. Keep your fatless bodies! I have better balance.

Back at the family unit I manned up, ashamed of my porky, shapeless torso, and went into the water for a swim. And was glad I did. It was refreshing and pure. It felt strange though, in a good way. I was swimming in a natural stream and the water wasn't salty. One doesn't usually swim in British rivers. I was used to the sea but I preferred the *garganta* by far. Petri then joined me and berated Elena for being too cowardly to get in the water. Time was swiftly moving on and Angel dropped a hint that it might be a good idea if we carried on with our tour before we ran out of day.

Our next stop was the wee little mountain village of Guijo. We rolled through Cuacos de Yuste, famous as being the centre of the *pimentón* – paprika – industry and Angel continued to honk and wave at people.
'We used to come here on camping holidays,' he said, noticing my quizzical look.
'I thought you were famous or something.'
'Haha, maybe!'
Of the villages I visited, Guijo was nearest the peaks. It felt distant and aloof. We had a drink in a bar full of older men.
'This is real, old-fashioned Spain,' Petri whispered, 'all the men have the free time and go to the bars together and talk while the women are still at home doing the work.'

Elena returned from the counter with some of the coffees we ordered giggling to herself. She held up a finger, 'one moment', went back for the other two coffees, returned, and sat down.

'At the bar a man had a magazine with a bare-chested woman on the front. I picked up our drinks. He glanced at me, looked apologetic, and turned it over. He wasn't embarrassed, he just didn't want a girl to have to see that!'

Guijo was very pretty and had a couple of fine artisan shops where we purchased some regional goods. After a few minutes of walking there were the village limits. Some old, but still not grey-haired, ladies were sitting on wooden chairs outside of a fairly featureless house – square brick doorway and whitewashed walls – knitting, well, embroidering what looked to be tablecloths. I walked past but Petri stopped to talk. She bought a little punnet of fresh raspberries off them. Elena and I walked back to where her mum was chatting.

It was commented that I was English and it was mentioned I was living in Spain, with Elena. I accidentally said that I had 'my own place' whereas I meant to say I rented a place. That was enough for the old girls and they started focussing on Elena in a 'Hark at you' way.

'Now listen love, don't let this one get away. He's got prospects'.

'He's not my boyfriend.'

'Shush, shush. Now, you need to make plans for the future.'

'And marriage,' said the other.

I didn't intervene. It was too much fun. Despite all evidence to the contrary, these ladies were convinced I was a well-to-do Englishman living in private property with my Spanish girlfriend. Elena seemed to enjoy it too. I think the women knew what the truth was and really just enjoyed a spicy bit of banter in what was otherwise a probably quite sedate and simple day.

Munching on squelchy, sharp raspberries we descended back into the La Vera valley and visited one more *garganta*. It was the biggest one yet, surrounded by cafés and cars and with scores of people using it. We watched adolescents drop metres from a bridge as we cleared our fingers of the remaining berry-rouge. The air smelled of forests and leaves. It was a shame to leave La Vera. The green subsided and the topography settled to flat as we shot back out into the dry, yellowing brutality of Extremadura proper.

I packed my bag and sat with the family a while. I got myself a drink from the fridge and smiled when I noticed one of the shelves was completely covered with tomatoes. How fitting. An Andalucian fridge would be full of cold tomato soup and a Valencian one full of paella no doubt... They drove me to Cáceres so that I could take my overnight bus northwards. We ran into some problems though. Earlier at the house I wasn't able to print out my e-ticket. This in itself was no problem, as one could get the people at the ticket offices to print it out, there in the station. However, the bus, being an evening bus, was to leave at around 10 o'clock. The workers had left at 7 o'clock, leaving the station a quiet, glassy wasteland. I started to panic, and panic quite a lot. I didn't know if they would accept me on the bus with just a scrap of paper and some details.

Petri and Angel then started to worry for me. We found a guard sitting in a little room and asked him. He shrugged and said he hadn't a clue. Angel, in that oh so dad-like way, started to get angry with Elena. He blamed her for the mess. Elena then got angry with her father for getting angry with her. They fumed and paced while Petri gave a 'Here we go again' look. I continued to think and remembered that Angel had a blackberry, so I managed to find my emails and bring up the e-ticket. Then, to make matters worse, the bus itself was delayed, thus prolonging the uncertainty. Angel talked to a driver on another coach, who said it would be fine,
'He just needs to show his passport. He'll be on a list.'
Tempers were tempered a little. Elena shot vitriolic glances at her father when he wasn't looking and Angel's chest was still puffed out like a silverback after a ruckus. Finally the long-distance ride arrived.

It had come from Cádiz and would, for more than ten hours, take me all the way north to A Coruña in Galicia.

The Extremadura leg was over and it was a whirlwind.
'Well, I'll be off then,' I hated goodbyes.
Angel shot out his hand with a smile. I looked at them.
'Hugs are in order I think,' and I embraced him, then Petri and finally my dear Elena. It was oddly emotional.
'You'll always have family in Extremadura,' said Petri as I got onto the slumbering bus without problems.

Clambering over and shuffling past various body parts that were sleeping and snoring in the aisle, I sat down, waved goodbye to the family and set off for cooler lands.

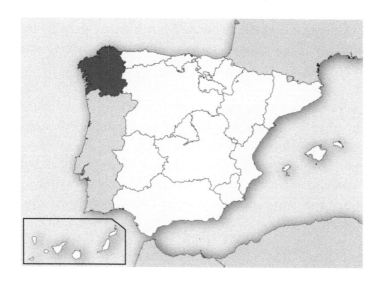

Morriña

A Coruña – Cambados – Santiago de Compostela

Overnight bus. Slight backache. Read Lolita for a while sitting in a yellow cone of light as the dark of night closed in around me. Heads and legs lolled out into the aisle as travellers slept. After a couple of hours we silently glided into my much-loved starting point, Salamanca. There was that cathedral all lit-up and showing off as we purred into the station. At Salamanca a fair-faced beefcake walked on and took the seat next to me by the window. For the next hour he imperceptibly but, to me, immensely, encroached on my space. The skin of our arms had begun to stick together until finally, somewhere near a corner of sleep I was looking for, he moved to another free double-space. For the next hours I drifted, uncomfortably and achingly, in and out of dreams. As soon as I got

231

into a pleasing position I was either bumped awake by a stop, or my muscles or bones or tendons or whole skeleton started to cry out. There was only one stop. It was a service station in Castilla y León. It was 11 degrees outside. I shivered but laughed sleepily. It was the first time I had felt cold in months and had clearly forgotten the sensation.

Bleary eyes blurred at a growing light far off in the sky and into my dormant head came the warped fuzz of a tannoy 'Ourense', then 'Vigo', then 'Pontevedra'. I had arrived in the region of Galicia. I had finally arrived at the North. Only in Pontevedra did the light finally describe itself to me as something worth waking up for. I rubbed my eyes and came to my senses as we left town and blasted into scenery.

The first thing that hit me, the first thing that probably hits everybody who goes there, was the green. It was like the North had had a bigger pot of green hues than the rest of Spain and that Mother Nature, not really knowing how to handle it, had just thrown it everywhere; spinaches, peacocks, viridians and chartreuses all muddled together. Not that I have been there, but it reminded me of Scandinavia as clean, white buildings, moderately modern and with red roofs, speckled visibly and looked welcoming amid the hills and valleys and rivers, and everything else natural. Pools of morning mist were collecting smoothly and ebbed and flowed through the curvatures and prongs of mid-west Galicia. We entered Santiago de Compostela and all but two of us got off. I saw pilgrims, rosy-cheeked with walking sticks and the faint towers of the legendary cathedral sticking thick in cloud, hiding its beauty for another day.

Leaving Santiago, the mist decided to eat our road, and us, almost all the way north to A Coruña. It was a light grey soup that often cut visibility down to metres. All texture of the land, all trees, all colours, all slopes were bound tight in its silken embrace. So thick was it that I could see the cloud brushing past the window, bumping

the glass. Almost as soon as we escaped it, the brimming northern
port of A Coruña fog-horned into the picture.

I found my way to the port area quite easily, thanks to an
exceedingly helpful gentleman at the information desk who was all
but climbing out of the window as he continued to offer help as I
left the station. The *Corunense* morning air was cool and crisp and, by
the time I had reached the port itself, reeked pleasingly of fish. Gulls
were screaming and darting about in the air as fishermen in big,
yellow waders sorted out their nets. Little painted and peeling
trawlers bobbed alongside small yachts in the marina. Fronting it
was a near unbroken line of fine looking flats. One could hardly see
any wall, just lots of tall windows broken into small, translucent
squares. Their borders were usually white and wooden, regardless of
the chosen colour of building below. It looked like something that
had fallen out of 1920s Paris into somewhere wetter.

One of A Coruña's nicknames is 'The City of Glass'. Galicia is
home to a particular style of balcony construction, called *galerías*.
This was what I saw on the line of flats. And A Coruña was a
specialist. According to the Galicia Guide website:
'*A galería is nothing more than a balcony, but one that is enclosed in a glass
frame protecting it from Galicia's cool winters and making it usable all year
round. Galerías can appear at first floor level, or on the sixth floor of a six
storey building and there are many variances on the basic design.*'

It goes on to give the reason for their prevalence in A Coruña. On
the one hand, the *galería* design was popular during the modernist
period of the late nineteenth and early twentieth centuries and on
the other hand, it was a structure that was easy to replace or build
on the original fisherman's houses that lined the port and harbour.
The effect was quite debonair.

The friendly tourist office, full surreally, but wonderfully, of young,
good-looking Galician girls, helped me finding a hostel with both a

map and their Sat-Nav knowledge of the roads. After some duds –
'We're full lad', 'Cheapest room? 30 euros', blank sign *'completo'* – I
arrived at the rather dazzling praza (*plaza*) de Galicia, right in the
centre of the city. Finding a large, elegant doorway I walked up
some blue-grey, marble stairs. Inside a grand spiral staircase looped
up with gleaming surfaces. Apparently there was a one-star *pensión*
on the third floor of the gorgeous building. Fearing the inevitable
high price I nearly turned around and left. However I had to kick
myself and remember my motto – 'Not to try is not to know'. In
fact, inside was a musty, rusty, creaky, flaky, bent and chipped place
of wood and old glass. It almost had *too* much character. I
tentatively asked the cost of the cheapest room and was made to
hang on as she went to check. I hung on, and she returned.
'The cheapest room is 11 euros.'
I nearly choked on my own astonishment.
'Four nights please.'
My room was probably worth that much though: a hefty old iron
key; a tear in my blanket; a cigarette hole in my towel; but it was
what I had asked for and it was utterly perfect.

The long walk of the *'paseo marítimo'* heads around the coast towards
the city's celebrated lighthouse. The path was well designed and
constantly divulged interesting or dramatic views. Tall, strange,
loopy and calligraphic streetlamps lined the route for about 2.5km.
They were bright orange and each one had a small sea-scene painted
on it. Every so often a whimsical little tram would trundle cutely
past. I struck off from the road as the maritime path took to wilder
stretches, passing a strange Stonehenge-like arrangement that
signified some extinct Roman paraphernalia.

This area was seen as a very strategic point for trade as early as 62
BC when Julius Ceasar came to the city, known then as Brigantium.
After the fall of the Roman Empire the city was almost forgotten. It
was only during the Middle Ages that it returned to its status as a
prized settlement. It became a celebrated centre of textile

manufacture and, as Spain's sailing industry grew, the city was the setting off point for grand expeditions or European missions. The only memory of that time is a few information boards and some stonework.

Quickly the land took a turn for the very theatrical. A large set of rock shore bluffs burst out of the sea. They were pale and sun-bleached, some covered with a violently orange, rusty lichen that seemed to be the only thing able to withstand the brutality of the pounding squall thrown at the coast by the Atlantic. I sat for a short period watching a lone, wellied fisherman in shorts struggle to catch something while avoiding the spray from the breaking waves. A few podgy old men were beginning to strip completely and allow whatever sun that found them to cook their bits. I left at that point and flanked the coast round to the Torre de Hercules, a UNESCO Roman lighthouse that has been in continuous operation for nearly 2000 years.

It stood alone on a headland with strong winds whipping over fields of yellow heather and stout purple flowers. A wide walkway took me up to the foot of the thing where a fair €2.50 entrance fee was claimed by the tower. After first passing through a low-ceilinged exhibit of the original roman remains to a small arched doorway that gave way to an unexpectedly long and quite strenuous set of stairs, I climbed up the four-walled *faro* until another doorway spat me out onto an eagle's nest 55m up. From that vantage point wind, sun and everything blue and green was laid out beneath.

As I let my heartbeat find its resting rate, I heard a sound I had hoped to hear. Bagpipes. The north of Spain historically has a Celtic aspect similar to that of maybe Scotland and Ireland – some Celtic tribes settled in the area before the Romans got there. Nowhere along the top of the country is this stronger than in Galicia. Their regional instrument, the *gaita de foles*, looks like a smaller version of a Great Highland Bagpipe. Although it appears out of place in Spain, it is very much their instrument, and they are proud of it. A little girl was watching the player, enchanted, until her parents shuffled her along, not wanting the embarrassing responsibility of having to pay. After I had drunk my fill of the excitable and noisy view I took a beeline back into town; the tummy wanted feeding.

I flipped and I flopped all over the city until chancing upon the bounteously attractive plaza mayor. I chose a side street at random and fortunately it was loaded with restaurants, all vying for custom. Different slants. Some offered competitive set menus, some tried to sell their range and quality of individual dishes, and some were bringing in the influence of the 'niche' – a kebab shop or a burger bar, all the more notable when surrounded by their piscatory neighbours. I chose, because of its cheap menu that allowed me to have lots of fish, the Meson San something-or-other. First course was succulent, fat mussels. They steamed with the salty subtlety of the sea and zinged with lemon. They were so fresh that that they had seaweed stuck to them and one even had some grains of sand in its shell. Next a plate of *parrochas*, deep fried sardines, arrived. Biting them whole – as the bones had been cooked soft – I felt like some Neptunian giant hurling creatures to their deaths. To accompany my meal was a glass of pale, white Ribeiro wine.

Galicia is a bit of a dark horse with regards to wine. Spain is basically famous for its big, juicy and powerful reds. And if we are being blunt, it is famous for Rioja wine. I hope one day that it becomes famous for its whites; notably Albariño and Ribeiro. Albariño is the most widely produced grape variety grown in the region. Oz Clarke's Encyclopaedia of Grapes states:
'It was presumably brought to Iberia by Cluny monks in the twelfth century. Its name 'Alba-Riño' means 'the white [wine] from the Rhine' and it has locally been thought to be a Riesling clone originating from the Alsace region of France, although earliest known records of Riesling as a grape variety date from the 15th, rather than the 12th, century. It is also theorized that the grape is a close relative of the French grape Petit Manseng'

236

In short, it isn't one hundred per cent clear where the grape comes from. Every sip is a mystery.

The fruitiness that was indicative of Spanish white wine snuggled comfortably with the lemony sea life. I left, very happy with myself, and walked it off by wandering through the old town that had started to put up banners and stalls to celebrate some day, as in Alicante, as in Logroño, concerning the historic quarter's medieval nature. At my hostel I had a siesta as I had been walking around, mostly in flip-flops, for about ten hours and my feet were burning and my legs screaming horrible, neuronal, things at me. I collapsed on my bed for a further ten hours. My original plan was to visit the Costa Da Morte and get a bus at 8:15 in the morning. I had to rearrange my plans in my sleep.

*   *   *   *

I arrived back at the bus station for just before ten o'clock in the morning, which was handy as there was a bus leaving for Santiago at ten. This wasn't my destination however, and at 11:30 I was sat on a slightly stumpy bus to the town of Cambados on the west coast. We were driving through the Rías Baixas (pronounced 'bye-shass'), an area of lush green that is located on the Atlantic coast directly above Portugal. *Rías* means estuaries, so the Rías Baixas are the 'lower estuaries'. The five large *rías* in the area are the Rías de Corcubión, Muros e Noia, Arousa, Pontevedra and Vigo. It was on the Ría de Arousa where I would find Cambados.

We skirted along the green Atlantic coast and passed through various towns: Vilanova de Arousa, Vilagarcia, Catoira. Apart from the fairly attractive Padrón – where the green Russian roulette peppers come from – the places were not really pretty enough for the surroundings. The broad Ría de Arousa speared into the land. Little boats, occasional sandy beaches and one bulky naval warship added flavour to its turbulent blueness. I alighted at Cambados thanks to a fifty-something German lady and her companion. They had been conversing fairly loudly and at the key moment, hearing what was presumably 'This is Cambados', I scurried off.

The lively tourist office offered a map with a couple of short walks to do around the little fishing town. The diminutive sea wall took me to a walkway leading out to a tiny round island, barely 50m in diameter. On one side, a sliver of sand looked after a few sunbathers as the wind punched waves into the bay waters. On the other side, barren, algal rock was choked by manure coloured seaweed. At the end of the heathy, wind-whipped, coral-less atoll an old ruined tower stood as if it were about to topple into the water.

The bay swooped around, occasionally breaking apart and leaving small, inhabited islands. The seafront was a line of small joined houses that looked like they could be from some Bumptington-on-the-Twee seaside village in England. Old strands of seaweed hung from chains holding grimy rowing boats in place. At the end of the maritime promenade the fact the Cambados was the centre of the Albariño wine region started to become visible. I had noticed it on the drive in as well. *Bodegas* aside, so many gardens had their own trellises spilling over with vines and bunches of compact, light green, marble-round grapes. I managed to pinch a dainty little fruit from its family. It burst in my mouth. Around the seeds was a taste that was both intensely sour and amazingly dry. It occurred to me that this was probably why supermarkets didn't sell punnets of wine grapes. They weren't for eating.

Just away from the sea front was the old quarter; a compact area of fine, clean, stone buildings, houses, shops, restaurants and churches. On the western tip of the zone was the Prazo de Fefiñans. It was low-key but it, in contrast to the rest of the town, seemed shockingly overblown and grand. A large square with little bars and cafés lined two sides of it while the other two were left unhindered for the viewer to enjoy – as long as you didn't look at the irritatingly positioned, bright-red, toy-town tourist trains.

In the never-ending search for typical food that had become such a large part of my trip, I found a quiet place in some miniscule little square. There was a sign that read *'con cada consumpción se sirve una necóra'* – 'with every drink we serve a *necóra* (type of crab)'. I ordered the necessary Albariño and received a plate with two small, crimson, and entire crabs. I wasn't prepared for that. The first, and smaller, of the two crabs cracked and fell to pieces in my big hands. I barely got any meat out of it and probably didn't approach it correctly. I'd never eaten a whole bloody crab before. A little annoyed at my failure I then ordered the most famous of Galician dishes, *Pulpo Galego*, Galician octopus. Served boiled and cut up on a wooden plate, the octopus pieces were coated with oil, salt and paprika, and nothing else. For a key dish though, it was a little underwhelming. It tasted like chicken trying to be fish and the texture was creamy. But it was almost too subtle to be worth making a fuss over.

The final route that I was given led to the 'high part of town', past a couple of leafy churches to Cambados' national monument, the Santa Mariña de Dozo ruins. It was quite a spiritual place. Now I am not religious, as you may have gathered. Not at all. But sometimes – a grand, sweeping vista of snow-capped peaks; streetlamps reflecting at night in shiny, tar-black, rippling water; an old, creaky house where the lights don't work and dust is everywhere – a view can give me a feeling of awe, romance or fear. In the ruins it felt very hallowed and revered. The church had lost most of its innards and looked as if some avatar had wrenched the roof off, just leaving some sombre stone beams forming a sequence of skeletal arches. There were crumbly rocks everywhere and a bleached Jesus Christ by the pulpit. It looked like a dying church, taken care of as it shuffled off its mortal coil. Vegetation had started to take over and all around the outside and inside was a cemetery. A field of tragically poignant graves. The death of the church combined with the death of man. I left feeling oddly at peace but sure it had nothing to do with a supreme being.

Cambados' Museum of Wine was due to open at 16:30 so with time to kill I went up to a viewpoint, the highest spot in the town. The air was syrupy and thick with the smell of hot pine and toasted ferns. It sank into my throat and made me cough. On some plinth-like boulder, surrounded by pine needles, a seven-step staircase led to a granite cross and the viewpoint itself. Yes, there was the town and spin and yes, there were the vined hills. The view was a little overly populated with trees so one couldn't actually *see* much. It was more of a half-viewpoint.

At 16:30 on the dot I strolled back down past a little chapel in the woods and found the *museo de vino* still locked. I waited in the shade on the other side of the street. A pluckier couple tried shoving the door but to no avail. They too went and sheltered out of the sun. About fifteen minutes later a fast-walking man approached the museum, looked at us, looked at his watch, and threw himself a sheepish grimace. Upon entering the sweaty, but friendly, bloke gave me some material and a quick explanation of the different exhibits.
'So, you're interested in Albariño wine then?' he asked.
'Of course,' I answered with a goofy, toothy smile.

In the second room of the museum, while reading usual information panels about the fermentation process, he came bounding over to me and gave me a cartload of more information, mostly relating to the *'rutas de vino'*, a wine route that you can tackle by car. Holding all my bumf, we then discussed wine for a bit.
'It's a shame that Albariño isn't widely sold in the UK. And for me on my teacher's budget it's a little expensive,' I said.
'The thing with Albariño is that the grapes are very small and give little juice. So ultimately the resulting wine is of quantities far smaller than what you get in La Rioja, or Ribera.'

240

I recounted my only Albariño based anecdote. When I returned to England for my grandmother's 85th birthday we dined in a fairly swanky restaurant in Bath. As with every restaurant dinner, there comes the point when somebody has to choose the wine. My father usually does it, grabbing something either not too expensive or of a grape variety that he and my mother are used to. Whereas I am a Hispanophile, my uncle Colin is a Francophile. He started saying 'There's a good looking Bordeaux or there's an interesting Chateau foux-du-fa-fa...' Clocking the Albariño I asked if maybe we could get a Spanish wine. Uncle Colin raised his eyebrows at me as if to say 'A Spanish wine? Here? In a nice restaurant? When there's French on offer?' Then, after some more menu perusing, he gave in 'Well, as you're travelling around Spain...' The Albariño arrived and proceeded to blow everyone away, as well as my uncle, with its svelte fruitiness and bold flavours. The man in the *museo de vino* swelled a little with pride.

'Well, overall only 3.7% of our production is distributed to the UK. Most goes to the U.S. and Japan' (I later found out that more than 6% goes to Panama!).
He asked me when I was leaving and told me that I would be missing the Cambados festival of Albariño. To alleviate my obvious disappointment he gave me a business card 'If you ever come back let us know'. He then walked off and returned with two bottles of Albariño wine giving them to me with outstretched arms.
'The best wine is from the little *bodegas,*' he said, almost secretly and, lowering his voice added, 'and I haven't even heard of this one!'
I thanked him profusely, shook his hand and left. He yelled to me from the reception that he would see me next year.

At the station the German woman from before was looking at the buses with a confused face. Seeing me she struck up a conversation inquiring as to which was the correct one. Her name was Inka and she was from Munich. She had done some of the Camino de Santiago, walking up with friends from Portugal, and had seemingly travelled a lot in Spain and had been almost everywhere I had chosen on my northern leg. She was a short woman, with clipped blond hair, a light mauve shirt and khaki walking trousers. On the journey back she helped me augment my plans so that I didn't waste my time.

'Unless you are at Finisterre with friends, at sunset and with a bottle of wine, there's nothing to see. So don't go there.'

She was probably right and, in a heavily accented and blunt conflagration of English and Spanish, made a lot of sense. I heeded most of her words. Inka and her optimistic, lined face got off at Padrón and waved goodbye 'Maybe I see you in Santiago,' she called as she walked down the steps.

My memories of the journey back to A Coruña after leaving Inka are fragmentary. I recall a little granite cottage consumed by grapes; the setting sun having a God moment as it threw vast beams of light from behind a silhouetted cloud; a nearly full moon sitting in blue as the sky beneath softly tinted pink and fir-treed hills below slowly removing their bright clothes and slipping into their dark pyjamas.

*   *   *   *

The following morning didn't go according to the new plan I had made for myself. I desperately needed the Internet but as it was Sunday, and as this was Spain, everything was shut. I rang my friend Nick back in Madrid. Waking him up with my call he groggily agreed to look at a website for me. According to the guidebook, on the third weekend of July an international pipe music festival was held in the forest town of Ortigueira. I was a few minutes away from the station when Nick informed me that it had already come and gone, two weeks prior - another Rough Guide balls-up. Angry and disappointed I counted myself lucky that A Coruña was, at least, an enormous city and not some tiny village. There was still a lot left to do.

The city's beach was the stylishly named playa de razor. The port and marina trawled along one side of the peninsula, while a golden arc swept along the other. Venturing down I discovered it wasn't particularly smooth sand, neither was it particularly nice to walk on. Half-naked bodies, a mild sun and a blue sea; it looked welcoming. There were glistening joggers, noisy families and strolling old-folk enjoying the day as an extraordinary sea wind bashed about and fluffed up my hair. Leaving the beach, a large building with a big, semicircular stone dome and an imposing granite staircase came into view. This was the 'Domus' or the *'casa del hombre'* – essentially a human body science museum.

It was very modern and interactive and had a 3D cinema in it. The combined ticket also allowed a visit to the city's aquarium, which was a strange place. It was extremely high-tech and wonderfully educational but – and this was what kind of put a dampener on things – there weren't many fish. No tropical section or freshwater section or 'monsters of the deep' section. Not many varieties were there either. Those which *were* swimming about were also quite dull. One exception included a tank with a flurry of octopuses swimming, hiding in crevices, and sticking to walls, surrounded by pink algal blooms. Another was the slightly strange recreation of the Nautilus from Jules Verne's '20,000 Leagues Under the Sea'. The visitor walks in through a representation of a leaky submarine then down into the viewing room that clung, glass-walled, below, as fish circulated. Again, all show, not great fish. One lazy sand tiger shark spiced up the shoal, but it was too little, too late. The aquarium reminded me of a pop-up book with a dazzling front cover, painted by Monet and paper protrusions designed by Norman Foster, footnoted by small captions. It was good, but I really wanted to read something. The aquarium was good, but I really wanted to see fish. I left feeling, well, nothing really.

With a sandwich, a packet of crisps and some bananas, I sat watching the port reflect everything. Families were having post-siesta strolls and young couples were walking lovingly hand in hand licking ice creams. A band of Spanish tourists were photographing every inch of the view, including me writing in my journal,

'Do you mind if I photo you?' asked a man, squatting, and holding a large camera.

I nodded it was OK. What pose do you want?

I felt both bored and sedate, comfortable and lonely, feeling like Galicia's potential would be fully realised with some friends and a car. The fishing boats, all lined up, looked like they were gathered at a US drive-in movie theatre: 'Return of the never-changing sea wall'. Fearing they were having more fun than me, I walked away and spent what remained of the evening spuriously aligning timetables and planning a couple of complex days that were fast approaching. For a learning holiday it was occasionally quite stressful. I texted my friend back in Madrid of my further plans in this most marine of areas.

'That sounds fishy to me...' he texted back.

Matt is a wit.

*   *   *   *

Galegos. The people in Galicia, and so far the North, certainly appeared different to their more southerly cousins. Faces were all kinds, often with bigger – not to say more unattractive – noses. There was a higher number of fair people with blonder hair and whiter skin and even some ruddy cheeks. They walked, as a general rule, faster and were more unforgiving to cars that were slow leaving the lights. However, they seemed a calmer and more genteel people, lots of smiles and unthreatening faces. Their Celtic blood was definitely apparent. I felt more at ease, or more at one, with them. I loved the Mediterranean Spanish, but I was nothing like them. There, surrounded by the wet and the green and the wind and the Celts, I felt at home. To this day I still inexplicably long for the place. The Galegos call it *morriña* – a sort of 'melancholic pining for Galicia'. It has no direct translation.

At 10:30, in a town called Carral, the Santiago de Compostela bus just stopped. The driver opened up a panel on the back and started telephoning somebody while holding a blue, oily rag. I had no idea what was going on, though presumably there was a problem with our transport. People started spilling out and lighting cigarettes. Many were smiling and laughing. I was seriously annoyed. The one day I wanted to get somewhere especially early and my damn bus had withered and died.

There was a flurry of unintelligible *galego* amongst some rough and ready local men. One was quite young with a t-shirt, cowboy hat and stubble holding a stick; another had a gold chain around his neck and sported a French nobility set of facial hair – one thick moustache and a goatee. As I watched them the bus fired into life only to conk out again thirty seconds later. I was stranded in some nowhere town, 50 km from my destination and was not best pleased. A few minutes later the bus roared again and the driver tried to encourage it with some revs of the engine. It sounded fine as the driver exited and walked round the back to check something. He then reversed a little and killed the engine.

It was nearing 11 o'clock – the time when I was supposed to be in Santiago. More people started to leave the bus. Now the smiles started to fade. A second round of cigarettes were lit. It seemed that having your bus die was bad for your health. I was contemplating alighting too when something big, yellow and purple whooshed into view – a replacement bus. The new, younger driver then proceeded to wrench the vehicle through forests and towns, occasionally overshooting stops with a 'Hey, stop!' from some passengers. He was making up for lost time and the remaining stretch to Santiago was nothing short of exciting.

After a short walk along obviously the wrong roads, but in the right direction, I found the first area of pretty, stone streets. I followed my nose east, or what my inner compass told me was east, and soon was confident I had made the right decision when I was added to a steadily increasing drift of pilgrims. They all looked the same. Shorts, t-shirts, dirty walking shoes, a medium-sized strappy backpack, sunglasses, a scallop shell hanging from somewhere and a Camino de Santiago walking stick. I liked to think I could tell the light walker from the real trekkers by the extent to which they had been bronzed and weathered.

Making a beeline through some honey-grey alleys, I followed the herd until the Plaza de Azabachería. The first building I saw was the Convento de San Martín Pinario – now a fancy hotel – which seemed to be growing as I entered the square. Then, all of a sudden a barrage of spectacle; hordes of people, and then the cathedral: a magnificently ornate, beautiful shamble of spires and stonework. The façade, sporting statues and the typical Galician overgrowth, seemed old and important. I wasn't happy with the crowd though, so I went through a portal into an even grander plaza, Plaza de Obradoiro, the focal point of the city. There was a roped off passage leading through the crowds from the exit of the cathedral to the Hostal de Los Reyes Parador. I didn't know when whatever was going to happen was going to happen, so I basically flapped.

'Luke!'
I heard a soft, musical voice.
'*Luke!*'
I spun like an idiot.
'Over here.'
It was Inka. She kissed me on both cheeks and explained that in a few minutes the Queen was going to leave the cathedral and walk through to the hotel. And she was right. A few moments later some officious and well-dressed people left the building. They were followed by some royal guards in decorative green tunics and a bevy of men in black suits flitting their heads around like sparrows: bodyguards. Then, subtle and understated, came the Queen, the

Reina Sofia, and her King, Juan Carlos – a man who had been in my studies for four years as he drifted in and out of history.

Everyone was cheering and clapping and chanting *'viva los reyes!'* The Queen, a still noble and beautiful woman, smiled and waved. The King, however, looked ill and old and tired but still he waved. They passed between the cathedral and the Presidencia de la Junta de Galicia where a large group of young people were holding banners and flags and posters to celebrate the Feast of St. James – *San Xacobeo* or Santiago in Castilian Spanish. I said goodbye to Inka and escaped before the exodus. I had my photo of royalty.

I joined a line that was slowly making its way into the cathedral, purely for the fact that it was making its way into the cathedral. Mass was taking place. No photos allowed. 'Dios, La Virgen, Espíritu Santu' and all that. Hundreds of people in prayer were talking along with the priest. They looked like automatons. The nave was lofty and quite bright and the fully golden reredos in the chancel was over the top. I admit I preferred the gloomier, gothic insides of earlier cathedrals but it was still very handsome.
'No photos at mass *please!*'
People still took them. I waited and waited.

'And now the peace.'
Hot under the collar, eyes, dead, cold, atheist eyes straight ahead. A lady kissed me. Burning embarrassment as I fumbled and shook her hand with a dumb Hugh Grant smile.
'And now the body.'
Priests filed out to the wings offering the little wafers of unleavened bread. Crispy, white Jesus flesh. All the attendants were occupied with making sure everybody got a crunchy bit of the God-child. I took my opportunity, snapped the chancel, and got out before I combusted via divine lightning bolt.

I strolled, neither here nor there, in search of nothing. It was nice to be surprised by turning a corner and being faced with some proud church or a gentle little courtyard with a café. The overall effect of Santiago was similar to Salamanca, only Santiago, despite the numbers, somehow felt a little more peaceful and musing. So many people were sitting and looking. Just looking at the buildings, occasionally swapping distracted sentences. There was a little restaurant with a free table. I wasn't famished but I decided it best to take the space while one still existed and before the acolytes spilled out of the cathedral, not content with only Christ in their gut.

I was going for Galego. My last supper in this region. A glass of Albariño, *naturalmente*, and a *caldo galego* to begin. The *caldo galego* is a spinach coloured stew comprising white beans, onions, potatoes, root veg, chorizo and some dark, leafy greens. It was surprisingly gentle and didn't bloat. After that came a portion of one of my favourite foods from the Spanish menu, *empanada*, a sort of squashed pasty filled with tuna, pepper, onion and spices. Sweet, light and delightful. Thoroughly happy with my gastric exploits I went to the see the cathedral from the Plaza de Orbradoiro again.

The altered position of the sun – meaning I could actually gaze at it without squinting – and the now free-to-wander square, added a new level of wonder to the building. A good half an hour was spent sat down gawping at the thing, making sure every inch of it was eternally burned onto my retina. I looked at the region's postcard. It had a view of Santiago from a bit of a distance and from where a range of towers, halls and buildings could be seen. I wanted that view. Walking out of town a little, in the direction of where I thought the angle might be, I walked up and into a small park and bought an ice cream. I am a firm believer in the mantra that you most definitely *cannot* stroll through a park without an ice cream.

The trees cleared, a fountain plopped and there was one of the most delicious city views you could ever hope to see. A staccato line of

248

dramatic granite buildings, spires and turrets, windows and arches and all topped with orange tiles. The centrepiece, around which all the other marvels flowered, was the cathedral. Once again I didn't feel I could do anything else but just sit and absorb. The estuary of shade cast by the trees ebbed with little islands of light that were fortunate enough to flow through the leaves. It was nice when doing nothing didn't feel like wasting time.

I was starting to get to grips with the geography of the place, but I still got thrown off right in the centre of the warren. The number of people made the streets lose their distinctiveness. Not being by the sea and full of bodies (the 'Pamplona effect'), the temperature was higher and the sun noticeably stronger. I tried my best to keep to the shade, as I was surviving on one thin coat of sun cream from that morning. My little factor-15 bottle was trying its best to cough up whatever protective fluid still remained in its plastic depths. And there was the enormous Monasterio e Iglesia de San Paio de Antealtares, which at 20,000 square metres was one of the largest religious buildings in Spain and outside which legions of protest groups were rallying. Just up the road from it I opted for an early evening drink outside a miniscule place at the confluence of three small streets. The Galego language bounced along behind me and occasionally a body 'plink-plinked' by with a stick in one hand and a fidgety map in the other. I finally let go of Santiago, catching a busy bus home to A Coruña.

At about 21:30 I was eating a sandwich by the beach as the sun was just starting to go down behind the buildings to my left. Swallowing my last soggy mouthful, I had a moment of clarity that threatened to stop the peristaltic process. I rearranged the map in my head and then clicked in place the one I had been given by the tourist office. A Coruña was built over a frayed headland and I was pretty sure that the part over to my left – with a viewpoint-topped hill on it – was the furthermost in that direction. It probably jutted out into the sea. Surely then if I headed out to it I would see the sun set over the

Atlantic sea horizon? I had to find out as I hadn't gone to Finisterre and I had never seen a sun set over the sea.

Walking north along the beach towards the headland I picked up my pace as I saw the sun drop quickly. And then it disappeared entirely. I became obsessed. I flip-flopped as fast as I could, muttering 'Come on, *come on*, just over there' to myself. The light was fading and a yellow hue had replaced it as the gassy beast sank. I started to think that I was going to miss it, that this was a silly waste of time. I would get round and the giant would have hidden himself. Then something glinted in the corner of my right eye. Somewhere a sun was reflecting in a block of flats on the opposite side of the bay – God bless you City of Glass! I picked up the pace and my heels started to burn. 'I can see you, come on!' – I made sure no one could hear me. I was racing a star. Trying to outrun the universe. The path bent left round the headland. Slowly the sky brightened, the yellow became more intense, and then, yes, there it was, a big ball of fire still making its way down into the darkness. There were some steps off the maritime path onto a bit of scraggy headland made accessible to the public. Venturing out onto bare rocks, I sat on the tip with a front row seat to a cosmic play. Slowly the big fiery giant fattened and reddened and finally – and I felt like I was the only one in the theatre – bowed and left the watery stage.

A gentle spectral sunset hued the west and a clear and large moon dangled low in bruised purple to the east. It was a very romantic end to a very romantic region.

Oh wild…
Oh wild green!
How the wind licks its chops and cools,
And spouts calms.

Oh wild…
Oh wild green!

Morriña

How you preen your blanket of trees,
And coat of farms.

Oh wild…
Oh wild green!
How your liquored lands offer up sweet
And heady balms.

Oh wild…
Oh wild green!
Mysterious verdancy paint far-off jewels
And a world of charms.

Oh wild…
Oh wild green!
Your name, on the zephyr, Galicia,
Into my arms.

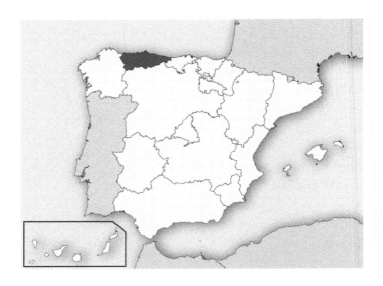

Pelayo's Legacy

Oviedo – Cangas de Onís – Covadonga - Cudillero

After a fitful period getting onto my Asturias-bound bus we were off.

[They said platform two; Shit, where's the bus? What…it's on platform five? Run, queue, ruddy cheeks, squeezing bags into the hold, take seat next to a fat, but not wide, man. Delayed leaving.]

'Are you going to Bilbao?' said the fat man.

'No, Oviedo,' I replied.

'What time will you arrive?' fat man.

'Two o'clock.'

'Four and a bit hours?'

'Yeah.'

'Joder!'

252

We left fifteen minutes behind schedule and notched up more delays as we slowly tracked east through windy Galicia. At a nowhere town some French people got on and walked to their seats at the back of the bus near me. Their allocated places were on the back row, however a couple were in their seats. Two smooching, inbred-looking, yobs. The girl was latently attractive but with a drunken gaze and slouchy shoulders. The guy, in a bright orange, sleeveless vest, was tall and muscular and had a face full of dumb gormlessness.

'*Perdón*, these are our seats,' said the French lady.

'Well, there are people in our seats,' responded the girl contemptuously.

'Yes. But these are *our* seats.'

'I know. It happened to us. Find other seats,' and she turned back to her boyfriend.

Finally my fat man swivelled his bulk and turned to show the Frenchies some nearby free seats. The brief standoff was over.

As the sun continued to pour in through the window on my side of the bus I was treated to kissing sounds until finally dumb and drunk went to sleep. As our vehicle cleaved through the wooded glades and skirted epic, green valleys from hillside roads, I also felt the intoxicating pull of sleep. Handsome town after handsome town warped through me as I struggled to keep awake. I wanted to *see*! Mondoñedo, Luarca and Avilés struck a chord. That's all I remember. Overall the bus was forty minutes late on arrival in Oviedo. I gratefully clambered out of the tepid shell and was surprised by the city's heat; one thermometer read 25°, another 28° and another 32°. Somewhere in between there was a temperature that was hotter than A Coruña. Briefly, just for a second, I missed that cool, Atlantic blast that whirlygigged around the torn-up headland.

I perspired all the way down the swanky Calle Uria, sweated past the delightful, but small, city park, tried to forget the 1.5kg of wine I was burdened (or blessed) with and finally found Fran's place. Fran was a gentle, ageing, hippy-type who had graciously offered a couch on which to surf. I'm not a man to pry, but I figured out – while he smoked weed for medicinal reasons and pushed his long, greying ponytail out of the way – that he had a daughter, didn't seem married, was retired, and spent as much time as possible travelling. After only a few minutes and some casual introductions we went to a little local restaurant to eat.

And how well they eat in Asturias! My first course was the very traditional, and in Spain, as famous as paella, *fabadas asturianas*. It's a heavy stew made from white beans, pork shoulder, black pudding, chorizo and sometimes saffron. This was followed by some fried steak-meat lathered in a naughty *cabrales* cheese cream sauce. *Cabrales* is a spicy and salty blue cheese that is produced in the traditional artisan way up in the Picos de Europa and aged in natural caves. As the product is *denominación de origen,* the milk must come exclusively from the herds that roam the mountain range. The resulting cheese is very rich. The only downside with lunch was that for the following afternoon, night, and indeed next morning, I was cursed with an orchestra of wind instruments and made a more than normal number of visits to the facilities.

The 'Old Town' wasn't particularly big in comparison with some other places I had visited, so I planned to take this one easy with the crumbly old map Fran gave me. Old Oviedo was, comparatively recently, given a series of facelifts – it took a bit of a bashing during the Civil War – and the result is dazzling. I think you would be hard pressed to find a more constantly swish-looking area of buildings in Spain. Not only were they clean and nicely arranged but also almost no two adjoined buildings were the same colour. It was like some exploded toy town. Spanish Noddy.

The odd, pastel green market sat like a curled-up cat by the honey-coloured San Isidoro el Real Church that, like a faithful golden retriever, stood primly by its owner, the flag-covered, fawn-ochre city hall. All around the area streets flew off with a dizzying array of cafés and bars. Oviedo took drinking seriously. There were two streets, with signposts, dedicated to wine, one to beery pubs and one street with a neon sign called the '*boulevard de sidra*' – Cider Street. Dotted amongst churches and little squares were university buildings and campus residences and in the belly of the old town was the cathedral.

Something I liked about these Spanish cities was the way they used their holy houses as orientation spots. Everything fans out from them. This one was pleasant, posh-looking but unremarkable. Like Oviedo's streets it was clean, smart and not kitsch in any way. One cream-coloured spear shot up out of a standard atrium. Tidy. Some local police were monitoring a group of artistic children in the cathedral square. One was doing some tasteful graffiti; another kid was piping an oboe whilst another was levering a bow over the strings of a violin. I didn't know why the police were there. Maybe they were there to stop members of the public interfering with what otherwise might look like delinquency.

A way out of town offered a glimpse of a tiny Asturian church. It was nothing to look at, but intriguing. It was a remnant of the Pre-Romanesque architecture erected in the period between the 8th and 11th centuries. At that time Asturias was the only Christian realm in a country beleaguered by Moors, Visigoths and Vikings and run by a messy continuum of infighting, early-dying, and oppressive Kings, so it was quite something that some of them had managed to survive.

The newer side of town with its swish promenades and shopping streets brought me to a monstrous church. Beautiful in a frightful way, it was all light grey granite and red domes and sculpting. It was the San Juan el Real church and was the place where the little dictator Francisco Franco married Carmen Polo. Of course outside and inside there were no traces of the man, but I got a feeling his fingerprint, a financial one, had been left. I had rarely seen such a 'bling' church. Inside was clean and colourful. The walls were light grey and the ceiling dim, sky blue. Off to the sides were a couple of cemeteries, or mausoleums, where the remains of no doubt very rich people were lovingly interred. A statue of some saint hovered on a plinth as a staircase led down into a cube room where all the walls and floors were composed of swirled marble slabs dedicated to someone.

A mass had started. A white-robed priest was dryly mumbling mantra into a microphone whilst a handful of old women – who, collectively, wouldn't have even filled one pew – were crossing themselves and murmuring responses. Another tiny, grey-haired, lady entered with what I presumed was her granddaughter. She wore a smart, blue suit. *'San Antonio'* she said quietly to the girl, patting her hand. They slowly shuffled arm-in-arm over to a selection of slots, above each of which was a saint's name. She began to drop coins into it. I didn't know what this saint meant to her – maybe she was called Antonia – but I was all but certain the coins were showering into a communal box that the church would then dive into in order to upgrade the lights, or give some wall a paint job whether it was San Antonio's choice or not.

Fran wasn't in the flat. After a brief period of being lost, I met him by a little square near the town hall. The bar he told me to meet him by wasn't open,
'It's Monday and it's closed!' he apologised.
We went to a quiet little café out of the way of the main hub and talked some more about his travels and different peoples and cultures we had encountered. He told me that one of the reasons he liked couchsurfing, and travelling and meeting the locals, was that it helped him to break stereotypes. The rolled up Rizla paper fizzed as

he inhaled. I had a genuine Asturian, a real Oviedo *carbayón*, in front of me.

'So what is it to *be* Asturian?'

'I'm just part of this world *hombre*. I don't consider myself 'Asturian'. I could have been born anywhere. I was born in the West, so for that I guess I'm lucky.'

It carried on in this vein for a while, until he stopped and took another drag. It was a nice answer, very liberal and democratic, but not useful to me in any way. Apart from a naïve dislike of England, and a belief in the tired myths that seem to fog the view of what I sincerely believe to be a pretty, bloody good country, we agreed and shared a similar viewpoint on most things. As he was providing me with free accommodation I decided not to press the regional point.

At the house he brought out some arrows and a bow he had made in the Peruvian forest. I didn't know what to say. In this we had no common ground. He had experienced things and travelled and stayed in places I had only seen on the BBC. After a, thankfully, small plate of pasta and with my head filled with tribal imagery, I zonked out on the sofa.

*   *   *   *

Covadonga is a very important little village indeed. It was there that the *Reconquista* of Spain is considered to have begun in 722 AD. The Battle of Covadonga pitted the Kingdom of Asturias against the Umayyad Caliphate – the Arabs. Pelayo, the founder of Asturias, had been the man to kick-start the rebellion against the Moorish invasion of 'his' country. He began fairly small by refusing to pay tributes and by assaulting Berber garrisons that had been set up in the area. After a while he made quite a statement by managing to expel the Muslim governor, Mununza, from the region. Despite this, the Moorish lords, based in Córdoba, all but ignored him. Asturias wasn't particularly important to them economically or strategically. It was only when Anbasa ibn Suhaym al-Kalbi had been beaten soundly by the Franks, during the Battle of Toulouse in the south of France, that Pelayo faced his greatest task.

Anbasa was reluctant to return to his masters in Córdoba with such bad news, so he decided that quashing once and for all the rebellion in Asturias on his way home would give him an easy victory, make him look better in the eyes of the Caliphate, and, if nothing else, raise the flagging morale of his men. After a failed brokering of surrender Pelayo and his force, of maybe only three hundred men, retreated deep into the mountains, ending up in a narrow valley flanked by steep walls. Nobody knows the exact number of fighters at Pelayo's disposal, but we know it wasn't a lot. A Moorish chronicler described Pelayo and his force as 'thirty wild donkeys'. Wild is a good description of them for, as the Asturian men opened fire on the invaders, Pelayo personally drove down into the valley with some of his soldiers and all but slaughtered the attackers, causing them to flee. As news of the victory spread it sparked uprisings in villages all over the region. That was the last time that the Muslims seriously challenged the independence of the Kingdom of Asturias.

The bus stopped for a few minutes in a town called Cangas de Onís before rising to Covadonga. Through the heavy matt of trees I could make out a basilica jabbing into the blue, sitting on a cliff. The bus carried on past the few houses that made up the dispersed village and deposited us at the top, at the basilica complex. Dramatic, large and grand-looking – for the lack of comparative structures – and all but rusty-pink, the basilica was a building that looked very out of place sitting in the centre of a bubble of heavily treed hills, literally miles from anywhere. Inside was boring. The main star of the show, at the complex, was the strange and tiny chapel crammed into a passageway in the side of the mountain, the *santa cueva*. I walked through a slender tunnel, trying to restrain myself from punching the idiot woman tourist in front of me – she was taking bad photos of everything she saw; plaques, crosses, walls, more walls, a wooden beam, another wall, the idiot – and approached an iron gateway. On the other side of the gateway were a few pews, a cliff face and shrine to my right and open air to my left. In front was a small, stone chapel big enough for three or four standing clergymen. A lady was kneeling at the shrine, crossing herself over and over again. The flow of visitors led up to it, shuffled in front of the pews, and then came back past everybody who were sitting down. A faint tickle of self-consciousness ran down the hairs on the back of my neck. 'Heretic!' they were surely all thinking.

At the bottom of a long set of steps was a small freshwater pond, its *fuente de los 7 caños*, and a viewpoint of the chapel cliff. Instead of sticking around and crossing myself, I bought a ticket to visit what it really was that I had come to see. It wasn't two homeless Asturians fighting over a bottle of cider but the twin glacial mountain lakes of Enol and Ercina.

The air walking down through the shadowy park to the ticket office smelled of hot mint and bark. From Covadonga the bus, a full size coach, heaved itself up an absurdly steep and narrow road, which seemed to keep going on and on and up and up for ever. After a preliminary hill, the view exploded open and there were the peaks. And we were driving through the air higher and higher. We carefully passed cows, goats and other buses in order to try and crash into fleeting clouds. All around us was majesty. About fifteen minutes later we arrived at the stopping station that sat round the corner from Lake Enol, the smaller of the two. While helpful information girls were mobbing anyone disembarking with white paper maps of the area, I hurried off eager to distance myself from the irritating summer throngs.
'If you could just come in, please. That's right, just in a bit more.'
She took the attentive visitors through a couple of the 'and then follow this well signposted obvious footpath' walks. I slipped off, unnoticed.

There was a busy and ultimately underwhelming viewpoint where scores of idiots – I know I'm unfairly critical of what are just normal people and their loved ones – were lined up, shoving and shouldering each other to have their photo taken. Their faces blocking a beautiful bit of mountain. I continued up a little away from the paved trail up more of a dirt track. Cattle were everywhere. Milk chocolate coloured dairy cows. Scores of them. Drinking or plodding round the lakes, munching grass, and batting their long lashes over their big, pretty eyes. They were incredibly docile, even the bulls. As the cows moved, either to find a fresh batch of grass to mow, or from scratching their heads on posts, or craning their necks round to fend off some overly interested flies, a constant soundtrack of bells jangled in the air.

The lake sat placidly below, bright blue. Instantly around it some mountains pushed up while in the distance an enormous flurry of peaks rose, grey, no trees and with some patches of ice. If you removed the tourists and added a busty Swiss milkmaid swinging pails and yodelling, no one would have thought her out of place. Delving down through a large herd of cows, I made sure I didn't get between an angry mother and her calf whilst attempting not to annoy the bull. The grass near the lake was caked in cowpats and the air was crisp but often bore the scent of vegetative dung. Sitting by a rock a little way down Lake Ercina, so that I was surrounded by vistas, I ate tortilla and ham sandwiches while a family of coots floated about. Every couple of minutes the mother would dive down and the cootlings would start baying. She would then pop up and they would rush to her, quacking a relieved sort of quack.

Having had my fill of what I was eating I left my seat, and a very inquisitive bouncy crow, and went for a walk. The land was decidedly rougher down the lakeside away from the crowds and towards the mountains. One rocky path went up, one carried on more downwards. Up was good, I thought. A few minutes along the path there was a surprising, small pigsty containing a pair of chubby, pink beasts. A little way round was a tiny house, a basic one or two-room affair. A walker and his family greeted the owner with a familiarity denoting a probable friendship. Further up still was another miniscule, stone house where a group of Spanish hikers were chatting to a prim, old farmer who was sat, crossed-legged, on a little stool just outside his front door.

'Yes, this is my house. These are my cows,' I heard him say.

The farmer's wife inside called, offering to sell them some cheese they had made. A chicken clucked avidly by my leg as I filled up at the farmhouse's tap.

On circumnavigating the peak that sat between the two lakes, Ercina slunk out of view. I was aware that the Spanish walkers were behind me and I passed another couple, who also started to follow my track, applying some sun cream in the shade of a boulder. I didn't want to walk with people, especially not leading the pack, constantly thinking that if I slowed down they would catch up. The path went through some jagged white rocks and then arched down into a small bowl with some farm buildings – probably owned by the farmer. The ubiquitous cows ding-donged to my left by some cliffs of the Mosquital peak and to my right was an even deeper bowl of green grass. From there a bar of cliff rose to a thick layer of pine trees seeming to cover everything in view until those magnificent iced peaks again topped the scene. It looked like someone had 'copy and pasted' a view from 'The Lord Of The Rings', and minimised it. As I came out from the small enclave I had a choice, albeit an easy one, to make: along and round the path with the others or up what could barely be called a path that shot up the Mosquital mountain. Up was good, I thought. The path was steep and after a few minutes dissolved into nothing. As I later found out, going 'off-piste' can really become quite a dangerous affair.

The side of the Mosquital mountain was rugged but oddly easy to traverse. It was a tough incline but constantly jutting out bulbs of rocks made a sort of stepping-stone sequence all the way up. As long as I avoided the sharp nastiness of the gorse I was all right. My brow was glistening and dripping quite severely with sweat by the time I reached the top. A little post indicated that it was the definitive point, 1289m. A plaque was engraved into a slab:

'Recorrí muchos caminos buscando paz y belleza y subiendo a la montaña disfrute su grandeza' – 'I travelled many paths searching for peace and beauty and, climbing up the mountain, I enjoyed its majesty.'

I agreed with the sentiment of the plaque and it was a similar sense of awe that broiled under my skin as when I had seen the Catalunyan expanse at Montserrat and the leagues of outstretched blue at Gibraltar. Only there, 1289m up and seemingly higher than everything but the monster to the west, the drama simply depth-charged the other two out of the water. A 360° panorama poured into my eyes. I kept spinning and turning, unable to decide which part to focus on. Both lakes were in shot, click; then our Tolkienesque behemoth, click; then the cascade of bumps and humps that filtered down to Covadonga, click; and finally a slender spine of very sharp peaks all pushed up together but just too far to walk to, click. I wanted to sandpaper down Mosquital and put a house there, or a hut, or just a bench. The now was too fleeting.

Something pricked my toe. A gorse spine had speared through my shoe and was bothering my feet. I removed my trainer and felt around inside. Something then pricked my finger, a sharp sting. Yes, so it was there. I took my hand out and moved my shoe about a bit, trying to see inside it. Then I noticed a slender, yellow thorn sticking out of my right index finger. I dropped my trainer angrily and tried to pull it out. Snapping it off at it the base entombed the blasted tip in a spongy bed of flesh. It stung. I applied pressure to either side, hoping it would pop out like flavoured ice from a Calippo or goo from a spot. It didn't. An almost unnoticeable blanket of dark purple blood rushed around it. My skin was light enough so I could see its body hovering in the translucence of thin epidermis, just under the surface. I then attempted to scratch it out but my nails were too blunt. All my efforts did was make it hurt more. I thought it best I make my way down back and see if anyone had a needle.

Descending the east flank back down towards the darling lake Ercina I soon realised why there was distinctly no path leading down this side. It started off much like the south side ascent with its stepping stone system. It was a little trickier using this method downhill, but it wasn't too bad. Things gradually got hairier. The bulbous stones had swiftly evolved into fins of rocks and more jagged and sharp. In between the fins the spaces grew and deepened. Often much deeper than a leg. This in itself wasn't a problem. The problem was that the vegetation was thickening. A perilous mass of ferns and heather and grass collected in the miniature ravines. I didn't therefore know what was probably solid ground and what was potentially a minor crevice waiting to snap my legs like a pair of dry twigs. Both hands and both feet were used to go over those stabby rock ridges that prodded out of the dangerous sea of green. I swung my camera round and put it in my bag. Things were getting out of hand. Dripping face. Exhale. Concentrate. It would have been a terrible idea at the best times but it was worsened by the grey satchel around my neck, swinging about this way and that, in a theatre where balance was key. I neither wanted to be impaled nor hear my bones whine and crunch as I was bent out of shape by nature. I slid and hopped and grappled my way out of the sea on to flatter land and blew sweat off my lips. Shit. There was a cliff in front of me.

I could see where I wanted to be but was having a hard time getting to it. Some 50m or so below, the area of families and cows and relaxation was unaware that some slightly adventurous, stupid tourist was somewhere maybe few people, maybe no-one (and for the now obvious reason) had been. There was a way off to my right that seemed like it would take me towards a gentler area with a goat or two. I smiled and approached it. Far from being a nice, natural path, it was a narrow, natural passageway that was a sheer drop – a good 20m – on one side and a flat, slightly out-pressed cliff wall on the right. I decided I couldn't safely walk it without a harness for fear of falling off. There was a tingly vertigo feeling in my feet. Maybe I could crawl. Someway in the cliff-face bulged a little into the passage. I could get to that. I whimpered once to myself. I could go back, but didn't want to. The green pastures were so close, a few metres away. First just to deal with not accidentally falling into a messy heap down below.

I steeled myself, once again swung my bag onto my back – please don't get caught or decide to slide off – and got onto my belly. I was breathing heavily through fear more than exertion. Inches to my left was a drop at which I dared not look. It was not 'Cliffhanger' but it was more than I had bargained for on a touristy stroll. To my right were thick grasses and the looming cliff wall. Thick grass that I near strangled to death. Those were my lifelines. I felt the weight of my body, all my blood and organs, veering left towards the drop. Thank Christ the grass held. I pulled myself into the tiny cave and kneeled up into a ball, soaked with sweat. Wiping away the perspiration from my red eyes, I tasted salt. I was halfway.

The sheer drop had reduced in height. I was faced with the other half of my route. Either a narrower belly job or a jump. Directly in front of me was somewhere I didn't want to land. Sure, the initial fall would only be about three or four metres but the ensuing tumble down the mountain would not have been conducive to survival. Slightly to the right was the closest space of green pasture, a small perch and a couple of rock walls. I threw my bag. It landed a couple of metres down with a dull 'thunk'. I slowly edged towards the 'edge'. I could try lowering myself down. There was a little foothold there. I tried it tentatively and my leg slid away.
No, not that way.

I bunched up and eyed my trajectory, shuffling slowly closer, almost at the tipping point. A couple of false starts and no goes and swear words under breath. My bag was there for God's Sake, do it! A tilt and then the briefest moment of freefall and then a thud and a fleshy 'thwack' as I collided with the wall. I was alive. Picking up the bag I descended down slippery scree that grinded and crunched and echoed, occasionally giving way under me. I didn't care if I stumbled, there was no drop. I headed for a freshwater spring with a tap. No one was near. No one was there to see the state I was in. I drowned myself. It was the coldest, freshest water in the world – like the Denia spring. I showered my head and neck and then basked a while on a rock with my feet in the lake, giggling to myself and muttering, 'Idiot'. A cow was sipping at the water, bathing in the radiant surroundings, oblivious to its beauty. I must have looked like a sweaty mess when I made the easy trek over to Lake Enol. Mosquital raised a wry grin with its dangerous grandeur. I had made up my mind; without serious hiking, the views that I got that day were not going to be topped.

I found no needle to remove the splinter in my finger so I returned to Cangas de Onís where I had an hour to kill. A town, which was, until 774, the capital of the aforementioned Kingdom of Asturias and was the site of the first church built in post-conquest Iberia. Despite this, the hour I had didn't allow much room for it to shine quite like Covadonga. It has a pleasant, but frankly – and especially after the mountains – dull town centre and a *Puente Romano*, a charming and impressive high arch bridge. Underneath it flowed the river in which young people and families were swimming and playing. To the disbelief of some visitors, and the tutting disapproval of a few older folks, a couple of young *chavales*, probably showing off to some attractive bikini-clad floozies, were leaping off the road bridge into the river.

*   *   *   *

I had planned the following day to be a more relaxing one and it was so. The FEVE was the elected mode of transport for the day. The FEVE is a northerly section of state-owned, narrow-gauge railway that burrows through the countryside, usually alone, and stops at all the tiny towns and almost-villages that probably only just make it onto a map.

In the station at Oviedo I, in my old English manner, helped a girl, who didn't sound Spanish, carry her very heavy bag down to the platform. After the rather bumpy, and at times violent, train pulled into the transfer station of Pravia – a middle of nowhere town – the girl and I got off and hurried onto our connecting train. She was clearly French.

'Tu es francaise non?'

'Si..er..oui.'

'Je suis anglais.'

We took our seats next to each other and she leant over to an elderly couple to ask them if we were on the train to Cudillero. They shook their heads, we shared a quick fearful glance and scrambled off as another train pulled in.

We entered, saw a lone old woman – the majority of people on the FEVE seemed to be silvery-haired – and asked her the same question. This time it was a nod. The girl and I talked for a while mixing Spanish and French. She had been living in Madrid too. Originally from Lyon she was off to visit a Spanish friend of hers in the weeny village of Muros de Nalón. At the stop after Pravia the old lady got up and I thanked her again. I didn't know why, maybe she was charmed by our highly linguistic, mostly Spanish conversation, or maybe she just liked manners, but she gave me a squeeze on the shoulder and one of the most subtle, but well-meaning and heartfelt little smiles I had ever seen. The train slowly lurched into the little station at Muros de Nalón with the small, yellow FEVE building.

'What is your name by the way?'

'Luke.'

'Luke.'

'And yours?'

'Violette.'

She heaved her bag out and waved to her Asturian friend who was signalling from the road. Violette was diving into her own, private Asturias.

The train continued to buckle and bang through the leafy valleys and ravines, through unknown settlements and over rickety bridges. *Hórreos* flitted by the windows at every village; handsome wooden granaries usually on stilts that housed either animal feed or crops. And by every house were numbers of Asturian apple trees, bearing red, juicy fruit that one would day be turned into the region's peaty cider.

The station at Cudillero was, like almost all FEVE stations, a couple of rail tracks and a cute building just big enough to house a ticket machine, a toilet, two barriers and a man at a desk. You were often left quite distant from your actual target and this was the case with Cudillero. The warm air was full of earthy aromas and there were roads sloping off downhill to the screams of far-off gulls. It had to be that way. One narrow road, barely wide enough for two cars, led away from the floral hill I was on, with its views of woods and private residences, and wound downwards as it was sucked into a corridor of buildings. The seagulls were getting rowdier the further down I went. I passed a selection of spanking clean baby blue, yellow and pink flats that looked amusing among the faded, but not ugly, old grey lines that surrounded them. The buildings started to get more attractive and tiny cafés were springing up at their feet. Sea air, salty air, then hit the nose. The small, but stately, town hall stood next to an oddly large, but old-looking, yellow church. I walked up the steps between them and round the back. The view was extraordinary and like nothing instantly recognizable as Spanish.

Portmeirion and memories of feeding sea gulls at New Brighton, across the Mersey from Liverpool, with my granddad were the first things that fluttered into my head when I looked out. From the floor, and built up in a near circle stuck onto the walls of a small cove, the houses of Cudillero rose in imperceptible terraces forming a constant wall of homes. All were different colours and well maintained. Down below the road had widened and a *'plaza'* had formed out of cobbles. Restaurants had swooped all over it with tables and chairs and umbrellas. Music was coming out of a doorway, people were watching the world go by from their windows and gulls sat on chimneys. A perfect place to have a picnic.

The day before I had bought some provisions and kept them in Fran's fridge. A blue cheese from Cangas de Onís, a loaf of sliced granary bread, and a bottle of cider. With no knife I had to break off chunks of the softening cheese – it had started to lose its firmness in the rising heat – with my fingers and press it over the bread. The cider, due to its size – 70cl – had retained its coolness. I sat, feeling a little bit roguish, globbing and pasting fat hunks of cheese onto slices of nicely sweet bread and washing it down with the earthy apple juice.

The blue cheese of the European peaks was salty and potent. The slender blue lanes that traced through the chalky white pillow added a subtle smokiness. The cider was the only bottle I could find with a *'denominación de origen'* stamp, which is the stamp that certifies both its quality and its place of birth. It opened with a gratifying pop. It was like a good farmhouse cider from Somerset: acidic, flat, peaty and a perfect rustic accompaniment to the cheese. I tried to drink the cider as subtly as possible, as members of the public were also occasionally making use of the viewpoint. I even took out my camera so they wouldn't think me some impoverished urchin who had fallen to the devil's sauce. He might end it all in the sea! But not with a camera like that. I finished about 200g of cheese and the whole bottle of cider and stood up feeling both decidedly content and decidedly fuzzy. The houses were not spinning but were instead gently rolling and oscillating.

A few moments walk out towards the sea and I intensely needed to urinate. This burning irritation, coupled with the need to keep pulling up my shorts from around my apparently receding waistline must have made me appear slightly troubled. After finding free toilets – always a moment of grand personal triumph on the trip – I walked onto one of the arms of the port and received a nice view back to the town. It looked like some Roman amphitheatre, with blue and white, red striped, green dappled, and painted houses where rows of seats and shouting crowds should have been.

Paths, narrow as a person, and a half-formed network of multi-level routes burrowed up and down the hillside like some giant ant nest. It was a struggle to imagine living there; it seemed too cramped and petite. I couldn't really see, or know, where I was in it all. Up, up was good. In only a few minutes I was spat out of the nest, right at the top, above everything. And there Cudillero sat, a circular ball, curled up like a cat. It was all very lovely. Lovely from every angle. On the way down, traversing round the hillside, a man stopped me to inform me of another viewpoint further on. It was a good viewpoint, full of orange roofs holding up the blue sea where little boats bobbed. Cudillero was a seaside charmer and although I didn't try any of their fish, I did pop into a local bakery to buy an *avellanito*; a little sponge cake flavoured with hazelnut and speckled inside with chocolate dust, and a *bretzel*; a twisted rope of pastry covered in chocolate and honey.

During the FEVE ride back I had to enjoy the views of the rivers and forgotten villages by myself. I wished I still had Violette as company. Finally, in the evening, and for my last moments shared with him, Fran prepared some little omelettes. I mentioned to him how I found omelettes fascinating
'I often think about eggs', I said in a pensive manner.

He snorted and started giggling to himself and I instantly realised my mistake. 'Oh Fran! Not those types of eggs!'

The Spanish word for eggs, *huevos*, also translates as balls or testicles. 'I often think about balls.'

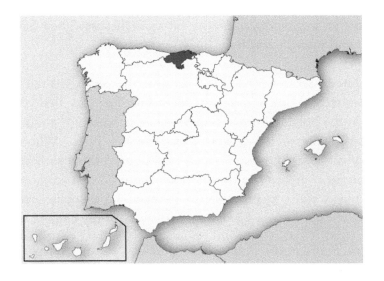

A Green and Pleasant Land

Santander – Santillana del Mar - Comillas

Four hours on the FEVE. Four hours jolting and banging through some deliriously beautiful scenery. Four hours punctured by enormous interchanging groups of school kids on adventure holidays or grubby French scouts larking about or falling asleep in their blue shirts while others painted phallic lines on their dormant faces. Four hours as we melted unnoticeably into Cantabria and gradually left the mountains. The last view of them, a final goodbye flourish, was a dramatic twenty-minute long fin that slowly lost height and petered out into normal hills. Cantabria, visually, didn't distinguish itself much from Asturias. Not until the train went further east did a shift become apparent. It was still green but the land was less rugged and overblown – though I knew the region

271

shared the Picos de Europa with Asturias and was not 'flat'. Nature had decided to seek out gentler paths for itself. Smooth undulations, less forests and more cows and grassy fields were what I saw. It was pleasant but a little duller than what came before. Then Santander arrived and ruined everything.

We entered past a series of ugly suburbs that strangled the scenery that they were scoured into. My first impressions, the first couple of hours in the bulging hub around the station, were not good. In fact my first couple of hours were a definite low point. Whoosh, the smell of hot dogs and greasy fried food clogged the breathing space. The sun was out and the air was thick and fetid. I spent a hazy and disorientated forty minutes or so looking for a couchsurfer's flat with only a photo of a Google Maps route on my camera to guide me.

It was the house of Belén and Manuel. They had offered me a night in the city and there I was, by the door sweating and stubbly. I rang the bell on the intercom. No answer. I rang two more times. Still no answer. I brightly texted Manuel that I was downstairs and that his bell didn't seem to be working. Wiping my forehead I saw the date on my mobile phone, the 29th. Why weren't they answering? Standing away from the buzzer I thought back. Back to when I made the connection with them. They had agreed to house me when? Shit. The 30th. I was in the city a day early and there was no one home. Realising my gargantuan mistake I sent an apologetic text. 'Don't punish yourself' was included in Manuel's gentle response.

Trudging back to town through the stickiness I found a *pensión* near the station. Small, but very clean and smart. It was *Semana Grande*, a fiesta week, so I was lucky to find anywhere. A round-faced woman let me in and, sticking a key into a brown wooden door, exposed a spotless but tiny room.
'How much for one night?'

'35 euros.'

I exhaled audibly, emitting a faint surprised 'whoa!' which she heard. There was an awkward second as I realised my rudeness. I paid and put on my cheeriest face so that she wouldn't enter my room at night and try to stab me to death.

I found it hard, at the start anyway, to endear myself towards the place. The horrid area around the station aside, I was walking darkly along the port and marina thinking 'A Coruña did it better'. It was difficult to look at Santander objectively through the black ink that was my foul mood – a mixture of desperation, irritation and anger. I felt like smothering tourists and their families: 'I'm English too, let me stay with you!' Looking back, the sea front wasn't unattractive and the occasional statue (my favourite being the children jumping into the sea) and views across the water to hills and fields helped lift my mood. However, I still think that A Coruña does it better.

I soon bored of the centre with its few attractive buildings, one or two nice streets and shoddy, squat cathedral. I should concede a point of pity to Santander however. In 1941 it fell victim to an evil fire that, fanned by strong southerly winds, ravaged the city for two days. Only one man died, but the majority of the medieval town was irrevocably destroyed and the city's cathedral was defaced. It was a victim of nature's violence. Like some beautiful woman scarred and beaten in an accident, it wasn't her fault.

With no plan in my head I walked down the coast towards the Magdalena peninsula. In retrospect it was lucky I did, for it saved Santander from finding itself on some synaptic list in my head of places that are a bit shit. My mood reverted to its normal, sunny self and the city managed to promote itself up to the list of 'not bad, worth a visit if you are in the area'.

Construction on the peninsula area was started in 1908 and it was envisaged as a 'pastoral residence' or 'Palace for the Kings'. Alfonso

XIII spent seventeen consecutive summers there claiming it a fine place for sports and hunting and staying in the vast mansion relaxing. A bulky building with windows to every direction, it is catalogued as having the definitive style of 'eclectic picturesque', which encompasses styles from England, France and Northern Spain. It sits and surveys an area of 28 hectares that fans around it. The park has since been claimed by the City and is open to the public whilst the building, declared a 'historical artistic monument', has been converted into a place to hold conferences and meetings.

The path took a variety of routes throughout the small outcrop of land and the all-encompassing perimeter path conducted me to all the necessary 'sights'. The first of them was a weary, empty, and rather miserable 'mini-zoo' where a couple of Humboldt penguins looked around aimlessly and a small selection of sea lions floated and laid about in a fittingly bored manner. To the left the waves were crashing about the bare, grey rocks and a male sea lion was bellowing mournfully.

Things improved from then on. There was a line of small, wooden, replica ships and a white stone sea barrier that could have been stolen from a British pier. Yet more delights awaited on that strange little bluff as I skirted round: an arched wooded corridor that snuck round right out of sight from the palace with trees that looked like giant broccolis; a v-shaped dip in the headland and white-water rocks that drew the eyes up to an island with a stumpy lighthouse on top; and the bikini beach, happy holiday-makers, distant hills, sailboats silently slicing through sparkling sea, while the body of Santander rose from nothing to a grand-hotel up by a high-level promenade.

There were lines, queues of kids, mostly dressed in black, waiting for the evening's rock concert. My feet were starting to ache in that dull, tired, flip-flop abused way. It was a fairly long walk back to the *pensión* and a fairly unremarkable one through town, though I did see one interesting thing. A small group of people were tossing heavy balls through the air to land on, and knock over, some hefty skittles. It was a Cantabrian sport called *bolos celta*, or *'bolos de tineo'* and a team was practising as darkness drew in. Families were taking evening strolls, as they always do in Spain, and tapas bars and restaurants were firing up. I dined alone, in my room, with a bottle of orange juice and an *empanada*. Ever so slightly lonely.

*　　　*　　　*　　　*

At the university of Alicante, for my Erasmus, I was enrolled on four courses: Spanish, Russian (*in* Spanish), Publicity, and Prehistory: Hunters and Gatherers, along with all the other Spanish students. After our first prehistory lecture the professor pulled us (my friend Nicola and I) aside to see how we had coped. He then uttered the now immortal words 'No foreign student has ever passed this course. Most drop out', to which I cockily replied something along the lines of 'Don't worry, we'll pass.' We did, and well. It was a lot of hard work, but was very rewarding – many hours were spent honing Spanish language essays on the subject of stone tools or writing reviews of museums and even book critiques. Of the long chain of human history we studied – from the origin of man (my personal favourite) to the end of the ice age and the dawn of modern *sapiens* – one thing rang a bell as I was reading about Cantabria; the caves of Altamira at Santillana del Mar. More precisely, the fifteen thousand year old cave paintings at Altamira.

The town sits buried in a verdigris alcove of rural pastures – all cows and warm haystacks. The caves were 2km up a hill. I walked there, sweaty, but glad. The original caves are now no longer open to the public – they were closed in 2002 – so instead the museum has faithfully, and impressively, recreated the entire painted cave system artificially. With clever lighting and a no doubt impressive budget, the overall effect is as if you were in the caves themselves. Albeit with snazzy information panels, video screens and holograms.

In the caves section I was told off quite publicly and forcefully by a guard *not* to take photos *anywhere* in the museum. I had understood the opposite. Fortunately the dark carmine of the bison and animals above outmatched the burning rose flower stains of my embarrassed cheeks. I hurried away feeling a funny mixture of smugness and geeky immersion as I walked around the museum. My thoughts harkened back to our bouncy lecturer Javier who was so proud and impressed with his two English students.

It was a shame the original caves were shut off but it really was for their own good. There were thoughts about opening them at the end of 2010 and in an endearing comment Miguel Angel Revilla, the head of government of the Northern region of Cantabria, stated that he would love for US President Barack Obama to be the first visitor when they finally re-open. He said:
'I have already written the invitation letter, and in English!'
For now though they are safe.

The pleasure didn't stop with the caves, as Santillana was a gem in its own right. A medieval village that never grew up, I had never visited anywhere that felt so contained and genuine. Trujillo came close. A core of cobbled streets flurried around gorgeously maintained, honey-coloured buildings, including mansions and a church that seemed far too big for the settlement they were in. Maybe it was expected to expand beyond a ten-minute diameter walk but never got the chance. It was like some architect in the 14th century wanted to design a village that made you want to pinch its cheek, 'You're sooo cute, yes you are, yes you *are*!' It was quite adorable, despite the summer crowds. I could so easily have imagined – turning my gaze away from the constant hotel, restaurant and artisan shop signs that seemed to be all that filled the place – knights and their armour clanging, great stallions and their hooves clopping off the cobbles and peasants lining the streets selling rotting vegetables and wearing sacks.

Another intriguing, but not out of place, thing in Santillana was the museum of torture, a theme I was sickly fascinated with. I don't know why. Some insightful psychologist would probably tell you that I have some latent anger issues and shouldn't be near people. I think it's just a fascination with man's capacity to inflict the most horrid atrocities on his own kind. It was interesting because in no way could I relate to it. The museum contained various nasties from the hollow metal bull into which people were stuffed and under which a fire was placed, to the more typical snappy, bendy, pully, cracky, stabby, slicey things so loved by the torturer.

Whilst eating my typical *cocido montañes* (a meaty stew not dissimilar from *fabadas Asturianas*) in a little family restaurant, I mused on the town. Sure, it was pretty and ornate. Sure, it was historical and attractive. Sure, it was a precious, glittery stone in a grassy crown. But its name didn't fit. In fact, its name is a joke. There is a cheeky saying in Spain relating to the place they call the 'Town of three lies': '*Ni es **santa**, ni **llana**, ni tiene **mar**'* – It's neither a Saint, nor flat, nor does it have a sea.

In the early evening I got the bus back to Santander and at 20:00 I once again found myself outside a certain Spanish family's house ringing the buzzer. This time however I was in after the first ring. I had been preparing my entrance for some time and, feeling really bad for having messed them about, apologised in the most emphatic Spanish at my disposal. I arched my eyebrows and everything. They weren't bothered at all. Manuel was a chain-smoker, walked slightly hunched, had a fluidic cough, grizzly short beard, a husky laugh and was sardonic but informative. Belén was buoyant, long mahogany-haired, instantly friendly and passionate. They were both the most wonderful and necessary people I could have met right then. They are prolific users of couchsurfing who, in a little over two years and a half, have had over 240 guests. They let me organise myself and then took me into town.

A couchsurfing girl who was staying with them, just prior to me, had left some earrings at the house. Belén found them under the bed along with a multitude of other couchsurfers' accessories whilst cleaning – 'It was lucky they didn't go up the hoover!' The girl in question had an emotional attachment to them so they had agreed to meet her, as she was still in the city, and return her jewellery.

'Is there a strong Cantabrian identity?' I probed as we stood in a busy square waiting.

Belén looked unassuming, shook her head, and shrugged, 'No'.

'Is there a...a Cantabrian character?'

'No, not really.'

'It's nothing like Cataluña or País Vasco,' said Manuel, 'Some of the regions are maybe similar to the relationships you have in your country, between Scotland, Wales and England. But some just aren't.'

Manuel extracted a cigarette from a weathered little packet and kicked a football back to some children who were running around. Seeing him light up Belén slapped him on the arm.

'Manuel, enough smoking!'

He giggled breathily and then starting coughing. It was busy because of the *Semana Grande* and an expectant stage with microphones and speakers had been set up. We waited.

Belén and Manuel told me about some of the traditional food in the region: *cocido montañes* (the hearty stew I had tried in Santillana) and *sobao* (a sort of lemony sponge cake with a dash of *anís*). We spoke about languages, tourists, manners and the couchsurfing phenomenon. I was impressed by the way they, just like Fran, were so passionate about it. They spoke about how it needed to be looked after and cared for, like a plant. Both parties disliked free-loaders.

'At times,' started Belén, her finger jabbing the air, 'I have felt like knocking on the door and asking for five euros.' She stopped, tutted at Manuel for lighting another cigarette, and carried on. 'Sometimes, rarely, people use it like it was a hotel so I feel like treating them like hotel guests.'

I found myself checking my own intentions. Was *I* a free-loader? I decided, due to my conversation skills, want to learn, and my interested manner that I wasn't and relaxed again.

The English girl, whoever she was, never showed up. The temperature was dropping and the noise of the animated evening was increasing as the Santander festival upped a gear.

'What is it for?' I barked.

'It started a couple of years ago and was so popular that they have kept on doing it,' said Belén over the ruckus, 'it's just to celebrate the city, you know?'

A band had started to play: a 50s style rock and roll group called "The Puzzles", pronounced *puth-less* in Spanish. English is 'cool' you see.

We moved away a little to have a drink and some *pinchos* at one of the many food stalls that had opened up for business.

'The bars around here hire them out and sell their products out on the street,' Manuel informed me, slyly putting away his lighter, 'Let's try here.'

First up was an anchovy, cheese and pepper *pincho* with a *caña*. The Puzzles, singing in perfectly written English, were getting a large crowd bopping and bouncing on their feet, knees upping and downing, hips swaying. After they finished to applause, Manuel rushed around to ask them if they had any CDs I could buy, 'Only vinyl' was the response. During the encore when the band descended into the crowd for an unplugged acoustic number, we moved on, further into the town and further into the crowds.

One of the most entertaining stalls was hired out by a very popular place called La Pulpería. It had decorated itself in a British theme with lots of flags and caricatures of famous people like Mr. Bean and Prince Charles.

'We have to go there!' I announced.

Another beer and a battered, fried, pepper stuffed with meat and lathered in a tomato sauce.

'I notice that Santander is up for the European city of culture. Do you think it has a good chance?' I said sipping my cold *caña*.

'I think not,' said Belén, despite loving her city.

'Granada is also part of it!' added Manuel snorting a kind of you-know-what-*that*-means snort.

In a straight race between the two cities I had to agree. Granada would win, simply and easily. I took a photo for a group of pretty girls, Manuel giggled, Belén told Manuel off for attempting to light his umpteenth cigarette and we moved on to a third and final place; *caña* with hog roast and apple *pinchos*.

Belén continued to slap Manuel's hand as he reached for his packet of fags while hills and steep roads pulled us home. I breathily exclaimed that it was a lot hillier than I had expected. They informed me that this is a well-known fact and that the Cantabrians even have two words, *pindio* and *sincio*, specific to the area and meaning 'steep incline'.

'That is why girls from Santander are famous for having great-' said Belén slapping her backside.

Biologically speaking I am sure there is truth in that. I endeavoured to produce a more detailed report on the matter in the next few years after some meticulous countrywide research.

'I am a scientist at heart and one has to be sure,' I asserted.

At the flat there were brief introductions to their eighteen-year-old daughter, Paula, who was in her room with a friend, and then to the wonderful and friendly family cat, Figaro. I sat on the floor with him a while in the hallway where he instantly flumped himself into my lap. The beast knew exactly what he was up to and it worked. He purred, padded and fidgeted and curled up.

'Figaro, I need to sleep.'

'Figaro, Luke wants to go to sleep,' added Belén as if addressing a child.

'I haven't the heart to move him.'

'Figaro! Fi! Come.'

The cat's ear flickered and he toddled off into the kitchen mewing sonorously. Before bed Belén handed me a nice notebook.

'If you want you can write a message here. Like a guest book. It can be whatever you want, a comment, a story. Some people have even drawn pictures.'

I was charmed by both them and the idea so, in my room I placed the book on the writing desk, took out my biro and wrote (including mistakes):

Manuel y Belén,

En un mundo lleno de maravillas — montañas besadas por los nubes, el mar brillando en el sol, cascadas tirando arcos de color en el aire, una familia caminando con sus niños, playas de oro cubiertas con cuerpos contentos, un tren viajando solo por un valle verde, las ondas golpeando las rocas nudas de la costa, viento silbando por las ramas de un arbol, los músculos del culo de una Santandrina, jovenes jugando en una garganta, el cielo azul como una piedra preciosa, bares de tapas llenos de gente y comida y vida, muros antiguos como la historia — en un mundo lleno de maravillas son las conexiones humanas que son las cosas más valuables. En un período breve habeís confirmado este hecho 100%.

Gracias a vosotros, mil gracias (y a Figaro),

Luke

It translates as:

In a world full of wonders — mountains kissed by clouds, the sea shining in the sun, waterfalls throwing arcs of colour into the air, a family strolling with its children, gold beaches covered with contented bodies, a train travelling alone through a green valley, the waves crashing against the naked rocks of the coast, wind whispering through the branches of a tree, the arse muscles of a Santandrian girl, young people playing in a stream, the blue sky like a precious stone, tapas bars full of people and food and life, walls old as history – in a world full of wonders it is the human connections that are the most valuable things. In a brief period you have confirmed this fact 100%.

Thank you, a thousand thank yous (to Figaro too).

*   *   *   *

The next morning goodbyes were shared over a conversation about the weather – the North was always bearable whereas Madrid and the South were almost unliveable in the summer.

'Here it's never too cold and never too hot,' said Belén.

'But it's humid,' added Manuel.

'That's true. Southerners often come up to escape the heat but then suffer with the humidity.'

'I guess sometimes in Spain in July and August you are just screwed, plain and simple,' I added as we embraced.

Leaving baby-blue in left luggage again I made the little trip to a strange town called Comillas. On a basic level the town is a fairly smart beach settlement, sitting on the coast, with a large supply of nice flats and large private houses. In itself not inherently interesting. But, when walking around the place, one can see why it was in the Rough Guide. It had been a modernists' playground. All over the town architectural flourishes were visible. They ranged from broken, coloured tiles wrapped around columns to a full university complex. It was as if bits of Barcelona had been carried off in some tempest and had been scattered amid the far off countryside of northern Spain. The map from the tourist office, even once I had found where north was, was fairly useless. There were no road names on it and it wasn't very accurate. Having said that, mapless was something I did quite well.

Three minor disappointments occurred throughout an otherwise fantastic few hours of wandering. The first was the Gaudí building called *El Capricho*, one of the three centrepieces of the town. It cost

€5 to go in and see it, both from outside and in. Refusing, out of principle as well as poverty, I instead found a side road leading up to some houses where I was able to photograph most of what there was to see through a hole in a gate. Gaudí built this as a summer residence for the brother-in-law of the Marquis of Comillas. The by-product is a cubic-looking house with one main tower and bricks of many colours: bold reds and greens mixed with browns, creams and whites. The resulting, intriguing mess looked like it had been made out of Lego bricks by some hyperactive, genius, child-architect.

The second disappointment came from the Universidad Pontificada. According to the map one could walk up to it. Well 'one' had a little trouble and never managed it. The main access road through the Puerta de la Universidad Pontificada, designed by Gaudí's contemporary Lluís Domènech i Montaner (who also designed the University), said 'sin paso: no acceso a la Universidad'. Further along private drive after private drive prevented me from climbing the hill, so I had to make do with viewing it from afar. My thanks go out to whoever invented the zoom lens.

Joan Martorell's Palacio de Sobrellano was the final disappointment but which, from outside at least, looked extraordinary. A strange granite-grey/pink mansion, in a modernist style combining English Gothic and Moorish, it sat perched in a salad of trees offering entry with a guided tour at specific times. The next one was eight minutes before the bus was supposed to return to Santander. Not ideal. This didn't bother too much however as I doubted the inside would have outshone the outer shell.

Sweating and badly in need of the loo, I sat at a nice little café/restaurant, offering the standard competitive menú del día attempt to battle with the many enemies that surrounded it, and used their facilities. Beer and olives; bill and toilet; supermarket and a bag of mini doughnuts; shiny green apple; lunch in the half sun;

overcast to a point; waiting on the warm grass; bus to Santander; twenty-five minutes wait and then another bus; and that was the quiet end to Cantabria.

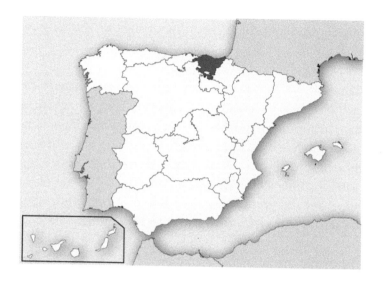

Euskadi

Bilbao (Bilbo) – San Sebastián (Donostia) – Vitoria (Gasteiz)

Entry into the Basque Country couldn't have been more obvious. A road sign with the words 'Cantabria: Have a good trip!' flashed and was followed by one with the word 'Euskadi', meaning 'Basque Homeland'. From then on in all the signs had funny, foreign names on them. Speaking ironically of course.

The Basque language is spoken by the people of the País Vasco, the Pays basque français, and Navarra. It is a hard, strange language full of consonant sounds – '*ek*', '*iak*', '*zki*', '*zu*', '*tx*', '*tz*' – that doesn't lend itself to playing well on the ears of soft Englishmen. Basque is considered a 'language isolate', that is to say one with no discernible relationship with any other language. Speaking evolutionarily, it

285

seems to share no common ancestor with any other extant tongue. Experts have been trying for years to match it up with something. It has been likened to Aquitanian; an ancient language spoke in Aquitaine in the south of France. Some suggest this as a precursor to Basque.

Other hypotheses have included: Iberian, an ancient peninsula language; Northeast Caucasian languages, like Chechen; and the Vasconic substratum hypothesis, which states that Basque is merely the last survivor of a larger linguistic family that once extended throughout Europe and for this reason odd words are similar to those used in other Indo-European languages. Whatever the truth, and I hope one day we found out, it is a lot more exhilarating to see and hear all over the place than it was to see and hear Catalan.

Then, bursting through the romance of the new language, came power plants stitched into gorgeous green landscapes of rising, cloudy hills and flat estuaries with little humming boats.

From the *termibus* station I caught the Bilbao metro to the *casco viejo*. As with the Madrid metro the trains ran on the left. This was probably, in Bilbao's case, due to the architect being a Brit, Norman Foster. The metro itself was a bit glum and downbeat – lots of modern concrete and grey-colours. It was a far cry from the brightness and colour shocks to be found in Madrid and Barcelona. A wild mix of people was travelling on it with me. Gorgeous, amply bosomed model-types sat paces away from biological failures that stank and distracted the noses of other passengers. It was stark.

The *casco viejo* in Bilbao was the most unnecessarily disorientating one I had visited. Unnecessary because it wasn't very large, nor did it have an excessively twisted web of streets. Somehow – and judging from the quantity of map-squinters, I wasn't alone – it had fostered for itself the singular capacity to bamboozle the visitor. I reckoned that the reason was that the small, busily surrounded cathedral couldn't be used as a focal point. I just couldn't seem to marry up the map to which way the building was facing so it was initially impossible to know where I was.

Overcoming my '*síndromo bilbaíno*' I bumped, by chance, into my road, the ironically named 'Lottery Street'. A bouncy and ebullient woman showed me around the very acceptable *pensión* and its room with a double bed.
'25 euros.'
'Absolutely perfect.'
I could never truly relax until I knew that there was a bed for the night and that my bag was sat somewhere, safe, and not on my back. This had time and time again formed part of the arrival procedure at every Spanish town or city on my journey. And from my experience in Santander it was clear how negative the effects could be on my judgement if I were to have problems fulfilling my criteria. With a map, a key and a still slightly chubby wallet, I ventured into the city.

I didn't want to 'do' Bilbao in the remaining few hours of the day so instead I just decided to try and get to grips with that devilish and fiddly *casco viejo*. I never managed to. I sat inside a little tapas bar called Soiz for it was cool and overcast enough not to crave the outside. *Pintxos*, the Basque spelling of *pinchos*, were present and abundant. It is a style of tapas principally eaten in the north-eastern communities. Essentially they are fancy concoctions on a piece of bread and País Vasco is famed for having the best. They sit, beaming at the visitor tastily from the counters. I ordered a drink and was handed a plate.
'Take what you want!' smiled the men behind the counter.
Croquetas of little squids in their own ink; ham and mushroom; and meat wrapped in aubergine coated with a tomato sauce didn't last long on my plate.

Around 10 o'clock the *pintxo* culture was in full swing. The signs were lit and the wooden doorframes gleamed and were loud and open. Every bar was seemingly full and many had spilt out onto the streets. Groups of friends sat on the curbs or around upturned barrels, laughing and smoking and eating and drinking. Children were hiccup-laughing as dogs scurried around after balls and parents watched with comfortable smiles. No cares. No worries.

*   *   *   *

I awoke naturally at 8:40 and about twenty minutes later was making my way along the Nervión river promenade, round to the star of the show, Bilbao's gleaming celebrity, and the financial saviour of the community, the Guggenheim Museum. It is a remarkable thing; for what it did, for what it is, and for what it has inside it. The walk was pleasant enough, even though the grey sky had robbed the world of its colour, but there was nothing much to note – apart from the Bilbao city hall – until the museum came into view.

It both commanded the attention of the viewer and trumped all surrounding architecture. Looked at entirely from the side-on, it appeared like some post-modernist representation of a shark. It was all waving titanium panels bent into shining sheets. It must shimmer in the sun. It was both shiny and matt – due, in part, to some brickwork. Different weather conditions affected how it looked. It was really the first work of art I saw at the museum – designed by Frank Gehry in 1997 and built as a do or die regeneration scheme for the city.

Approaching the entrance I passed Jeff Koons' 'Puppy' – a giant dog sculpture created with flowers – that was originally a temporary exhibit but proved so popular with the locals that the museum kept it. I was there at around 9:50 and joined the small queue waiting for the next ten minutes to go in. Not many people had decided to show up this early and I imagine that the high Spanish summer is more likely to draw the throngs to the beaches rather than to the North. My insides jumped up and down when my gaze fell upon a sign hanging above the entrance. One of the guest exhibitions was one I had wanted to see in London that year but couldn't for the obvious reason of me living in Spain. It was the solo exhibition of the British artist Anish Kapoor.

At 10 o'clock prompt the doors opened, I bought my thirteen-euro ticket and instantly took a glass lift up to the second floor and had Anish's exhibit more or less to myself. Three hours passed there exploring the various offerings: Robert Rauschenberg's 'Gluts' prompting a little girl's comment 'but it's just bent metal'; Rousseau's cutesy paintings; Richard Serra's enormous 'The Matter of Time' installation; some bullshit expressionism; and some modern art including Andy Warhol's 'One Hundred Marilyns'. It was spacious inside, airy, and, after the final photo of the inside building, which was nearly prevented by a security lady, I left.
'No photos inside please sir.'
'Thirteen euros to enter? Internal architecture? I'll take whatever photos I damn well want!' I didn't say.

I continued round along the river, past an eerily quiet, and mostly shut, modern shopping centre and through a charming park offering what all parks should offer: green grass, trees, benches, a pond, fountains, ducks and pigeons. The colours were desaturated and the sky was low and steel grey. Then there was the main street, Diego Lopez, where I was struck by how quiet it was even though it was Sunday afternoon. A great long street that cleaved through the city all the way back to the *casco viejo*, it was wide with large vacant pavements and lined with expensive-looking flats and offices. Sapped to dourness by the lack of sun.

Having completed a funicular train ride up a hill, which offered a broad view of Bilbao – terracotta colours and flats surrounded by big green hills – I was back in familiar territory. After a long, long meander around the old quarter I made my way to the subtle and colonnaded plaza nueva. There were similarities between the old part there and the one in Pamplona. They were both good-looking but with an undercurrent of griminess that you get from a place that is truly lived in. Only once did it verge into unpleasantness when a drunk man urinated into a bin. At least it was in a bin... I got the impression that the Bilbao government was focussing less tourist attention on plugging the *casco viejo* and more on the museum. In a way I quite liked it like that. Sometimes it was good to see a peeling wall and locals calling to each other from balconies.

I chose a bar according to the parameters I had set myself each time I wanted to eat. A place that looked good, and with not too many people inside that I would look like some 'Billy no mates' and not too few that I would feel uncomfortably obvious. And, if possible, with a table or place to write. I needed my leather-bound, paper-filled friend out on show even at this stage of my trip. I think it reassured people that I was supposed to be alone and not just some well-groomed drifter looking for Spain at the bottom of a glass. *Pintxos*. Basque specials: cod and pepper. The former was smoked and topped with an oily, vegetable garnish, while the latter was stuffed with meat and dribbled over with mayonnaise. They were washed down with something else typical of the region – *txacoli* (pronounced 'chakoli'), a crispy, slightly sparkling, very dry and fragrant white wine with the clever attribute of being able to hug lovingly to the flavour of any *pintxo* placed in the mouth.

With my buccal cavity rejoicing and my taste buds flashing like excited fairy lights, I took a final stroll down to the Guggenheim, sitting on the opposite side of the river watching the museum as the crowds thinned and the day ended. In different stages the lights of Bilbao came on but never, not even when night had fully laid its dark claim over the sky, did any light appear on the Guggenheim. To this day it strikes me as odd, a missed opportunity. I like how cities' night-time personalities differ from those of the day. Every city, town, village and hamlet; every road and alleyway, and every cathedral and shopping centre changes. All civilization is schizophrenic.

The streetlamps cast shimmering oblongs of light onto the river and fish jumped to catch flies as hints of wind rustled through the hairs on my arms. Bilbao evoked London in many respects. Modern and progressive but with intact history, cut through its belly by a smartly promenaded river and with a palpable air of hustle and bustle but with the required areas of 'social' and 'residential'. I didn't know if Bilbao had enough to make me want to spend a considerable amount of time there, but it was certainly a very positive introduction to the Basque Country. The exciting, but at times unattractive, mix of industry and history and countryside.

*   *   *   *

Very early the next morning I took a quick bus to San Sebastián and was up and around the provincial capital by quarter past nine. The journey had been uneventful and the region once again proved to continue its trend of sprinkling mostly ugly-looking towns onto a green cake of handsome countryside. Low pulled-cotton clouds were sliding over the hills making the land appear aflame, some white blaze. Green gorges full of destitute buildings confused beauty and beastly and meant that I couldn't work out if I liked what I was seeing. Another sign: 'Welcome to Donostia', San Sebastián's Basque name. Donostia sounded noble and mysterious and I felt a pang of pity for Bilbao whose Basque name is Bilbo. If only the *vascos* knew that their largest city and industrial powerhouse was actually a furry-footed, literary midget hero.

It was a straight line from the surprisingly small bus station (I would say 'stop') into the centre. The weather was overcast and spitting with rain. Grey again. It was good searching-for-a-hostel-with-a-heavy-rucksack-pulling-apart-my-back weather. I found the hostel recommended by the Rough Guide. *'Completo'* read a little sign on

291

the downstairs door. That wasn't the *parte vieja*, it was a smart area of flats surrounding the slender and pretty, but not overt, cathedral whose main spire-side faced out the back end so, when looked at from the required angle, appeared not like a cathedral but just one spike growing out of the ground. I took the road all the way from the spire-face into the old town past the city hall on which a white a blue flag fluttered next to a banner that read: *'No to ETA. Human rights and living together in peace'.*

People were having breakfast and some shops were starting to show their innards but it was still quite sleepy feeling. An hour was spent in the fine spray walking around aimlessly trying to find somewhere to stay. Most had the same 'full' sign.

Buzzer sound.

'Si?'

'Hullo, do you have any free rooms?'

'How many people?'

'Just the one person.'

'No.'

Buzzer sound.

'Hola?'

'Hullo, any free rooms?'

'Yes, come up;' door opens.

'Oh, you are one person?'

'Yes.'

'We only have one double room, and that's 65 euros.'

Exasperated sigh.

'Sorry,' she said.

'Do you have a map?

'Yes, of course. Really sorry.'

'Don't worry.'

Buzzer sound.

'Hi, do you have any free rooms for one person?'

'Let me see…yes we do!' door opens. Jolly woman lets me in. She gestures at a crummy room.

'How much is it?'
'45 euros.'
Desperate wheeze.
'I might have to go and check my bank.'
She guffaws.
'You see I am at the end of a trip and don't have much money left.'
'You should have come here at the start! It's August. A busy month!
You'll find that for a single room that's the going rate.'
'Right, I'm going to see if I have enough.'
'Have enough!' She snorted energetically with a big smile.
I couldn't just say 'no', that's too much for an Englishman
'Goodbye'. Curse you manners!
Buzzer sound.
'Hullo. Free rooms, one person?'
'Yes,' door opens.
'How much?'
'Well…35 euros.'
'Perfect!'

The *parte vieja* was all identical golden Labrador coloured streets —
decked out with *pensiones* and tapas bars. In a little plaza I had some
much-needed breakfast with the locals: coffee and two small
omelette sandwiches, fresh and squidgy. I loved to watch locals: two
middle-aged women, with styled hair and covered with the eager
paws of two naughty dogs, knocked back espressos at the bar; an
old lady slowly sipped a *café con leche* and watched the world flicker
into life out of the window; a well-fed and slightly rosy man in a
prim shirt read a morning paper with a glass of red wine. No
tourists. Not yet. Just me. It was a great feeling having so many
hours to play with.

The winds of providence carried me back to the cathedral and
through the door to find a sedate mass taking place. There was
always a mass taking place. A small woman was on her knees by a
box confessing her sins to an invisible priest in a gloomy side wing.

'I killed my husband with a ham.'

'God forgives you.'

The door opened again as a couple more people shuffled in.

She stood there with a gobsmacked smile splashed across her face and my heart leapt up to lodge itself in my throat as the bottom fell out of my stomach. She prowled towards me with a face of incredulity. I was still knocked for six. Wrapping herself around my neck she squeezed.

'Oh my God!'

I pulled away.

'Outside,' I said.

Outside we looked at each other again.

'Is it you?' I joked and we hugged again. Her name was Carina and as coincidences go she had just blown whatever may have previously been at number one way out of the park.

One night in Madrid, my friend Euan – who the reader will remember – was invited to try out DJing at the party of a friend in a small underground club/bar in one of the funky areas of the capital. I was wearing my brand new t-shirt at the time and a cardigan, doing the best I could to look cool; to look like someone a girl would like to be looked at with. I am not going to lie, I hung around the DJ area with Euan, feigning interest in the music with the hope that people would ogle. And they did, to a certain degree. There was a girl there who I was hoping would notice me, a slender, chestnut brown haired girl with a beautiful face and a comfortable smile.

My only tactic up until that point had been my flawed, long-winded and childish technique of waiting to 'accidentally' bump into a girl. This would be the spark for conversation and it worked. As soon as the match was lit I could operate better. I met Carina a couple of times after that night and she occasionally quipped that I was too young for her. Nothing ever led anywhere. I found out on a later rendezvous that she didn't have a boyfriend but was 'sort of going out with this American guy'. That was the nail in the coffin in terms

of technicalities of course. Eventually the fire inside me calmed down and we met a couple more times. I wanted to grab her and hold her but knew it was futile. Sharing a final coffee together a few days before my trip, we didn't quite say goodbye.
'Oh I'll see you one of those days before you leave finally'.

In my heart I knew I wouldn't, which is why her appearance at the very end of my trip in the beautiful San Sebastián caused waves of emotion from a long forgotten crush to break over the rocks inside me. She had only entered the building to collect her dad who was looking around inside. He then came out. A smiley man with a little moustache. We shook hands and I agreed to meet them later. She hugged me again and planted a kiss on my cheek. I probably blushed after. We parted and I walked off with sunbeams shining out of my face.

Out of the noble and expensive streets came the promenade that sidled alongside the main city beach, the Playa de la Concha – 'shell beach'. The rain had given the sand a colour not dissimilar to maple syrup. It looked dark and sticky, like a paste. The beach followed well-to-do seafront hotels and apartments round the inside of a bay. On the beach itself some activity mornings were being held for kids; beach football and table tennis, children shivering in a little swimming pool, sand castle making. Further along a row of closed twirled-up blue and white beach umbrellas stood like giant lollipops while out in the water windsurfers and canoeists streamed out past scattered private boats. Despite the grey sky the water was still blue. To me it felt, due to the comparatively near closure of the bay, more like an open lake or lagoon than sea. On the other side of the beach, buried past indoor tennis courts and amongst some attractive houses, was the unassuming entrance to a little funicular railway.

In my carriage was an irritating couple (I think grandparents) and a child. They were sweet, maybe too sweet, but they kept singing songs, which just seemed to make the little girl cry more. I couldn't work out the language and instead looked out of the window to watch the tracks lengthen from out of the back window. At the top of Monte Igueldo was an inviting view over the whole of San Sebastián. Also on the top was a tacky fairground-like theme park, which didn't seem to fit in with a place so near the classy city down below. *'El río misterioso'* for €1.80 – a little canal that had little boats that went on a little trip round a little bend into a little cave and lasted two little minutes. I didn't partake in its shot glass of fun. By *not* doing it I guess that made it all the more mysterious. So in a way it was better that I abstained, for the sake of the river's *raison d'être* – something that was definitely important to me from the moment I reached the summit.

The walk down offered personal views along País Vasco's wild, wind-lashed coastline to phantasmal, dark hills off in the west. Plants and trees and rainbows of flowers glittered with drops of rainwater that were fighting off the laws of gravity. A spider's web, grey and thread-like, had caught liquid pearls, while snails and slugs were shining across wet rocks. The air smelt of nothing.

At sea level I sat on a bench and watched the beach activate. People began populating the cafés and the first brave swimmers took to the water. It was muggy even though I *had* just walked for half an hour down a hill. Some Camino de Santiago pilgrims trotted past. They were fresh-faced and strolling comfortably. They had a long way ahead of them – about 730km in fact. It was one of those afternoons that were clouded over but still very bright. My phone buzzed. It was a text from Carina that she and her dad were done and ready to eat.

Meeting by the Basílica de Santa María, Carina took us to a place she had been to already on a previous visit to the city. Bar Aralar was a typical *pintxos* restaurant: orangey, yellow lights, wooden tables, many people and a counter about to break under the weight of so much food. A *pintxos* bar was a place you could go wild. As long as it fitted on a skewer or a piece of bread it was fair game. In Aralar I treated myself to a pickle and tuna skewer and a ham and tomato mayonnaise mixture on bread. The plate filled, I handed it back to the barman who tallied up the prices. At the same time the drinks were ordered. Then we paid. It was a fun and quick, if a little hectic, way of ordering food and the people working there invited the customers to look at everything on offer and ask questions. The most common being 'Um…excuse me, what is that?'

Carina's dad, Pedro, turned out to be one of the jolliest and easy to like people I had ever met. He was constantly laughing and cracking jokes in the best English he could muster. Outside Aralar Carina asked him to take a photo of us together. He backed up, backed up, crouched down, and then fell over backwards nearly knocking over a small child. He got up sheepishly, brushing himself off. All of us were laughing.
'And this is only my first beer!' he shouted, whisking his finger up into the air.
'Your second, pa!'
'Oh yes, I had one on the hill!' he snorted.

Searching for another place to try we entered the first bar that had life, but not too much, and ordered more exciting *pintxos*: seafood *croquetas*, stuffed peppers, *bacalao al ajoarriero* – a local speciality of salted cod with a garlicky, tomatoey vegetable mix. There were groans of pleasure as the squidgy snacks succumbed to our jaws. I regaled them with the story of when I almost fell off a mountain in Asturias. Pedro was laughing all the way through it.
'Are you understanding, papa?'
'Yes, he uses his hands a lot. If I don't know the words I can *see* what's happening!'
After suffering a few Luke Skywalker jokes we strolled together down the beach, toying with the surf and getting sand in our shoes. I kept asking when they needed to go, how much time did they have left.

'Haha, are you sick of us already?' she quipped.

So much the opposite, I thought to myself.

We shared a final coffee out of the rain in a little café that was busy and noisy, full of babies screaming and throwing their toys onto the floor near their parents. At the bus stop I felt like something was opening me up and throwing butterflies inside. This may well be the last time, I thought. Neither of us said it. Just like back in Madrid. The bus came. Her dad shook my hand heartily and, with a laugh, said 'Remember Luke, I'm *not* your father'. Carina gripped me and peppered my cheeks with hard kisses, each one a cannon exploding fields of violet-filled balloons that hovered inside me. On the bus. Hand on glass. Goodbye.

Recovering from my melodrama, at around 9 o'clock, I made my way to the northern tip of the city for no other reason than because I hadn't been there yet. Another sea-facing promenade. This time, and without the need to perform a *galego* run, a sunset had begun to rip apart the sky. The ball itself, still quite high, was hidden behind some tattered clouds but hurled mighty and dense arms of light down to the sea forming dazzling pools of radiance. As the orb started to lower, the orange and yellow intensified. The torn flesh of the clouds had been struck with galactic napalm. Star-burn. The rays vanished. Blood-red, the sun finally showed his beautiful face. He perched in a slender space between a silhouetted cloud line and the choppy ink of the sea. Flexing the last light of his flaming muscles as the final batch of trawlers came in, he flooded the horizon with scarlet and then dived into the depths. The temperature soon followed him. I left with the lights of the city igniting the air.

*   *   *   *

The last day started off, and sporadically continued to be, wet. I arrived at the station soaked to the bone with my curling hair dripping and got on my expensive ALSA Supra+ bus to Vitoria. I wanted to go to my last destination as early as I could so that I would be able to return to Madrid the same day and at an agreeable time. Carina had told me that, as I was alone and not planning on having lunch there, I would only need a couple of hours to look around the centre. A few mountain tunnels later and the blanket of green and height that was 'the North' was gone. A few foothills lingered and that classic Spanish colour – yellow – ferried my eyes to Vitoria. The change appeared quickly and in a low-key manner in tune with the personality of the city.

I was sure that the weather – first overcast and then rain – affected the feel of the place, but still it was quiet and there seemed to be no tourists. The *casco viejo* was compact and wrapped itself around a small hill. An amusing and helpful aspect about Vitoria's old zone was that if you were aged, an invalid, or it was raining or you were just lazy, there was, shooting up on either side, a snazzy moving walkway split into various stages leading all the way to the top. It wasn't a particularly strenuous climb but I opted for the travelator. It was something that stood out amid the otherwise standard and at times dishevelled area.

I couldn't be bothered with a detailed inspection of the map as long as I more or less knew where I was. By choice of somewhere that looked attractive, I descended again past a church, half-submerged in the ground, and down towards the Plaza de la Virgen Blanca, which housed the stylish and colonnaded Plaza de España. Up above on a path overlooking the plaza was a statue of a man, a typical man of Vitoria. He was called *Celedón* – the 'spirit of the city' and was supposed to represent the ideal of how the Basque should be. Minutes later I saw him in human form sat on a bench, hands in his lap and just watching the world go by. I suppose it was due to their proximity to France but a lot of old Basque men sported berets, usually with variable combinations of dark wool cardigans and a light blue shirt. There were pale colours all around, washed out by the lack of sun, but it was handsome.

Rough Guide quote: 'the heart of the old town is the venerable Catedral de Santa María'. To be honest *that* cathedral was a waste of time. It was a shabby box covered in scaffolding. What did surprise me was that the book failed to mention the city's other, enormous, Catedral de María Inmaculada, a twentieth century catholic church that was never finished. An enormous neo-Gothic hanger. Inside was something unexpected. It was almost empty and all but silent. No visitors. It was the first big cathedral I had been in that felt like it was mine. Also the nave itself was surprising. It must have been one of the highest vaulted ceilings of any cathedral I had been in, except perhaps the one in Liverpool. Awesomely spacious and hollow. Outside small gardens sat awaiting the sun, an old lady beat the dust out of a blanket, and a modern tram buzzed along some tracks.

Another feature in Vitoria, that spiked an interest both in my camera and me, were the many decorated walls. Sometimes known as '*La Ciudad Pintada*' – The Painted City – Vitoria has entertained, for the last three decades or so, a muralism that is now a part of the city's DNA. It all began in 1982 when the City Hall promoted a competition in order to improve the image of an old central school called La Florida. The winners, José Antonio Martínez Arbulo and Antonio Cipres, won 70,000 pesetas, which is about 420 euros. 500 probably would have been today's rounded-up offering. Since then various local artists and many anonymous art creators have been rejuvenating the urban landscape in the city. This artistic reclamation has also been aided, or added to, by graffiti artists, whose edgier and more outspoken art sits, sometimes side-by-side, with lush and more technical works. Far from trying to put it down, this public initiative has been encouraged. The result is an interesting modern twist on an old area. Grey walls suddenly give way to a side of a building coated in images and paint; representations of instruments and creativity, food and agriculture, or clothing and fashion; and all using the brightest, most vibrant colours.

Vitoria felt like the real Basque Country, not the holiday Basque Country. There were a few more regional flags here and there, as well as more pro-autonomy graffiti and posters. I doubted there was a heavy tourist industry there making sure everything was spic and span for the foreigners. What was noted was the distinct, and very different, characters of the two coastal giants and the inland capital. Bilbao was edgy and modern; San Sebastián was leisurely and cultural, while Vitoria felt quiet and stately.

What I never got in Vitoria, or in the other two cities, was a feeling of threat or danger. Since 1968 ETA has been blamed for over 820 murders, the majority as a result of explosives or direct killings. They usually carry out their attacks in either the northern regions of Navarre and the Basque country, or hit populous areas, notably Madrid, Barcelona, and coastal tourist resorts. Vitoria may not have suffered the worst but it had in no way avoided attack. Indeed a few days after my visit a string of attacks spread through the region. It started on the 7th of August in Ondarroa and on the 17th came to Vitoria with a spree of rubbish container fires. Despite all this, and despite the comments sprayed on some walls, it felt safe.

Carina's estimations were right and after a couple of hours, and in the pouring rain, I found myself back at the bus station. Realistically I wasn't going to get much more out of Vitoria whilst on my own. Two idiots, a queue of more than thirty people, a missed bus, a two-hour wait, and a new ticket later and I was leaving the País Vasco and leaving my last region. It was a soggy and subdued end to a diverse and busy trip.

However, Spain had a final treat in store for me in the lands between Vitoria and Madrid. There was a rest stop in Burgos, which granted enough time to run out into the sun, hurry to its *casco antiguo* and behold the other great cathedral of Spain – León's sister. A massive, spiky, spirey, gothic wonderland, all light grey stone, Burgos Cathedral was similar to the one at León but had squatter haunches. Happy as a collector who had got that stamp for his set, I hurried back to the bus purring in the station and trudged back once again through the Castilian plains to the capital.

Capital Conclusions...

The trip was over and so was my time in the country. I spent one evening with my friends in our local pub – the ever-friendly La Solera – and bid farewell to Diego and Flo.

'We will need one less barrel of cider each week,' he laughed as he shook my hand.

'See you when you come back!' added Flo kissing me on both cheeks.

I hugged and kissed all my friends and tried not to be too emotional. But the potent La Solera beer and the heat made everything a little Hollywood.

A last lazy and sultry evening was spent with Elena and Carlos in the small, hot flat, with a dinner of mussels, fried pork steaks and *gazpacho*. It was that perennial limbo moment when no one really wanted to dwell on the fact that one party was leaving. Jettisoning out of a life.

'I have a feeling you will be back. Maybe sooner than you think,' she said with a sad, but hopeful, smile.

Flying home I glued my face to the window, squinting in the brightness, wanting to see my beloved Spain for as long as possible. There was the country, a patchwork blanket, in all its expansive grandeur. I kept looking until the last fronds of the coast disappeared behind the wing and all that was left was ocean. With a tender heart and a smile smoggied by both happiness and melancholy, I left Spain, a country that had both opened itself up more than I could have imagined but still retained a beguiling level of mystery.

Spain is a land full of contradictions. It is both a frighteningly easy place to visit but also sometimes near impossible to journey through. The people are at once absurdly giving and helpful but also blunt and a little intolerant, pensive and educated one minute but loud and verbose the next. The country has one of the richest cultures of any nation – artists, musicians, writers, directors – yet modern music and television in Spain remain some of the most unbearable things around that human beings can experience. They are a nation of food lovers and for a couple of years it was even home to the number one restaurant in the world 'El Bulli'. They talk about food in the way British talk about the weather. At the same time however they are fairly dismissive of the food of other cultures and are not particularly concerned with broadening their culinary horizons. They have impassioned discussions about tortillas, like we do with rain. We all have our Talking Points.

'Hi, my name's Ramón.'

'Hey. I'm Sofia.'

'Nice to meet you Sofia.'

'Nice to meet you too Ramón.'

The two looked deeply into each other's eyes. Sofia blushed and looked away with a slight giggle, lightly flicking a curl that bobbed just behind her ear. Ramon, smiling, looked to his feet. They caught glances.

'So Sofia...' Ramon, serious, penetrated her with his gaze

'Sí Ramon?'

He inhaled and his heart trembled. He exhaled heavily and looked at her.

'Tortilla. With or without onions?'

'With.'

'With?'

'With.'

He kissed her.

It is also a very openly sexual nation, thanks in part to the 'La Movida'; a counterculture movement, well, hedonistic explosion, during the late 1970s and early 1980s, after Franco had popped his clogs. It was a period characterized by a challenging and transgression of the taboos that had so long been in place and also a newfound freedom of expression. As a result television channels nowadays will show bare breasts at any hour of the day, fairly explicit sexual activity is shown as early as 6 o'clock and I even once saw full nudity, in the form of a striptease, on a standard entertainment chat show. The young people, if blessed with good looks, go above and beyond to try and advertise that fact.

Having said that, the Catholic roots of the country, and the cultural zeitgeist having shifted towards stigmatisation, have instilled in the nation a mindset in young people that is quite opposite to that in the UK. From a 2006 UNICEF league table of 'Teenage births in rich nations', Spain scored 'very well' with only 7.9 of every 1000 women between the ages of 15 and 19 getting pregnant. In the United Kingdom, and this was four years ago mind, it was 30.8 of every

1000. If the media coverage and various news reports are to be believed, which on the whole I think in this case they should be, the problem has worsened in my home country. I never saw anything relating to teenage pregnancies on Spanish television. This fact, coupled with the 'living at home' aspect, has led to a nation oddly famous – amongst the knowledgeable – for *not* having sex. But these are statistics. Benjamin Disraeli once said that there were three types of lies: 'Lies, damned lies, and statistics'. Whereas this is fairly extreme, I think it's true that they often don't reflect day-to-day truths.

What else did I learn? As well as contradictions I found that Spain has so little in common with the image in everyone's head – mostly fostered by the tourism agencies of the world. Sure there's sangria, sun, beaches, bulls, paella and flamenco, but, to be honest, that's mostly either Andalucía or the country's east coast. The Spain I saw was only three fifteenths that. The divides and differences that permeate the country alter the stereotype to countertype. The north/south divides that split the region into three horizontal strips; Andalucía, the central *meseta* and the northern coastal regions are a showcase for how geography can alter a culture; the coastal towns with their rampant tourism and frightening over-development are jarring reminders of the wants of man when compared with the countless forgotten and unknown towns and villages further inland; whereas the financial divides between the wealth of Madrid, Catalonia and País Vasco and the financial struggles of Andalucía and Extremadura show how those regions drenched in 'Spanish' history are still just victims of circumstance.

Everything changes: the flags change, the food changes, the accents vary, the countryside morphs, the climate fluctuates greatly, the architecture adapts to its history and the people distort in and out of what I understood to be Spanish. Having said this, '*hola*' is still '*hola*' wherever you go. It just may sound a little different or be met with a varying degree of warmth. If there *were* constants that could lend themselves to forming a country stereotype they would be, in my eyes, the following.

Their cities tend to have a concentric architectural planning, with a central historic quarter – usually beautifully preserved – and with the more modern buildings fanning out from there. They seem to care about where they live; a trait I wish had been present in the genetics of the planners of the great British towns and cities. My thoughts turn to the Hulls and Sloughs of home. Places in Spain are often just pleasant. To look at, to walk around in, and to photograph. If you type Segovia into the Internet you will see what I mean.

The people, wherever you go, have a natural warmth, openness and intelligence. It's a broad generalisation based on experience in the same vein as saying that British people, in the general scheme of things, are polite, reserved publicly and have a good sense of humour. While with Spanish people I was also oddly reminded of the Irish on witnessing how even the most brusque *chulo* knew his country's history better than I knew my own. Not only are we English somewhat demonised for being culturally and linguistically unaware, but also, it seems, we are historically unaware too.

The people, and the culture, have an intense passion for food and regional products. Their pride is infectious. Every Spanish person waxes lyrical about 'Oh, in my area, we have [like everyone says] the best cheese/ham/wine' and so on. Britain has pockets of regionality but it's simply not in the same league and I bet no one could list the regional delicacy of Suffolk or describe what the flag or coat of arms of Lincolnshire looks like. Similarly, I bet every Spanish person, *every* Spanish person, will know at least one regional product and will know what their flag looks like.

As a nation I noticed that, in comparison with the British, there is a fundamental lack of moaning and bitchiness. Of course it exists, but it isn't, like it is back home, the same kind of hobby. I rarely caught

Spanish people badmouthing somebody else. And in the year living with Elena, rarely heard anything worse than 'God, sometimes so and so gets on my nerves' or 'He's a bit weird'. It never turned into hour long slagging off sessions like in Britain. I found it refreshing. And I only noticed the difference because I bitched a lot with my English friends, and not with my Spanish ones.

They aren't a particularly fatalistic people. They have more in common with the optimistic fatalism of the Russians than the 'Oh, typical. Here we bloody go again. It never works; God!' moaning fatalism of the Brits. They seem, problems aside, to be a genuinely happy people who genuinely love being Spanish and living in Spain. They are proud and are by and large content with their lot. Flying a Union Jack or St. George's Cross in England may, to British eyes, be seen as something approaching nationalism, but in Spain pride is, on the whole, healthy and well-meaning.

Ultimately my love for the country started off as merely a school-era exercise in receiving acceptable grades in a subject I was good at. It then morphed into a holidaying admirer of their simple pleasures – good food and pretty cities, was consolidated by my time living in the culture and made absolute by my trip to the regions. As with every country, it is unique. Uniqueness aside, however, its list of positives is far longer than some other countries I have been to. Spain offers so much, for the casual tourist, the intrepid traveller and the enthusiastic inhabitant.

As the view from the plane window was consumed by blue – all sky and sea – I started to wonder if I had made the right decision in leaving. Would Russia be as forthcoming? And would I regret departing from a life so near to perfection? I got prematurely nostalgic 36,000ft in the air and thought about ordering a bottle of wine. Thanks to the air companies' outrageous pricing I didn't. My eyes were still stuck to the plastic window, flitting about in thought.

No. No regrets. I thanked Spain for its proximity to the UK and its ease of entry and smiled to myself.

It wasn't going anywhere and I had a whole life to try and get back.

Thanks

In Castilla y León: Peñafiel – thank you to Sergio for giving me my first taste of the Spanish wine industry and conversing so freely with me. Valladolid – thank you to José who saved my trip before it had begun.

In La Rioja: Logroño – thank you to Fran and your cats for giving me a place to rest my head and for welcoming to your region. Also thanks to Lara and Javier for joining us and fleshing out the tapas evening with your presence. Haro – an impossible thank you to María José López and her family members that run the Lopez de Heredia bodega for the lunch they treated me to and the ensuing hours of life-affirming conversation.

In Cataluña: Barcelona – massive thanks to my friends Caroline and Ben who gave me a flat and put up with me and my jokes for a few nights. Also, thank you to Kim, Debbie and Jesus who formed the Sitges group and provided much laughter.

In the Comunidad Valenciana: Valencia – my heartfelt thanks go out to my old friends, Imogen and Malou, who were kind enough, though they ethically had no choice, to house me. Denia – gratitude to Patricia and Enrique for letting me stay in their palatial house for a night and for showing me around the town and the mountain. Alicante – thanks to Rodrigo and the boys for giving me not only a place to sleep, but an unforgettable look into the Valencian bachelor lifestyle!

In Navarra: Pamplona – really grateful to Elena and Itziar, two girls that decided to take a poor, lonely, Englishman under their wings. Thanks to you and your Pamplonan friends for adding extra zing to my San Fermín experience.

In La Mancha: A huge thank you to Alfonso and Alfredo for driving me around the region to whatever took my fancy and for your endless knowledge. I hope all the money you're investing in the *bodega* pays off. Also, extra thanks to Alfonso and his family for allowing me to eat and talk with them like I was an extra cousin.

Thanks

In Extremadura: Hard for me to say thank you enough to my wonderful housemate Elena, her family and her boyfriend Carlos, who not only gave me somewhere to stay but also fed me and toured me round the region.

In Asturias: Oviedo – my gratitude to Fran, the pensive couchsurfer, who put up with me for three days, sharing both maps and anecdotes.

In Cantabria: Santander – thanks to Manuel and Belén who, even after my organisational errors, were so kind and giving in my brief time with them.

In País Vasco: San Sebastián – thank you to Carina and her father Pedro, for adding the cherry on top and really ending my trip in the nicest and most surprising way.

Extra thanks go out to Katrina Nelson, an old friend from my Alicante days, without whom this labour of love wouldn't have the luxurious and beautiful artwork it does. Thank you for my covers!

And lastly, thank you to my parents for their dedication, help and constant re-reading. The best kind of editor is a parental one!

Detours

What follows is a more or less unedited selection of the smaller trips I made during my time living and working in Madrid. They are extracted from my blog: http://lukemadrid.blogspot.com/.
Photos of the Sun Struck Upwards trip can be found here: https://profiles.google.com/115051411853999562927/photos

Day Trips:
Aranjuez (Comunidad de Madrid)
This place is green. I mean seriously green. If you took the colour green and then added another pot of green to it, upped the fluorescence and set brilliance to 1000, you'd get Aranjuez. It's only a short hour-long train journey south, but it couldn't look and feel much more different to Madrid if it tried. Sure, there are parks and trees in the capital...but they're not as green.

We (Anna and I) pulled into the station, disembarked and, mapless, started walking. The area around the station was – as the area is around almost any station in the world – a bit bleak and grimy. These were not the luxurious palaces and gardens we thought we would find. However, after a short walk, a vast creamy pink palace flickered into view through the trees. It was very casually placed. No massive signs or 'THIS WAY TO THE PALACE' boards. It just sat there, subtly majestic, ten minutes from the station. The Palacio Real was fantastically beautiful, maybe because of the contrast with the station and the way it sat adoringly amongst the gardens. It could have been more due to the fact that it was originally built by those Spanish bourbon monarchs to be a Spanish Versailles. It isn't, of course. Versailles is frankly ridiculous. Aranjuez is more quaint and shrunken. Nevertheless the building is gorgeous. Smaller, but more personable than the vast, cold Palacio Real in Madrid and un-touristy enough to feel like you are one of the few people enjoying it.

Around the place are the wonderful gardens. It felt like I was walking through England, like I had absent-mindedly tumbled into Much Ado About Nothing. There were copious fountains and benches and bushes and flowers and statues (my favourite being a naked Bacchus riding a barrel of wine). Lots of water in Aranjuez, clever irrigation and a lot of rain in winter made for a turbo-charged vegetative experience.

We had some cheap-o tapas at a franchise tapas joint, stole a glass, saw some more historic buildings and then bought an ice cream. On buying the ice cream the heavens finally opened. Why should we be allowed to remain dry all day? We scampered to safety under the archway of the palace where a few Spaniards were hiding. My umbrella took a beating – three-euro piece of crap.

When the rain finally stopped and when the little girl who was staring maniacally at Anna eating her ice cream had left with her parents, we walked back to the train station.

Nothing remarkable about the trip back, apart from a far off city on a hill that sat bathed in the sun's rays while everywhere else was cloudy and black. The golden city.

Alcalá de Henares (Comunidad de Madrid)

Another day-trip with Anna. Alcalá de Henares boasts one of the oldest universities in the world and the second oldest in Spain behind the larger one at Salamanca. We left the little modern station and wandered out into the town and its 28-degree sunny weather. Shorts weather had finally arrived [Note: it is currently making teaching almost intolerable]. We chose a direction, based on the other people leaving the train, and headed off. We had no maps. Maps aren't fun. We soon - after I expertly noted a bus with 'Universidad de Alcalá' on it going past - went along the road that led towards distant old buildings. Thinking back on it, buses can go one way *or* the other. Thank God for spires, they also help.

The main square and centre of the *casco histórico*, was like a toy town. A plaza with a bandstand and Cervantes statue in the middle, lined with trees and surrounded by low ornate buildings. Only the spires felt brave enough to try and touch the sky. The spires themselves weren't that tall, so the juxtaposition between this non-height highness and the apparently grand, small buildings made it feel like you were walking through a large miniature. Then there were storks flying heavily through the cyan blue sky and crunching down on their massive nests that clung to the old Catholic crosses like mistletoe on a tree. The roads were mostly unpopulated and we walked for over an hour around the academies and holy buildings almost alone.

We then attempted to locate a tapas bar I was tipped off about prior to coming. Around 4 o'clock the main street had burst open. Scores of restaurants down its length had spilled their guts out onto the pedestrian area that passed Cervantes' birth home. Chairs and families and friends all tucked into their lunch (except the chairs of course, they tucked into the ground). We found our place - Indalo. Why did I want to go there? Well, you get free tapas with drinks almost everywhere in Spain. Not usually in the Madrid Community does that tapas turn out to be toasted ham bagels or small hamburgers and chips. Bless you Alcalá. Fed and rosy we got an ice cream and lolled about in the remaining sun for a while before trudging back to the station.

Cercedilla (Comunidad de Madrid)

Sunday was spent in Cercedilla, a village in the north of Madrid in the hills. It was also this time when snow was a common daily sight in the beating heart of Spain. We took the C-8 *cercanías* train to Segovia and alighted at our designated stop, inhaling the frosty air. No map, no idea where to go or what to do, we headed up. Up was good. Up would take us to hills.

We walked for maybe 25 minutes. We, by the way, were me, Heather, Philomena and Matt (Anna joined us a short while later).

We perchanced upon a charming looking restaurant called Los Frutales. We entered. Log cabin-esque inside and quite clearly a family affair and labour of love.
'This'll probably be expensive.'
It was reasonable. And I had the best, biggest, most glistening and sumptuous leg of lamb I have ever had. Only 16 euros. Anna joined us at the restaurant in time to eat with us.

Full of dead animals we headed further up the hill. Eventually (having asked vague directions from the owner of the restaurant) we reached the tourist office. We were given a map and information about the different routes around the valleys and mountains. They varied from 1.5km to 15km. We chose 'El Camino de los Aguas' ('The Route of the Waters'); at 4.1 km. Starting our trek, we entered a forest. A winter wonderland, all virgin snow and ice. It started to snow slowly, lending a magical, serene air to the woods.
We climbed.

The snow came down heavier. We made snow angels, threw stones into a far away frozen reservoir, we fell over, we found abandoned buildings quilted with white, we shivered, we had wet feet, and we followed our map. About one and a half hours later we arrived back in the town. The ghostly peaks and cloud dandruff world we had just been in seemed unreal somehow. Far off. Mother Nature showing us just what she could do.
'Pretty isn't it?'
'Yes, yes it is.'
'How about if I just started snowing now, lightly, like a dream, would that be even better?'
'Possibly.'
'There you go...'
'I think I love you.'
'At least someone does...'

At 18:36 we hopped onto the last train of the day. Our feet were frozen and wetter than the sea, but at least we were cosy. We spent our trip back playing 'Guess Who' - the game where you all give each other names on a piece of paper and slap it on your forehead. I was both Hannah Montana AND William Shakespeare. And that ladies and gentlemen, is a talent.

Cuenca/Ciudad Encantada (Castilla La Mancha)

A writer called Giles Tremlett ('Ghosts of Spain') said this of a particular Spanish trait:

They like the warmth, the solidarity, the sense of belonging that groups give them. That, perhaps, is why their towns and cities pack people together, ignoring the acres of open space around them. Individuality, I discovered when my own children reached school age, can be viewed with suspicion'

Whereas I can't relate to this quote from the point of view of having children, which I don't, I think, I can find truth in it. They do have a tendency towards grouping like sardines. It's natural. It's a family-based lifestyle, like Italy. Big groups, big get-togethers, patriarchs and matriarchs and small streets. Also, on the subject of individuality, I think he may have a point. Last week, from Thursday to Sunday, we had the Easter holidays. On Thursday I had a 'me' day: watched some films, went for a long walk in the milky sun to a lake, watched quiet families herd their unsteady children around the perimeter on feet and bikes. I read my book and watched the silky water play with the light that tinkled through the lolling arms of my private tree, while parrots and sparrows showed off and sang for my attention. Here was individuality without suspicion.

On Friday we decided to make the most of the little time we had and went on a day-trip. There were five of us in total: me, Matt and his girlfriend Raquel, Euan and his girlfriend Mahal. I was a welcome fifth wheel. We took Raquel's car and drove at an alarmingly breakneck pace to Cuenca, a small city (large town really,

316

though the locals are proud of its status) some 160km east of the capital. On arrival we raced up through the town, dodging the aforementioned locals and screamed along impossibly narrow streets, lined clumsily with badly parked cars. Raquel wasn't used to this style of 45 degree uphill driving and thought the best course of action was to speed up. Matt closed his eyes, I thought we were going to violently make friends with a wall, and the wing mirror took a bashing. We parked and walked down into town, our legs a little bit more jellied than before.

It was the *viernes de Pasion*, the Friday of the Passion (of Christ), and the town was bulging and straining with the sheer number of people in it. Hundreds, maybe thousands were there. Half were tourists and locals and maybe half were participants in the city's processions. People walked through the streets, some barefoot, in differently coloured robes and cloaks, topped with a traditional (now aggressively lampooned) Klu Klux Klan style hood. They hauled large wooden icons of Christ's struggle and stamped staves to the beat of the band while locals looked down from their windows.

It was all very strange, but impressive and at times clearly quixotic. Something that made me laugh was that people were trying to walk along the pavements by the procession, like we were, but with difficulty. Logical option? Cross the road. I mean, if you have to cross the road, you have to cross the road. A road's a road and surely I can cross it. Some people tried this, but were quickly reprimanded and chased away by one of a variety of tall men in full robe/hood combination brandishing a staff and sweeping his clothing authoritatively. It was ridiculous of course. It was probably José Fernando, father of two, mechanical engineer. But today he was something else, something more. Empowered by purple.

We finally freed ourselves from the procession and its noise and its confusion and went to look around the old part of Cuenca and the famous '*casas colgadas*', hanging houses. Rickety old houses perched on cliff faces, with makeshift wooden balconies that bravely hung over nothing. A local tourist attraction. The city had a rustic, golden charm that was so reminiscent of many *pueblos* in Spain. Cuenca and Valladolid are rather sad tales though. They are considered forgotten towns. Once great, they are now places for day trippers and quick holiday seekers. Still, I found it charming and would happily return.

Our next stop? 34km away to Ciudad Encantada – 'Enchanted City'. Ciudad Encantada has the status *'Sitio Natural de Interés Nacional'*, natural site of national interest, and it deserves it. It is a 20km squared Natural Park of limestone formations formed by a 90 million year old karstic process. It is a landscape spat out of true fantasy, full of rock mushroom blooms, arches, columns and great blocks. It was in fact used in the classic film 'Conan the Barbarian' with Arnie yelling and running about with a big shiny sword.

This brings me neatly back to the quote from Tremlett. The Spanish tourists in the park seemed to travel in herds. Now, of course, in a park with arrows you tend to follow the arrows. But this was no UNESCO World Heritage Site with strict signs. You - as far as I know - were allowed to walk around wherever you liked. The Iberian flocks stayed to their paths. Sometimes small groups would venture a few metres from the route then gravitate back. Now, I don't know if this is a particularly Spanish trait but it seemed to coincide with what Giles was saying in his book.

As the fifth wheel I thought I would give the couples some privacy and go and sate my sense of adventure. I walked off and climbed to the tops of the large karstic arms. Eight metres up and alone, there was a sea of scratchy stone before me. The wind was blowing hard and brought me smells of dusty pine and sun-baked rock. I ran around for hundreds of yards above the throngs below. I jumped over deserted gulfs between the arms of stone. I regarded the moon-like surface that was once a roof over this entire park. I contemplated the tourists below in what was first solid rock, then a limestone cave and now ground. I then thought I might not actually be allowed up there. I descended in a precarious manner, rock-climber mode, camera slung round my back and all limbs in use. I later burst out of the undergrowth covered in needles and earth and confused a group of sightseers. I was back with the hordes. For a moment though, just a brief moment, I had the craggy, spiky, top of this park's world to myself.

Chinchón (Comunidad de Madrid)

The road in drifts through blood red, poppy-stained fields. I entertained the hope that the pretty girl behind me would strike up a conversation and we would get together, live with each other in a village and have curly-haired, blue-eyed, olive-skinned children. They would run around wielding their names Tarquin Baltazar Sanchez Darracott and Eva Emily Sanchez Darracott - Sanchez being the imaginary family name of my imaginary wife. We would spend lazy afternoons getting tipsy with chilled wines and olives in the sun, as we had no other worries but to remember to take the roasting lamb out of the oven before our friends arrived for the cool evening dinner. That didn't happen. Instead I got off the bus at the first stop that indicated my arrival into Chinchón and blasted away my silly thoughts. I walked in the direction of the large church that I knew, with the help of Google Images, loomed dramatically over the famous picture perfect plaza mayor. The square in question is more of a ring. This is no accident as in the summer it doubles up at the town's *plaza de toros*.

I then spent about 40 minutes wandering around the beautifully beaten streets. There are whiffs of the prettiness of Cuenca's lanes and Toledo's back streets but with more of a genuine, naturally scruffied and inhabited air about them. This day was hot and I stupidly chose a black t-shirt. The annoying science behind why dark hues are a bad choice in the sun was present, although it wasn't as potent as I thought it could have been. I started to need things: water, a place to go to the toilet and a bank so that I could recharge my phone. I was about to call it lunchtime when I spotted a castle over in the distance, on the other side of the town. I like castles me. It wasn't open, or that impressive. It was a - more or less – large, square, 15th century blob of stone and turrets. What it did do well, however, was command a good view of the bullet-wounded poppy hills that formed the outer stretch of Madrid before it flumps into La Mancha. I found a water machine and headed back to the main square. I then found an ATM - always tricky in a small place - burnt my fingers on the sun-heated metal buttons and sent the texts I needed to send.

I finally buckled to the whim of both my belly and my bladder and found the most populated outdoor café on the main square - La Taberna Conrado, helmed by a waitress as ugly as she was efficient. And my! she was efficient... I ordered a beer, some *patatas bravas* and two *croquetas*. The potatoes had one of the spiciest *bravas* sauces I had tried and were also coated with coarse salt. I don't really like all that much salt on my food but I found these little golden starch cubes strangely moreish. My nose ran and my belly filled as I relaxed, reclusive in my little pool of shade.

There is something inexplicable in the way one is able to pick out one's countrymen before they even speak. I think it's two parts physical and stylistic appearance to three parts mannerisms and body language. I thought about this as I regarded the green and white multi-tiered balcony-laden inner walls of the square. I was reminded of the hanging houses at Cuenca. I saw a prowling cat, walking like John Wayne, under the tables, well-fed and well-kept. No collar. Maybe a pet. Then I asked for the bill and an *anis de Chinchón*. This a sweeter version of anisette liqueur that you can find anywhere. The famous, harder version is Sambucca. *Anis* is a typical drink of Chinchón. In fact it is *the* product of Chinchón. In fact it is the only product for which the Madrid Community has a *denominación de origen,* giving it the same status as Rioja wine or Manchego cheese.

The smell is a heady mixture of vodka and liquorice. The taste is pleasant and delights in curling up around ice cubes.

The sky couldn't have been bluer as the hundreds of sex-mad swifts danced around the heavens trying to impress and catch and fight each other. My head started to spin lightly as the heat and alcohol cushioned me. I asked where the bus stop was, got on my number 337 and slept most of the way back to my capital.

Touring with visiting parents:
Consuegra (Castilla La Mancha)

After negotiating the melee of roads that wind, cross, overlap and get tied up in the centre of the capital we managed to find the exit route. The road leaving Madrid led us out of the glum, lonely looking outskirts of Madrid - massive advertising boards and washed out warehouses offering furniture - into the low, green plains of Castilla La Mancha. Our first stop was my request, for Consuegra is the home of those famous white windmills that show up in that perennial Spanish classic *Don Quixote De La Mancha* (the old knight of the book attacks them thinking them giants...silly knight). I wanted to see them and my parents, who were driving, didn't mind.

They sit proudly, 11 of them, on a ridge that stands on its own surrounded by lowlands. Chalk-white and perfectly preserved they provide a quixotic (*ha ha*) contrast with the rusty orange town below and the coppery red and green fields in the distance. These little sail-bearing teeth share the jaw of land with a bulky 12th century castle. When you managed to squeeze past the four separate groups of school children being scared, taught and spellbound by actors in costumes, the view from the top was superlative. If it weren't for the coaches the view would have been as classically Manchegan as a slice of cheese, with a glass of *Valdepeñas* wine and a few lines from the great book.

Úbeda and Baeza (Andalucía)

These two little Renaissance beauties are a couple of often unknown and little visited towns. They are World Heritage Sites and are just, quite frankly, delightful.

The road took us into the community of Andalucía and through Jaen province. Jaen is the major olive-producing region in Spain and you can see this if you just look out of your car window at any time and any place in the area. The hills, rolling and broad as they are, are studded with little olive bushes. If you imagine a roast turkey studded with so many cloves, you can imagine Jaen. Rarely visited reservoirs surrounded by olive-bush dappled slopes with copper red, dirty white and green soils, dotted with farm buildings and everything tinkling in the limited sun, produced a scene worthy of literature. Unfortunately Quixote didn't get this far. He was too busy chasing sheep and staring down windmills in La Mancha.

So to Úbeda. Nestling up a hill and surveying the great Jaen valleys Úbeda is the bigger of the two sister towns. Its *'zona monumental'* houses an impressive array of Renaissance palaces and squares. The small town was shut up and closed due to the time of our visit - the Spaniards will have their siestas - but we could still see the bulk of it. A little visit to the 'Jaen' shop meant that I could procure a 1.4kg plastic jar of Jaen olives. Lovely. We departed from sweet little Úbeda and drove 9km down the road to her little, maybe even sweeter, sister Baeza.

Baeza is really small. It's weeny. In fact were it clothing it'd probably be a yellow polka dot bikini. You get my drift. It too sports a selection of grand buildings, far larger and more ornate than its size would usually allow. It also really does have that 'Sunday morning' air about it that the guidebook mentioned.

Granada (Andalucía)

As the road drifted into the wide and high peaks of the Sierra Nevada we arrived in Granada. Having stayed in the city previously in 2003, my first thoughts were those of nostalgia. 'Oh, there's that bench I sat on with Ollie'; 'Oh, haha, there's that shop where we struggled to buy a bottle of water'; 'There's the square where we always used to relax'.

Plaza Nueva is in the heart of the city and sits by the river in the belly of the Darro Valley - the Alhambra perched on a hill on one side, the old Moorish (and World Heritage Site) quarter, the Albaicín, rising up on the other.

The Alhambra was our target the following day. In the sun it glows. The Alhambra (Arabic for 'The Red One'), for those of you who don't know, is a vast fortress and palace complex that surveys the whole of the city. This UNESCO site is full to bursting with towers, colourful gardens, glittering ponds, flowers, ochre walls and about two million arches. Beautiful. For us the day was slightly sullied by a prolonged and unforgiving weather system. The clouds wept on us for almost the whole time in Granada. Grand but greyed was our visit.

The brief moment of sun I did have I spent waking around the other UNESCO site, the Albaicín. Twisty, narrow streets, cobbles and white-painted houses create a near impossibly complicated, web-like district. It's fun to get lost though. And on my last evening I walked around alone and to the top in order to get a glimpse and photo of the big, beastly Alhambra by night.

Córdoba (Andalucía)

Leaving the climbs of the Sierra Nevada and the Arabic muscles of Granada we sped into the bowling, over-green hills of the Cordoban countryside. It was like some vast pod of harlequin, myrtle and straw-coloured whales breaching their way across the fields of Andalucía; never showing their heads or tails. After not much time we pulled into our horror-film, cheap, Cordoban hotel, with its peeling walls, creaking doors and flickering buzzing lights.

Córdoba, after its morning drizzle, was a glorious little pearl of Spanishness. The main calling card of the place is the Mezquita and surrounding buildings. You enter the city by crossing a big, clean, preserved Roman bridge. You are then faced with an historic area. You can walk around the majority of the buildings in an hour or so. Big, Gothic/Arab, yellow/brown, and dramatic. There are some words.

Before we went into the Mezquita, I popped into the tourist information office and got us a plan of another little shindig that was going down in the city. The week we had chosen to travel also happened to be one of the weeks that held the Festival of the Cordoban Patios. It is a festival where the luckier members of the city, who have internal patios, open them to the general public and the competition judges.

Little fountains that dropped water serenely into little pools while little flower pots dotted little walls with many little flowers - flash purple, pink, red, yellow, colours of rainbows - and little tourists with their little cameras take little photos. These patios lay hidden inside small, pristine white houses - similar to those in Granada but statelier. We left this area, smacking with smells: flowers, pollen, warm leathers and hot boiling pork, and moved to the older barrio.

Prior to our 'history bit' we had some tapas in a sweet little café run by a very funny and animated chap. When we paid, he graciously told me that I spoke Spanish perfectly. I beamed modestly and truthfully informed him that I speak well, but hardly perfect. I then made a joke that I'm called a '*guiri-gato*' by my housemate. A *guiri* being that endearing term for a foreigner and *gato* meaning someone with both parents and grandparents from Madrid (basically someone who can truly claim to be 'from Madrid'). He laughed and told me that he once lived in Mexico and Miami and that in both places they called *him* gringo. I quizzed him as to why. He was Spanish surely. He told me to hang on. He trotted inside for a minute or so and then trotted back out. 'This is me when I was thirty'. He showed me some crusty old photos of a young man with wild ginger hair and fair features. 'This is why they called me gringo!' He also had lived with the Mayan people for two years, but that's another story...

The Mezquita was something else. Proof that sometimes a photo really just doesn't do it. You enter surrounded and confronted and wrapped up in a blanket of endless dark red and white stripy archways. They caterpillar away as far as perspective will allow you to see. Stunning. Mosque-y and stunning. Then, right in the centre, where you can't see for the arches, a massive ivory-white Christian cathedral rises up 50 metres to the heavens. You blink and try and work out where it came from. You walk back a few metres and you're back with the Muslim arches and its spongy half-light. Then back into the light and Christendom. It is, in the very literal sense of the word, unbelievable. And, you know, it's magnificent.

Calatrava La Nueva (Castilla La Mancha)
Our last stop before returning to Madrid (ignoring the normal but comparatively rubbish Ciudad Real) was a hilltop ruined castle complex called Calatrava La Nueva. The Calatrava Knights were a sect of Cistercian soldier-monks who went a bit power mad and caused the then king – Alfonso X – to set up Ciudad Real in order to keep the prayer/sword-wielding nutters in check. The Knights set up the settlement in 1216, in order to have a vantage point against the Moors. And they chose a cracking spot.

After driving up the precariously bumpy and badly laid stone road, juddering the car to pieces and causing my seatbelt to lock and choke me, we arrived at the small, empty car park. The weather improved for us and the views from the top were arresting. I spent the next hour and half running around the ruins alone but for my parents. It was like a private school trip, without teachers and with no 'Don't do this' signs. We hit the road again and drove through the flower-splashed fields of La Mancha, looking like so many paint dots of an artist thrown lovingly against a green canvas: white daisies, red poppies, yellow ones, pinks and purples spattered the world around the car. We were driving through a piece of landscape art.

Ávila (Castilla y León)

After a quick spell in Madrid we took a train to Ávila and its famous wind-beaten walls. I shall begin by saying that Ávila was cold. Absurdly cold. Bone-shakingly, arse-clenchingly, finger-numbingly cold. Why? Because I only took a cardigan. Why? Because I'm a crap boy scout. The city was not what I expected. I imagined something twee and preserved like the old quarters in Granada, Segovia, Toledo, Córdoba, Cuenca and other places I'd visited. Instead the town inside was a bit scruffy and bland. However, the star of the show and, in fairness to Ávila, the 'thing' to see, was the wall.

The whole town is surrounded by a perfectly maintained medieval wall. Tall, broad, attractive and imposing, the (so Spanish) yellowy fortifications wind their way around the 'old town' forming a large oblong perimeter. After lunch (the famous *chuletón de Ávila* a.k.a. the big face-sized steak of Ávila) I walked around the outside by myself. I ventured away from the town a little, in order to run up a hill (scrambling through a fence I wasn't supposed to and performing some amateur wall-climbing) in order to get more of an all-encompassing shot of the wall. It was really a marvel. UNESCO agrees.

Milton Keynes UK
Ingram Content Group UK Ltd.
UKHW011038131123
432477UK00001B/261